Geopoetics

GEOPOETICS

*The Politics of Mimesis in
Poststructuralist French Poetry
and Theory*

JOAN BRANDT

Stanford University Press
Stanford, California

Stanford University Press
Stanford, California

© 1997 by the Board of Trustees of the
Leland Stanford Junior University

Printed in the United States of America

CIP data are at the end of the book

Stanford University Press publications are
distributed exclusively by Stanford University Press
within the United States, Canada, Mexico, and
Central America; they are distributed exclusively
by Cambridge University Press throughout
the rest of the world.

For Terry, Ted, and Tim

Preface

Through an analysis of the writings of a number of poets and theorists often assembled under the "poststructuralist" label, this study aims to shed light on some of the recent reactions to the demand that both literature and theory respond more directly to the political questions of the contemporary sociocultural world. By focusing specifically on the problematic of mimesis in its linguistic, psychoanalytical, and cultural incarnations, I argue, in opposition to those who stress the political inadequacies of the French poststructuralists' "privileging" of language, that what leads to a theoretical or practical apoliticism is not the emphasis on language and mimetic representation. It is, rather, the failure to examine more closely the relationship between mimesis and politics that closes off the possibility of articulating an adequate response to any form of political imperative.

In order to make this point, I begin with a consideration of the "revolution in poetic language" waged in the late 1960's and early 1970's by the politically motivated revolutionary group of poets and theorists associated with the now discontinued French journal *Tel Quel*. I examine the impact of its political radicalism not only on the writings of the major theoretician of the *Tel Quel* group, Julia Kristeva, as well as on the work of two of the most important *Tel Quel* poets, Marcelin Pleynet and Denis Roche, but also on those more closely associated with deconstruction, whose resistance to the highly charged political rhetoric of the period led many critics to denounce the deconstructive approach for its failure to come to terms with the sociopolitical. In an effort to respond to those who claim that deconstruction's focus on questions of language and textuality constitutes a denial of history and of the political, the second part of this study considers deconstructive poetry and theory in the context of *Tel Quel*'s ultimate repudiation of its own revolutionary project. And it argues, through a reading of the theoretical texts of Philippe Lacoue-Labarthe, Jean-Luc Nancy, and Jacques Derrida, as well as the "deconstructive" poetics of Edmond Jabès, that the deconstructive approach, with its radical interrogation of traditional notions of the mimetic, presents possibilities for a reintegration of the political that, in many respects, exceeds the more highly politicized strategies of the *Tel Quel* group itself.

Moreover, by showing that the texts under consideration do not confine themselves to mere language games that empty discourse of its social and historical content, I hope to respond not only to those who insist upon the apolitical, ahistorical character of poststructuralist theory and practice (and this includes critics who insist upon *Tel Quel*'s so-called formalist perspective) but also to those who tend to consign modern poetry to the distant margins of contemporary culture. The term "geopoetics" was indeed chosen as the title of this work for this very reason. Borrowed from a relatively recent treatise on poetry by Michel Deguy, *La Poésie n'est pas seule*, it is a term that stresses the interrelatedness of the poetic, the theoretical, and the sociopolitical and thus reinforces the central argument of this book—that far from cutting themselves off from the political and cultural concerns of the modern world, poststructuralist theory and poetic practice have for some time now been actively engaged in real-world issues.

A greatly abbreviated version of my general argument was made in two of my recent articles, "Questioning the Postmodern: Deguy, Jabès and Pleynet," reprinted here with permission from *Studies in Twentieth Century Literature* 18, no. 2 (Summer 1994): 167–75, and "'Sharing the Unshareable': Jabès, Deconstruction and the Thought of 'the jews'" (forthcoming in *Borders, Exiles, and Dias-*

poras, ed. Elazar Barkan and Marie-Denise Shelton, Stanford University Press). The first part of this book also incorporates articles that have previously appeared in print. The two sections on Denis Roche in Chapter 2 appeared as "The Theory and Practice of a 'Revolutionary' Text: Denis Roche's 'Le mécrit,'" in *Yale French Studies* 67 (1984): 203–21. Chapters 2 and 4 incorporate portions of two articles on Julia Kristeva. One is reprinted by permission from the *Romanic Review* 82, no. 1 (January 1991): 89–104. Copyright by the Trustees of Columbia University in the City of New York. The other is reprinted from *The American Journal of Semiotics* 5, no. 1 (1987): 133–50. I thank the editors for their permission to reprint.

　　I am deeply grateful to Renée Riese Hubert for her helpful suggestions with regard to the final draft of this manuscript and for introducing me to the writings of the *Tel Quel* group in general. I am especially thankful for her unwavering support and encouragement throughout the years. I would also like to thank Carrie Noland for her careful reading of the manuscript during its early stages and for a critique that, in numerous ways, led me to clarify my own position. Ewa Ziarek, Nathalie Rachlin, and Michael Harper were also generous enough to read certain sections of this manuscript and provided me with many insightful comments and pertinent suggestions, for which I am very grateful.

　　Unless otherwise indicated, all translations in this volume are my own.

J.B.

Contents

Introduction: Deconstruction, 'Tel Quel,'   1
and the Legacy of Marx

PART I.   The "Revolutionary" Poetics of Tel Quel

1. Politicizing the Text   15
The Textual Politics of Théorie d'ensemble, 18.
Althusserian Marxism and Its Influence on Tel
Quel, 24. Tel Quel's Subversive Literary/Theoretical
Practice, 37. The Practice of an "Open" Text: Marcelin
Pleynet's Stanze, 42. Scissions, Ruptures, and the
Marginalization of Tel Quel, 52.

2. Textual and Cultural Enclosures   66
Kristeva's Revolutionary Poetic Language: The
Semiotic and the Symbolic as a Political Distinction,
73. Denis Roche's "Le Mécrit," 78. Theoretical
Closure, 87. Rereading "Le Mécrit," 94.

PART II.   Rethinking the Collective and the
Political

3. Dismantling the 'Tel Quel' Community   101
The Multiple Languages of Dissidence, 101. Love,
Psychoanalysis, and Religion, 104.

4. *'Tel Quel' and Deconstruction*   113

The "Other" Within: Kristeva's Passage Through
Narcissism, 124. A Politics of Otherness/An "Other"
Politics, 135. Reevaluating *Tel Quel*, 146.

PART III. Deconstructive Poetics

5. *Deconstruction on Trial*   159

The de Man and Heidegger Controversies, 159. Jean-
François Lyotard's *Heidegger and "the jews,"* 166.

6. *"Sharing the Unshareable": Deconstruction,*   172
Edmond Jabès, and the "Thought of 'the jews'"

Lacoue-Labarthe, Heidegger, and National Socialism's
Misapprehension of *Technē*, 177. Of Ashes and
Holocaustal Fire: *Technē*, the "Trait," and "the jews,"
196. The Cata-strophic Poetics of Edmond Jabès, 210.
A "Politics" of Community: Jabès and Jean-Luc
Nancy, 220.

7. *Of Hospitality, Responsibility, and the Democratic*   235
"Ideal": Derrida's 'Specters of Marx'

Notes   255

Index   283

Geopoetics

Introduction:
Deconstruction, 'Tel Quel,'
and the Legacy of Marx

With the publication in 1993 of Jacques Derrida's *Spectres de Marx*, any doubts concerning the political significance of deconstructive theory and practice should finally be laid to rest, for it is in this work that Derrida makes one of his most explicitly political statements in favor of a certain "re-politicization" of critical Marxism.[1] Finally abandoning a long-standing reluctance to address the question of his relationship to Marx, Derrida does not offer in this work an endorsement of Marxist politics, but he underscores, through his affirmation of Marx's "critical spirit," the political implications of what has always been one of the most fundamental but also most misunderstood objectives of the deconstructive project, that of rethinking the political itself. Indeed, in spite of a number of studies that make a compelling argument for the inherently political character of Derrida's interrogation of politics (not to mention the many works in which Derrida himself addresses this question), there are those who have remained and will no doubt continue to remain unconvinced that such an interrogation is anything more than a retreat from the political itself.[2] Nancy Fraser is, of course, one of the first critics who comes to mind in this particular context,[3] but a more recent work by Simon Critchley, which makes a strong case for the ethical dimensions of deconstructive thought, conceived in the Levinasian sense as an opening to the alterity of the Other, argues that deconstruction fails when it comes to translating the undecidability of that ethical relation into a course for political action.[4]

   In an effort to respond to the criticism proffered by Fraser, Critchley, and others, this book argues that it is precisely this relation to otherness inscribed in the undecidable "logic" of *différance* and supplementarity that constitutes not only what Critchley describes as the "ethical moment" within deconstruction, but that contains distinctly political possibilities as well, possibilities for assuming our political "responsibility to act" while rethinking the philosophical precepts upon which our concepts of political action are grounded.[5] In order to make this point, I consider the question of the political from a more historical perspective by examining the highly charged political climate of the late 1960's and early 1970's out of which deconstruction's interrogation of conventional notions of the political emerged. For what has up to this point received little attention from those who characterize poststructuralism's, and particularly deconstruction's "privileging" of language as an apolitical textualism or a perverse kind of nihilism is that those who are usually assembled under the "poststructuralist" label (as if they were part of a monolithic theoretical "movement") responded to the turmoil surrounding the student uprisings of May 1968 in very different but nevertheless "political" ways, with some, such as the members of the *Tel Quel* group, becoming increasingly militant and others, such as Derrida, resisting the revolutionary rhetoric of those caught up in the political frenzy of the period.

   Just why deconstruction and *Tel Quel*, whose interests were initially quite similar, moved in such different directions is a question that, I believe, is worthy of consideration because it has political repercussions that are still being felt today. Indeed, the struggle that continues to be waged by Derrida, Kristeva, and others to find new ways of thinking about the political can in a sense be traced to that highly volatile period of the 1960's when the more revolutionary aspects of Marxist theory were gaining an increasingly strong hold upon many French intellectuals, particularly upon those associated with *Tel Quel*, the avant-garde French journal to which Derrida was also an early contributor. Founded in 1960 by Philippe Sollers in an effort to challenge the major literary currents of the early postwar years, *Tel Quel* became a powerful intellectual force in the late 1960's when it served as a vehicle for the dissemination of many of the ideas of the newly emerging French theorists and literary writers, including such innovative thinkers as Foucault, Barthes, Kristeva, Lacan, and Althusser.

Although these writers joined in a common effort to call into question the principles of identity structuring traditional notions of language, literature, philosophy, and politics, it should be remembered that there were those who became increasingly alienated by the political radicalism that began to emerge at *Tel Quel*, where a failure to assume a certain "responsibility to otherness" was to have, as we shall see, devastating political consequences. Attacked and even ridiculed for its naive utopianism and its increasingly doctrinaire tendencies, the *Tel Quel* collective came, interestingly enough, to be repudiated by its own members. Openly criticizing, in 1981, the "romantic vision" that prevailed during *Tel Quel*'s politically militant period of the late 1960's and early 1970's, Philippe Sollers denounced the idea of a collective effort, claiming not only that the collectivity itself could be just as oppressive as the social order it opposed but that its goal of accomplishing social revolution through a revolution in language was an "illusion" that had structured the activities of many of the avant-garde groups of the twentieth century.[6] The demise of *Tel Quel* as perhaps one of the last of the politically motivated, avant-garde communities can thus be said to constitute the final stages of an important turning point in French intellectual and political history, one that saw the collapse of Marxism as well as a growing apprehension that the traditionally accepted forms of political confrontation were no longer workable, that no course of political action could be undertaken without a rigorous interrogation of the notion of the political itself.

If it is true, however, that the dissolution of *Tel Quel* coincided with the demise of political radicalism in the mid-1970's, the questions raised by the political activism of that period have not lost their urgency. That urgency is indeed underscored by Derrida's *Specters of Marx*, whose claim that we must assume our responsibility toward the legacy of Marxism carries an additional, unmentioned responsibility, that of examining the theoretical and literary writings of those who attempted to put the critical spirit of Marxism into practice; Derrida's work points, in other words, to the necessity of acknowledging and critically analyzing the legacy of *Tel Quel*. Indeed, in light of the call in recent years for a reintegration of the political into critical discourse, a reexamination of the *Tel Quel* experience becomes all the more necessary, for it raises questions regarding the very possibility of constituting a politically effective discourse in an age when the efficacy of representational language has been challenged, and of finding a way to articulate that discourse without succumbing to the more dogmatic expressions of theory and its programmatic imperatives.

The question of representational language and the mimetic precepts that structure it thus becomes one of the central concerns of this book not simply because language occupied a central place in the theoretical investigations and poetic practice of both *Tel Quel* and deconstruction, but also, and more importantly, because of the significant contributions these investigations have made to our understanding of the relationship between language and the political. This is what I consider to be one of the fundamental lessons to be learned from *Tel Quel*'s early collaborative efforts. For however extreme *Tel Quel*'s position may have become, it points to the importance of examining the extent to which the unifying logic of mimetic representation, with its denial of the differences between the model and its copy, between an original intention and the forms that reproduce it, provides the conceptual framework upon which conventional politics are grounded. By allowing for a thought of the unitary, sovereign subject as the coordinating center of political action and by viewing language as a transparent medium through which the subject shapes its reality in accordance with its political objectives, traditional mimetic principles (manifested most directly in representational theories of language but also evident, as we shall see later, in the sociopsychological identificatory mechanisms constituting psychic and communitarian identity) acquire certain structuring and regulating powers that have obvious political implications. It is, of course, for this very reason that representational language, conceived by *Tel Quel* as an instrument of political domination and exploitation, was placed at the center of the group's preoccupations, with the desire to break open the repressive "closure" of discourse providing the motivating force for the entire *Tel Quel* project, leading its poets to write "open-ended" often nonsensical poems and inducing its theorists to pit the prelinguistic realm of "semiotic" heterogeneity against the "repressive" linguistic, "symbolic" order of representation.

The group's inability, however, to fully pursue some of the implications of its own linguistic investigations is what, in my view, lends support to one of the central arguments of this book: that it is not the focus on language and mimetic representation that leads to a theoretical or practical apoliticism, for that term, as we shall see, can hardly be applied to the activities at *Tel Quel*; it is rather the group's failure to examine its precepts more carefully that accounts for the political inadequacies of the *Tel Quel* project. I try to show as we move from *Tel Quel*, through Kristeva's later work, to the writings of those associated more directly with deconstruction, that deconstruction's more probing analyses of the fundamentally unresolvable contradictions inherent in the structure of mimesis itself have important implications for political thought in that they point to the possibility of pursuing practical political goals without succumbing entirely to authoritarian, narrowly programmatic directives.

A consideration of the different approaches to the problem of mimetic representation and its relation to politics thus provides the focal point around which this book is organized. The first part offers a historical overview as well as a critical analysis of the *Tel Quel* phenomenon in terms of its revolutionary politics and its poetics as they developed before and after the student uprisings of May 1968. By tracing the numerous changes in the journal's perspective, I examine the impact of its political articulations on the writings of the major theoretician of the *Tel Quel* group, Julia Kristeva, as well as on the work of two of the most important *Tel Quel* poets, Denis Roche, who resigned from the editorial board in 1973, and Marcelin Pleynet, who served as the journal's editor-in-chief. My emphasis on the highly collaborative nature of the *Tel Quel* effort thus differentiates my approach from those of previous studies undertaken in the United States, which tend to focus on the individual members in isolation from the activities of the *Tel Quel* collective.[7] When, for example, the writings of the *Tel Quel* poets have been considered, they have often been cut off from their theoretical and sociopolitical context. Conversely, although much has been written about Kristevan semiotics as it relates to feminist issues, little attention has been paid to the ways Kristeva's theory of a revolutionary poetic language may or may not have been carried out by the poets with whom she collaborated as a member of the *Tel Quel* group. Moreover, through an examination of the historical and political context in which Kristeva's thinking took shape, this study seeks to shed light on a debate that continues to be generated by those who still question the ethical and political implications of Kristeva's writings.[8] Whereas some analysts criticize Kristeva for her essentialist notions of the feminine, others imply that her questioning of identity is not essentializing enough because it deprives us of the notion of agency upon which our action-oriented expressions of the political are based. In this study, I try to resist the tendency to categorize the totality of Kristeva's writings, to place them definitively on one side of the opposition or the other, by tracing, particularly in Part II, what I consider to be important modifications in Kristeva's thinking as she moves away from her focus on semiotics toward a more psychoanalytical perspective.[9] Although my purpose here is not to construct a rigid distinction between an "earlier" and a "later" Kristeva, and thus deny the possibility that ambiguities and contradictions exist in all the different stages of Kristeva's writing, I believe that there have been certain changes in emphasis that need to be examined more closely, changes, I would argue, that accompanied the breakup of *Tel Quel* and that stemmed from Kristeva's growing interest in psychoanalysis, when her more thoroughgoing analysis of the narcissistic (that is, mimetic) identifications structuring psychic identity led to new and, in my view, more fruitful ways of thinking about the political.

In the second chapter of this section, Kristeva's writings continue to occupy a prominent place, but at this point I consider them through a more direct encounter with deconstruction. The chapter begins with a brief but necessary analysis of the initial relationship between Derrida and those members of the *Tel Quel* group who attempted to revolutionize Derrida's notion of *différance* by making it conform more closely to Kristeva's concept of the semiotic. And I argue that the failure of *Tel Quel*'s political strategy stems not only from *Tel Quel's* uncritical acceptance of Kristeva's notion of the semiotic as a disruptive space of pure drive existing outside the symbolic and its structuring representations, but also from an unwillingness to embrace the more radical implications of *différance* itself, whose interrogation of traditional notions of the mimetic and whose confrontation with otherness far exceed the limits of what I would characterize as *Tel Quel's* rather superficial critique. Although the members of the *Tel Quel* group were among the first to provide a comprehensive, critical analysis of the relationship between the political and language by focusing on the role of representational discourse in shaping cultural and political identity, they did not see that their own identification with a political group and its revolutionary ideal was governed by the very representational logic they set out to contest, with the unfortunate result that traditional notions of the mimetic came ultimately to structure the thinking and the politics of the *Tel Quel* collective as well.

The way that the deconstructive approach responds to the questions raised by *Tel Quel's* "failed" experiment is thus the focus of the third section of this book. In an effort to continue the emphasis in Part I on the interaction between poetry, politics, and theory, it considers the "deconstructive" poetics of Edmond Jabès as well as the theories of Philippe Lacoue-Labarthe, Jean-Luc Nancy, and Jacques Derrida in the context of *Tel Quel's* ultimate repudiation of its own revolutionary project. Here I argue that these writers' more penetrating analysis of the logic of mimesis presents possibilities for a reintegration of the political in a way that was in some respects envisioned by *Tel Quel* but that at the same time goes beyond the more doctrinaire aspects of *Tel Quel* theory and practice. Moving, then, from the Marxist-Freudian perspective of *Tel Quel* to the perspective of what some have erroneously referred to as the "French Heideggerians," this section takes as its point of departure Jean-François Lyotard's contention in *Heidegger and "the jews"* that deconstruction's failure to assume its political responsibility by speaking out against the Nazi atrocities is due to its inability to liberate itself from what is an essentially philosophical/representational problematic.[10] In opposition to Lyotard's critique, I argue that it is precisely this concentration on language and its inscription of alterity that makes the question of our moral and political responsibility in effect unavoidable. By focusing primarily on Lacoue-Labarthe's *Heidegger, Art and Politics* and on Derrida's *Of Spirit: Heidegger and the Question* and *Cinders*, I try to show that these writers have not shirked their responsibility to confront the issue of Auschwitz: their interrogation of the principles of mimesis, which takes different forms in each of their texts, and their radicalization of the Heideggerian notion of *technē* allow for an examination of the very modes of thought that make the totalitarian discourses of fascism possible.[11] The work of Lacoue-Labarthe and Jean-Luc Nancy, who have written extensively in recent years on the mechanisms of fascism and its totalitarian logic, are particularly useful in this regard. In claiming that traditional notions of representational discourse are at the very root of National Socialism, where the formative or fashioning power of the German myth constitutes national identity, they underscore the extent to which the deconstruction of traditional mimetic precepts, which Lacoue-Labarthe undertakes through a rigorous analysis of Heidegger's notion of *technē*, has important political ramifications, for it serves as a means of destabilizing the myths of the Aryan state and thereby of resisting the totalizing logic of which fascism is a possible outcome.

What should become clear, then, as we progress through my analysis of the various practices of both *Tel Quel* and deconstruction is that the concept of mimesis itself takes on a different meaning. Limited by *Tel Quel*, in spite of its critique of traditional mimetic principles, to a more conventional notion of representation, whose unity of meaning and logic of identity must be undermined through the restoration of an excluded heterogeneity, mimesis emerges in the hands of those more closely linked to deconstruction as a process in which heterogeneity is "always already" inscribed. In this case, the emphasis is placed on those processes of depropriation that have not been excluded or repressed by representational language but that are always supposed by the act of representation itself. This shift to a more profound recognition of the contradictions and duplicities that are an integral part of even the most normative discourses has, in my view, considerable political significance. Given that, as both Lacoue-Labarthe and Nancy have argued, the process of identification with a political group or national identity is in itself an act of *mimesis*, involving the mimetic appropriation of some predetermined political model or ideal, deconstruction's foregrounding of the duplicities inherent in this mimetic relation to an other ultimately destabilizes the identificatory mechanisms that are essential to the formation of any political community. Such a foregrounding exposes within the very processes that constitute community, not the possibility of a closed, self-identical, totalitarian order, but the fundamental loss of the self-identical, the impossibility of closure that the duplicitous structure of mimesis necessarily implies.

Drawing upon Nancy's and Lacoue-Labarthe's analysis, Part III thus develops this argument through a reading not simply of deconstructive theory, but also of the deconstructive poetic practice of Edmond Jabès, a French/Egyptian/Jewish writer who places the Holocaust at the very "center" of his work.[12] This section argues, in opposition to those who denounce deconstruction for its so-called textualization of reality, that despite its constant questioning of language's capacity to represent history, deconstructive theory and practice at the same time show that language cannot be dissociated from its sociohistorical affiliations. Moreover, I maintain that only through such rigorous questioning of traditional notions of the mimetic and of the precepts of identity that underpin it, can an ethically and politically responsible discourse be assumed, one that offers a means of undoing the political program of fascism and of resisting the logic of identity structuring all forms of totalitarianism—including that of the *Tel Quel* collective itself. For if, as Sollers has indicated, "Telquelism" was indeed the outcome of the *Tel Quel* experiment, and if, as a consequence, it failed in the realization of its political objectives, perhaps its interrogation of traditional notions of the mimetic and of the subject did not go far enough; it never interrogated its own political practice or, more importantly, examined the extent to which politics itself is by its very nature dependent on notions of identity and representational language that the group called into question.

It could indeed be argued that the examination of the complexities involved in the very movement of identification is one of the reasons that the deconstructive approach itself has not led to the formation of a restrictive, ideological community of the Telquelian type; nor can it be assimilated to a uniform "Heideggerian" practice of deconstruction, given that Heidegger's own writings have, as we shall see, been subjected by both Lacoue-Labarthe and Derrida to a rigorous deconstructive analysis. Although Derrida, Lacoue-Labarthe, Nancy, and Jabès have all been engaged in a questioning of traditional mimesis and its metaphysics of presence, they appear to resist the idea of a mutually determined, common "practice of writing," particularly, I would argue, of the kind that shaped and ultimately came to dominate the activities of the *Tel Quel* collective. That resistance is expressed quite clearly by Derrida in his introduction to one of Lacoue-Labarthe's works, where he takes great pains to underscore the possibility that the various proponents of deconstruction do not necessarily think in identical ways. In so doing, he reminds us of the need to resist the demands for likemindedness that seemed so often to prevail at *Tel Quel*:

> What I share with Lacoue-Labarthe, we also both share, though differently, with Jean-Luc Nancy. But I hasten immediately to reiterate that despite so many common paths and so much work done in common, between the two of them and between the three of us, the work of each remains, in its singular proximity, absolutely different; and this, despite its fatal impurity, is the secret of the idiom. The secret: that is to say, first of all, the *separation*, the non-relation, the interruption. The most urgent thing—I'll try to work on this—would be to break with the family atmosphere, to avoid genealogical temptations, projections, assimilations, or identifications. . . . Assimilation or identificatory projection: these are what Lacoue-Labarthe constantly puts us on guard against. He uncovers their fatal character, the *political* trap they hold, even in Heidegger's "unacknowledged" and "fundamental" mimetology.[13]

Rather than joining, however, in the relentless "*Tel Quel* bashing" in which so many critics, even in the earliest days of the journal's existence, liked to engage, this study argues that, despite the many shortcomings of the *Tel Quel* project, something positive is also to be gained from the *Tel Quel* experience. The group's later reevaluation of its political position provides the basis not only for a rethinking of the political but for a certain reconciliation with the deconstructive approach itself. The demise of *Tel Quel* as a constricted "ideological collectivity" (Sollers) indeed lends support to Nancy's thesis in *The Inoperative Community* that this very dissolution of traditional notions of the communal as a closed, cohesive, fully integrated, collective Subject presents us with the possibility of understanding community in terms other than those of immanence and subjectivity and thereby of resisting the totalizing, mythizing logic upon which the traditional notions of community—and of the political—depend.[14] According to Nancy, the modern experience of community disrupts such logic by marking the impossibility of self-contained identity, by showing that being, in order *to be*, must be " 'posed' in exteriority," taken "outside itself" so that the self may exist. And he claims that it is not the totalizing language of myth but literature or, preferably, writing that gives voice to this shared state of incompletion. In exposing being in its necessary relationship to an other, literature shares in being's non-identity, and this includes the non-identity of literature itself. In an effort, however, to distance my argument from what might be construed as a certain privileging of literature on Nancy's part— even if he speaks, in this case, of a literature that is never identical with itself—I hope to show that literature (which is never "purely" literature) has no special or privileged status but is instead just one of the possible forms that this opening toward otherness might take and can thus work in conjunction with theory (which is never "purely" theory) in the exposition of being to alterity.

Moreover, in the context of Nancy's claim that writing interrupts myth by giving voice to this fragmented "being-in-common," I intend not only to examine the more recent work of Edmond Jabès, in which the duplicitous structure of sharing becomes particularly explicit, but to stress the importance of a reexamination of the "literary/theoretical" practice of *Tel Quel* as well. Although one would have to agree that *Tel Quel*'s emphasis on "writing" (*écriture*) seems to support those critics who stress *Tel Quel*'s formalism (and formalism is, of course, not what Nancy is advocating here), one should also recognize that the group saw its practice as a complex of intertextual relations conceived not in terms of the strictly linguistic but of the *translinguistic* in which social and historical complexity is also inscribed. In fact, despite the more doctrinaire aspects of *Tel Quel* theory, the group's effort to call into question the traditional concepts of closure related to the individual or collective subject anticipates in some respects Nancy's notion of "literary communism" as developed in *The Inoperative Community*. Nancy later rejects the term because of its "equivocal character," but this very equivocality is particularly appropriate in the context of *Tel Quel*, for it suggests both the "romantic vision" of *Tel Quel* as an immanent community and the possibility also opened up by the *Tel Quel* experience for another thought of community, one that recognizes the shared state of incompletion and finitude characterizing what Nancy describes as "la *praxis* de l'en-commun." The paradoxical nature of *Tel Quel*'s collective activity indeed points to a concept of community that the group itself, especially during the highly political period of the 1960's and 1970's, seemed unable or unwilling to comprehend, and it anticipates the work of Nancy and, at a much later date, of one the members of the *Tel Quel* group itself, Julia Kristeva. In two of her more recent works, *Strangers to Ourselves* and *Nations Without Nationalism*, she, like Nancy, examines the dissolution of traditional communal bonds within contemporary society and finds in it certain ethical or political possibilities, for it joins us together in the recognition of our own limits and favors a tolerance for strangeness and difference that was clearly a part of the practice if not of the politics at *Tel Quel*.[15]

PART I

The "Revolutionary" Poetics
of *Tel Quel*

CHAPTER I

Politicizing the Text

The transformation of *Tel Quel* into a politically motivated collective would come as a surprise to anyone whose knowledge of the journal did not extend beyond the earliest years of its existence. The "Declaration" in the journal's inaugural issue in 1960 takes an unambiguous position against the Sartrean notion of a politically "engaged" literature by advocating a renewed interest in the literary text divested of all ideological preoccupations. As the unsigned "Declaration" announces:

> To speak today of "literary quality," or of "literary passion," let it appear to you as it may. The ideologues have ruled over expression long enough. It can now permit itself to go its own way [*leur fausser compagnie*], to become concerned only with itself, with its fatality and with its particular rules. . . . [W]hat needs to be said today is that writing is no longer conceivable without a clear idea of its powers . . . a determination that will elevate poetry to the highest level of the spirit [*à la plus haute place de l'esprit*]. Anything else will not be literature [*tout le reste ne sera pas littérature*].[1]

By placing the emphasis once again on the literary text unencumbered by "extra-literary justifications," the journal was not, however, advocating a return to the aesthetic idealism of the late-nineteenth-century Symbolists. On the contrary, its aim was to call

into question a whole range of outmoded literary practices includ-
ing not only the Symbolists' "sanctified" notions of the work of art
but also the politically committed literature that opposed it, both
of which, according to the members of the *Tel Quel* group, re-
mained subservient to a fundamentally "bourgeois" ideology.[2]

Although Sollers stated later that the journal abandoned rather
quickly the "aesthetic ambiguity" of this early period,[3] the notion
of the literary work as a "textual practice" was maintained with
considerable consistency throughout *Tel Quel*'s history, leading it
paradoxically away from its apolitical beginnings to embrace a
highly politicized notion of the revolutionary text. The course of
that transformation and the problems *Tel Quel*'s political "engage-
ment" ultimately generated have indeed been well documented in
a series of interviews given by Sollers himself and by a number of
those who were part of the *Tel Quel* circle at that particular period
in the journal's history. This included Marcelin Pleynet, one of the
Tel Quel poets and the journal's editor-in-chief, and Julia Kristeva,
who began contributing to *Tel Quel* in 1967 and served on its
editorial board from 1970 until 1983, when the journal metamor-
phosed into the more conservative *L'Infini*.[4] Although other mem-
bers came and went as they became embroiled in the controversies
and disputes generated by the political furor of the late 1960's,
Sollers, Kristeva, and Pleynet can be said to constitute the core of
the *Tel Quel* circle, with their collaborative activity emerging grad-
ually as the journal passed through what Sollers has described as
three distinct stages.[5]

According to Sollers's schema, which provides a brief review of
what might be for some a very familiar trajectory, the journal
functioned from 1960 to 1963 as a primarily literary venture that,
in its effort to articulate a radically new and subversive literary
practice, forged a loose alliance with the French New Novelists and
printed many of the previously unpublished works of the impor-
tant "subversive literary forces" of the past, including writers such
as Sade, Lautréamont, Mallarmé, Joyce, and Artaud. The first stage
of *Tel Quel*'s development thus was characterized by a certain
literary eclecticism, and although its spirit of contestation was
clearly evident from the very beginning, the journal's initial state-
ments of intent as they appear in its short publicity notices sound

very mild when compared to the highly politicized declarations of the late 1960's. Its goal at the time was simply to provide a forum for innovative, young writers who would bring "a new critical point of view to the literature of yesterday and today" and thus provide a new orientation for "the literature of tomorrow."[6] Without a well-defined theoretical position of its own but determined in its effort to negate traditional standards of aesthetics, the group had an open spirit of exploration, which attracted some of the most innovative and controversial novelists and poets of the period, including Robbe-Grillet, Claude Simon, Michel Butor, Francis Ponge, and two young poets who were to become members of the editorial board, Denis Roche and Marcelin Pleynet.

As the journal entered its second phase, which Sollers dates from 1963 to 1966, other writers were drawn to the group and its theoretical perspective became more focused. This period constitutes a major turning point for the *Tel Quel* journal, when it moved beyond strictly literary concerns to incorporate the works of those who were to become leading French philosophers and theorists, many of whom were still relatively unknown. Some of the earliest essays of Jacques Derrida were published by *Tel Quel*, as were the writings of Barthes, Foucault, Jakobson, and Ricardou. Sollers indeed credits the texts of Barthes and Foucault for providing *Tel Quel* its first solid foundation in theory, but he indicates that the work of Derrida actually exerted the greatest influence by changing *Tel Quel*'s approach dramatically. Derrida's critique of phonocentrism in his essay "La Parole soufflée," which first appeared in the 1964 issue of the journal, and his notion of writing as a process of differentiation or temporal spacing within language presented the *Tel Quel* group for the first time with possibilities for an integration of theory into their so-called literary practice. In the words of Sollers: "The first text by Derrida that we published in 1964, 'La parole soufflée,' . . . is for us one of the first explicit links between the field of philosophy and a field of the practice of writing. . . . It should be recognized that Derrida's work defines in a powerful way the general transformation that is taking place in this era."[7] Although studies in linguistics also contributed significantly to *Tel Quel*'s elaboration of a materialist theory of language, Derrida's and Kristeva's critical analysis of the formalist premises structuring linguistic theory paved the way for the articulation of a subversive *pratique tex-tuelle* that would, as the journal moved into its third phase, become increasingly political.

Tel Quel's initial receptivity toward many divergent theoretical approaches and its growing interest in Marxist and Freudian theory indeed laid the groundwork for the idea of a collective practice of writing that emerged in the late 1960's, just as France was nearing the explosive political events of May 1968. In contrast, however, to the earlier more "literary" years at *Tel Quel*, when the journal advocated a politically disengaged textual practice in an effort to challenge the major literary currents of the postwar years (domi-nated by Sartrean engagement and its instrumentalist view of lan-guage), the members of the *Tel Quel* group began to stress the sociopolitical implications of their collective *pratique scripturale*. They became engaged in a process of politicization that coincided with a growing commitment to Marxism, one that became in-creasingly intense as the discrepancy between Marxist theory and its practical applications both in the Soviet Union and in France became more apparent.

The Textual Politics of 'Théorie d'ensemble'

Reflecting its newly acquired political focus, *Tel Quel* began releasing a series of position papers beginning with the announce-ment of the *Tel Quel* "Programme" written by Sollers in the fall issue of 1967.[8] Its advocacy of the radical reversal of bourgeois culture's "fetishized" notion of literature was followed first by "La Révolution ici maintenant" (Revolution here now), a statement signed by seventeen *Tel Quel* members and associates (including Sollers, Pleynet, Roche, and Kristeva), which made a more explicit connection between textual practice and social revolution, and second by the publication of *Théorie d'ensemble* (1968), a collec-tion of essays that some regarded as the collective manifesto of the *Tel Quel* movement and that laid the foundation, according to Sollers, for the definition of its third, most politically militant period.[9] In this work, one finds the preliminary sketches of some of the major motifs that would structure *Tel Quel* activity until its break with Maoism in the mid-1970's. The group draws upon the diverse theoretical articulations of Barthes, Foucault, Althusser, Derrida, and Freud to formulate not only a radical interrogation of "literary ideology," and related notions of representation, meaning, author, reader, and the literary work of art, but also a revolutionary political practice grounded largely in Marx's analysis of the relations of production within the capitalist system.

The members of the *Tel Quel* group came to believe, on the basis of their readings of Marxist theory, that capitalist ideology is embedded in Western communicative language and the traditional literary text whose logic of meaning works to preserve the fundamentally constricting and repressive structures dominating almost every aspect of Western bourgeois culture. They argued in a number of essays that appear in *Théorie d'ensemble*, from Kristeva's "La Sémiologie: Science critique et/ou critique de la science" (which would later appear in her first major theoretical work, *Séméiotiké*)[10] to Jean Baudry's "Le Sens de l'argent," that the laws of exchange governing the capitalist marketplace could be applied to other social practices as well, for whether the reference is to the exchange of commodities or the exchange of messages, the focus is always on the goods produced, on the finished and immediately consumable product that hides the processes of production. Thus, in a capitalist economy, which measures the value of a particular commodity on the basis of the labor time necessary to produce it, the activity of labor is not considered on its own terms, but only in terms of its relationship to what it ultimately produces. Productive labor, as a consequence, is essentially denied by the capitalist system, concealed by society's fetishization of the product and of the money that serves as its sign in the system of exchange.

It should be pointed out that Marx himself was implicated in this critique. Although he was the first, according to Kristeva, to focus on "this productivity which precedes value" (that is, before it becomes part of the system of merchandise), his own emphasis on the circulation of values, on the *product* of labor rather than on the productive process, binds him, in Kristeva's view, to the capitalist system he investigates.[11] The attempt by Kristeva and the other members of the *Tel Quel* group to distance themselves from some of the more reifying aspects of Marxist theory did not prevent them, however, from embracing Marx's analysis of the modes of production within the capitalist system. On the contrary, that analysis was applied, in a manner that, as we shall see, should have been dealt with more critically, to other structures in the system as well, all of which were seen to follow this economic model, according to which the focus is directed exclusively at the goods produced. The family unit, which provides the manpower necessary to the survival of the social system and to the development of its productive capacity, is valued primarily for its procreative function, for its role as a producer of integrated, socially acceptable, and productive members of society. Literature and the arts as well become part of the system of merchandise as producers of messages to be consumed by a reading and viewing public.

Similarly, the logic of the sign and of representational language is also seen to obey the laws of the capitalist marketplace by suppressing the differential relations involved in the constitution of meaning in order to preserve the communicability of discourse and thus enter a system of exchange that is analogous to the circulation of commodities within the capitalist system. Western discursive language, which depends, according to Kristeva, on the unified structure of the linguistic sign—defined by Ferdinand de Saussure as a combination of a phonic signifier or sound and a signified concept or sense—thus constitutes what Kristeva later described as a process of "de-spatialization." In its effort to assure the absolute identity between the concept and the spoken word, it excludes the processes through which meaning is constituted and the pluridimensional spaces of the material world existing outside language by reducing the complexity of reality to a simple binary structure. "[T]he thought of the sign," Kristeva writes in *Séméiotiké*, "imposes a . . . structure on the exterior referent; it immobilizes it, makes it finite, orders it in its own image, makes it coincide with itself: space vanishes, replaced by the two sides of the page" (p. 79). The logic of the sign thus suppresses both its detachment from the real and the processes that interfere with the direct relationship between signifier and signified in order to affirm its unifying, traditionally mimetic function: "The sign silences difference in order to seek out an *identification*, a projection or a resemblance, *beyond* distancing [*au delà de l'écart*]" (p. 84).

Gathering together these various components, the social organization thus forms a system of productive or what Kristeva calls "signifying practices," all of which contribute to the productive and reproductive capacities of the bourgeois state and attempt to assure its cohesiveness and stability by emphasizing their own structural coherence and the self-contained and unified identity of what they produce. The activity of the various signifying practices thus reveals the emphasis within the capitalist social system on the finished product, on the concrete, unified, and therefore consumable entity that aims to preserve the repressive sociopolitical order by constituting a system of cohesive, monolithic structures. In this context, it becomes clear that Western discursive language, which Kristeva describes as "statique, didactique et finitisante," has a major role to play in the preservation of the sociopolitical order. As she later wrote: "[I]t is the structure of language that represents the ultimate ground of this constraint which establishes the one, identity and structure."[12] Its repressive operations seek to assure not only the unity of the social system but also the integrated identity of the principal support of that system, the individual social subject.

According to Kristeva in an analysis developed more fully a few years later in *La Révolution du langage poétique*, it is primarily upon the acquisition of language that the individual is constituted and that the cohesiveness of the social order is for the most part guaranteed.[13] Here, Marxist theory is combined with Freudian and Lacanian psychoanalysis in an effort to show that the relations of production, or the economic infrastructure uncovered by Marx, could be equated with the heterogeneous impulses within the individual unconscious that Freud discovered, impulses that have a role in the constitution of the speaking subject but that must be repressed in order for the individual to emerge as an integrated identity. As Kristeva describes the process, the individual establishes himself as an independent and conscious subject only after cutting himself off from and repressing the instinctual drives that lie with his prelinguistic unconscious. This occurs during the earliest "pulsional" stages of a child's life when his first sounds, rhythms, and intonations, which are uttered according to the needs of the bodily impulses, are repressed in order to establish the discursive function of language and the individual's identity. The child, at this point, must be weaned from his attachment to the mother so that he may become conscious of his own existence as a distinct and separate identity. This break occurs when the child has mastered normal patterns of speech, and only then is the individual as an integrated being actually formed.

Thus, because of its participation in the repression of the unconscious heterogeneous impulses that pose a threat to unity, discursive language came to be viewed by the members of the *Tel Quel* group as a principal guarantor of Western culture and of the individual "unitary subject" who supports and perpetuates that culture through its own subjective projections of meaning. And although the social and economic practices within the capitalist system were all seen as basically interrelated, with each one working to support the other by engaging in the same type of repressive activity, the *Tel Quel* group believed that it was in large part through language that the repressive social order and its principle of unity was maintained. For this reason, the linguistic operations of the literary text became the major focus for the members of the *Tel Quel* group. They believed that by formulating a revolutionary textual practice that would bring to the surface those material productive forces that had been traditionally repressed, they could undermine the objectivist, capitalist ideology embedded in Western discourse and thus help to achieve by indirection a transformation of the social order and its repressive laws as well. In *Théorie d'ensemble*, Sollers explained *Tel Quel*'s position in the following way: "[B]y accentuating *the text*, its historical determinations and its mode of production . . . we have touched the nerve centers of the social unconscious in which we live and, in sum, the distribution of symbolic property [*propriété*]. As far as 'literature' is concerned, what we propose aims to be as subversive as Marx's critique of the classical economy" (p. 68). Thus the group came to see theory and practice as basically inseparable. The so-called literary activity of its various members was looked upon as a working extension of the theory, as an attempt to transform social, linguistic, and literary codes by means of a revolutionary textual practice. This does not mean, however, that the text was to be viewed as a simple "expression" of the theory or as a reinstatement of traditional mimetic principles, for the text did not merely reproduce a preexisting theoretical idea primarily because there was no idea as such to be reproduced. As Julia Kristeva defined it in one of her contributions to *Théorie d'ensemble*, "Semiotics: Science critique et/ou critique de la science," which incorporates what Derrida later referred to as Marxism's radically self-critical "spirit," the theory, like the literary text, was to function as an open-ended, self-critical exercise, one that would perpetually seek to uncover and undermine the ideological underpinnings of its own operation, and thus never allow itself to take on the character of a closed, universal, and reproducible system.

This desire to maintain a perpetually self-critical stance explains, in part at least, *Tel Quel*'s recourse to Freudian theory, which, in conjunction with the more revolutionary aspects of Marx's critique of bourgeois ideology, was to provide a means of counteracting not only the more dogmatic uses of Marxism but the more conservative strains within Marxist theory itself. By incorporating Freud's problematization of the subject and notions of libidinal heterogeneity that were excluded by a strictly Marxist analysis, the group believed that it could, in a sense, save that analysis from falling back into the subjectivist trap from which orthodox Marxism, in *Tel Quel*'s view, had never completely liberated itself. Despite its focus on "struggle, contradiction and practice" (that is, on those elements that undermine the unity of the individual and social subject), orthodox Marxist philosophy, as Kristeva argued in *Revolution in Poetic Language*, falls prey to the "anthropomorphization" that characterized the thinking of its philosophical predecessors. But in this case the notion of "human unity . . . is represented in Marx by the proletariat, which is viewed as the means for realizing the total man—mastered and unconflicted":

[M]an is above all a *"mastery,"* a *"solution to the conflict."* . . . Within the machine of contradictions in production and class conflicts, man remains an untouchable unity, in conflict with others but never in conflict "himself"; he remains, in a sense, neutral. He is either an oppressing or oppressed subject, a boss or an exploited worker or the boss of exploited workers, but never a *subject in process / on trial* who is related to the *process*—itself brought to light by dialectical materialism—in nature and society. (pp. 138–39)

The importance of *Tel Quel*'s reading of Marx in light of Freud-
ian (as well as Lacanian) psychoanalysis cannot be underestimated,
for it allows the group to stress the more revolutionary aspects of
Marxist theory that place the subject "in process/on trial" by view-
ing it as that which is no longer *constitutive of* but is instead
inscribed within a set of productive relations. That reading was in
many respects made possible by the French Marxist philosopher
Louis Althusser, who, in turning to the writings of Freud, Lacan,
and Mao Tse-tung in an attempt to reconstruct Marxism in anti-
humanist terms, contributed significantly to *Tel Quel*'s Marxist/
Freudian critique. Although various *Tel Quel* members later crit-
icized Althusser for going too far in his denial of the subject, his
critique of the humanist ideology prevailing in Marx's early work
and his affirmation of Marx's "break" with the "idealism of the
subject," which he replaced in his later work with a concept of
"human practice" and its possible modes of production, provided
the theoretical basis for *Tel Quel*'s attempt to exploit the revolu-
tionary possibilities of the Marxist dialectic.

Althusserian Marxism and Its Influence on 'Tel Quel'

According to Althusser's account, Marxist philosophy or, more
precisely, dialectical materialism, emerges in its more radically
antihumanist form following the development, most notably in
Marx's *Capital*, of a "new *science* of the history of 'social forma-
tions'" (that is, historical materialism) when history and society
are viewed not as the products of a collective or individual human
subject, who constructs social reality in accordance with some
predetermined design, but as the processes or *practices* in which
subjectivity is itself situated. Dialectical materialism, as the phi-
losophy involved in the investigation and theoretization of these
various practices that shape a given society and its history, thus
conceived of the social organization in a radically different way. By
foregrounding *productive process* as opposed to the finished prod-
uct, it pointed to the possibility of a major disruption within the
capitalist socioeconomic system, contesting the unity of the social
order itself and of the principal support of that order, the individual
social subject, whose identity is undermined by the very processes

that constitute it. Althusser's concept of *practice* thus became central to *Tel Quel*'s revolutionary project. In its ability to contest capitalism's "unifying," "reifying logic," by focusing on the productive forces that disturb notions of identity, system, and order, it could undermine a culture whose structures they regarded as totalizing and repressive.

In the process of defining his conception of practice in *For Marx* (1965), Althusser drew upon the economic model outlined in Marx's *Capital* to describe the ensemble of social relations, which have four distinct practices—economic, political, ideological, and theoretical—all of which transform "raw material" into a final "determinate product":

> By *practice* in general I shall mean any process of *transformation* of a determinate given raw material into a determinate *product*, a transformation effected by a determinate human labour, using determinate means (of "production"). In any practice thus conceived the *determinant* moment (or element) is neither the raw material nor the product, but the practice in the narrow sense: the moment of the *labour of transformation* itself, which sets to work, in a specific structure, men, means and a technical method of utilizing the means. This general definition of practice covers . . . the complex unity of the practices existing in a determinate society . . . [including] political practice—which . . . transforms its raw materials: social relations, into a determinate product (new social relations); ideological practice (ideology, whether religious, political, moral, legal or artistic, also transforms its object: men's "consciousness"): and finally, *theoretical practice* . . . [which] works on a raw material (representations, concepts, facts) [given to it] by other practices, whether "empirical", "technical" or "ideological."[14]

But once again the "determinant moment" in each practice is not a human consciousness or will; it is not the men who are engaged in the activity of labor, since labor can no longer be viewed as a subject-centered process of production; rather, the process of production itself gathers together the raw materials, the men who utilize them, and the means of production. This notion of practice was to have dramatic consequences for theory, particularly for Althusser's and ultimately for *Tel Quel*'s own reconceptualization of dialectical materialism. In functioning, for Althusser at least, as a kind of "subjectless" theoretical analysis, Marxist philosophy (that is, dialectical materialism) would enable us not only to think the *process* of social formation unencumbered by the subjectivist constraints of traditional political and economic philosophies, which merely reduce social complexity to some underlying essence or simple causal principle, but also to examine and ultimately to revolutionize the very functioning of theoretical discourse itself.

Proceeding first to the implications of the Marxist dialectic for an analysis of the process of social formation, I should point out that Althusser arrived at his understanding of that process through an encounter between Marxist-Leninist theory and the writings of Mao and Freud. Indeed, this aspect of Althusserian Marxism was especially appealing to *Tel Quel*, since it aimed to subvert through Freud and Mao the logic of the Hegelian dialectic by challenging, as Sollers writes in *Sur le matérialisme*, its "idealist conception of contradiction."[15] Drawing upon Freud's notions of "overdetermination," "condensation," and "displacement" as well as on the "law of uneven development" advanced by both Lenin and Mao, Althusser stresses, as Sollers points out, the complexities involved in social development by showing that "reality is not a substantive and closed field" of the kind presupposed either by a predominantly capitalist ideology or by the subjectivist, idealist philosophies that ultimately support it; reality is instead, according to Sollers, "the opening (historical, natural, social, conceptual) *produced* by the struggle of opposites" (p. 140). In opposition, however, to the Hegelian model of contradiction, which posits, according to Althusser and Sollers, a "simple original unity" that then splits into two opposites only to be reconstituted, following the negation of the negation, as a "new simple unity," Marxism sees contradiction as a complex confrontation of forces, which are contained in all the practices making up a given human society and which are in a sense mutually conditioned.

A brief review of the substructure/superstructure formation as it functions for Marxists in the course of social development reveals that when the material forces of production have developed to such a point that they enter into conflict with the existing relations of production, which are essentially property relations controlled by the dominant class, there is a contradiction within the economic substructure, and social revolution ensues. As a result of these changes within the economic substructure, revolutionary changes within the superstructure (society's ideological, political, religious, and philosophical practices) also occur. What Althusser shows, however, as Sollers emphatically points out, is that in claiming that the economic substructure conditions the superstructure, Marx is not arguing that the process of social development can be reduced to a simple economic determinism. Although the superstructure is in many respects conditioned by the modes of production that shape human activity and thought, the reverse, as Sollers maintains following Althusser, is also true. Ideology and political and religious institutions help shape the economic substructure as well and thus do not deny but also testify to the role of human agency in the process of social change. This interpenetration of opposites is further complicated by the contradictions inherent in the economic substructure itself, which is more than a simple contradiction between two opposing forces (that is, between the developing forces of production and the existing relations of production, which attempt to obstruct further development). Although these forces are joined in a hierarchical relationship of subordination and dominance, they are at the same time mutually dependent, with each functioning as the condition of the existence of the other. As Sollers writes, citing Althusser: " '[C]ontradiction' is inseparable from the total structure of the social body in which it is found, inseparable from its formal *conditions* of existence, and even from the *instances* it governs; it is radically *affected by them*, determining, but also determined in one and the same movement, and determined by the various *levels* and *instances* of the social formation it animates; it might be called *overdetermined in its principle*."[16]

To this "reflection of the conditions of existence of the contradiction within itself" Althusser thus assigns the Freudian term "overdetermination" in an effort to distinguish the Marxist from the Hegelian dialectic. Used by Freud to designate the representation of multiple dream-thoughts in a single image, the term allows Althusser to emphasize the permutations and interdependencies that propel social history forward, permutations that are produced not simply by external conditions but that are inherent in the developing system itself and whose contradictory structures develop unevenly depending on their particular social and historical context. Add to this schema Althusser's incorporation of Mao's distinction between "principal and secondary contradiction," between "the principal and secondary aspect of a contradiction," as well as between "antagonistic and non-antagonistic contradiction," and "the Marxist conception of contradiction appears," as Althusser tells us in For Marx, "in a quite un-Hegelian light" (p. 94 n. 6). For social change is determined by a plurality of external and internal causes, producing an " 'accumulation' of contradictions" that "fuse" or "condense," if they have not been neutralized or "displaced," into a "ruptural unity"—with the result that a social revolution takes place (p. 99). Thus, by defining through his reading of Marx, Freud, Lenin, and Mao the specificity of Marxist contradiction as a process that is "complexly-structurally-unevenly-determined" (p. 209) (that is, in other words, "overdetermined" in its essence), Althusser sees himself completing the Marxist project by giving it a more precise, theoretical formulation, and in so doing, he claims to have "reached the Marxist dialectic itself" (p. 217) by describing it in all its complexity.

Although Sollers did not offer an unqualified endorsement of the latter conclusion, claiming that Althusser's approach was still too abstract, too theoretical, and too closely aligned with the academic discourses of the French Communist Party to fully account for the "process of contradiction posed by Lenin and developed considerably by Mao Tse-Tung," he did recognize that Althusser had provided "the only significant analysis of dialectical materialism" available in France at that time.[17] Althusser's reworking of Marxist theory not only permitted social reality to be seen as a "plurality of instances" whose underlying structures are complex and heterogeneous, but it also allowed a rethinking of theory itself. For theory too, as Althusser tried to show, is a form of practice that transforms a "given raw material into a determinate product." What is produced, in this case, is knowledge, and so the mechanisms involved in the production of that knowledge are also susceptible to analysis. Thus, going beyond the standard definition of dialectical materialism as "the science of the more general laws governing the development of nature, society and thought,"[18] Althusser extends that concept to encompass the practice of theory itself. In order to do this, however, he must make a distinction between two different notions of theory, one conforming to conventional "empiricist" epistemologies, which, despite their claims of objectivity, ultimately locate knowledge in the abstractions of a perceiving subject and must, therefore, be viewed as essentially "pre-scientific" and ideological; and the other referring to the more truly "scientific" practice of the Marxist dialectic, a practice that Althusser used the term "Theory" (with a capital T) to designate.

Defined more specifically as the "Theory of theoretical practice," dialectical materialism thus comes to constitute, in Althusser's mind, a revolutionary rupture within the practice of philosophy. Its examination of the mechanisms involved in the production of knowledge exposes the "ideological," "pre-scientific" philosophical foundations out of which dialectical materialism itself, following the "epistemological break," emerged. And it is this concept of the dialectic that the members of the *Tel Quel* group initially embraced. In *Theorie d'ensemble*, which opens with an acknowledgment of Althusser's influence on many of the essays in the collection, Sollers writes: "Theory should be understood in the sense that Althusser gives it so decisively. It is a 'specific form of practice'" capable of analyzing and ultimately critiquing not only its own ideological and formal conditions but the ideological conditions structuring other practices as well: "Let us cite once again this fundamental text *For Marx*: 'The only Theory able to . . . criticize ideology in all its guises, including the disguises of the technical practices of science, is the Theory of theoretical practice (as distinct from ideological practice): the materialist dialectic or dialectical materialism, the conception of the Marxist dialectic in its *specificity*.' "[19]

Although Althusser later rejected (as did Sollers) this early definition of the dialectic as "Theory," claiming that its abstract formulations inadequately addressed the political realities of the class struggle, his reinterpretation of Marxist philosophy and his attempt to construct a new theory of ideology provided the inspiration for *Tel Quel*'s revolutionary *pratique scripturale*. *Tel Quel*'s concept of practice, however, expanded upon the Althusserian version (in a way that ultimately worked both for and against Althusser) by focusing on the materiality of the text and by delving further, as a result, into the problematic of the subject and language, both of which remained within the realm of a fundamentally capitalist ideology. The question of language, which Althusser never seriously considered, was implicitly raised in his own definition of ideology. Describing it as a "system of representations (images, myths, ideas or concepts)" through which the subject constructs an imaginary sense of wholeness out of the contradictions that constitute it, Althusser seems to point to the necessity of the task, subsequently taken up by *Tel Quel*, of examining the structure of language itself and of thereby unmasking and destabilizing the ideological precepts structuring representationalist forms of discourse and other signifying practices as well.[20] To this end, *Tel Quel* proposed adding to Althusser's elaboration of the dialectic a "science of writing," which, in treating "different practices (philosophical, scientific, aesthetic, social) *as texts*," would uncover what ideology tries to hide: the materiality of textual production whose unmasking would have a "liberating" effect in many different domains. As Sollers writes in *Théorie d'ensemble*:

> To make "textuality" appear would thus be at the same time to liberate us . . . in relation to the archeological accumulations [*l'entassement*] of our culture (and to pursue more successfully, as a result, the dialogue with other cultures) but also to *turn them into* [*le faire basculer*] a more complex, more expansive practice. . . . The reflection upon the "preceding exteriority" [*l'extériorité préalable*] that is writing thus opens . . . onto a real, social practice encompassing at the same time the culture of the past—read, deciphered, rewritten—and its transformation into a new productive field, created today by Marxism. (p. 405)

An additional contribution to the group's emphasis on the subversive powers of Marxist materialism can be found in the theories of Vladimir Lenin, who, in stressing the more practical applications of Marxist theory, attracted the attention of Althusser as well. Indeed, Althusser's two essays on Lenin, "Lenin and Philosophy" and "Lenin before Hegel," reveal the extent to which his own thinking moved away from the abstractions of his earlier definition of the dialectic as "Theory" toward a more Leninist configuration, with the dialectic functioning, in this case, as a "practice of political intervention" in the realm of theory.[21] Following Lenin's claim that all philosophy is political, Althusser points specifically to the partisanship at work within the structure of philosophy itself which is marked, as Lenin argued, by an incessant struggle between two different epistemologies: idealism and materialism. Althusser saw the history of that struggle in philosophy as the expression of the historical division between the classes in a given society. Within the capitalist social system, for example, the dominant discourses of philosophy are produced by members of the dominant bourgeois class whose fundamentally idealist ideology is placed in opposition to the "proletarian [and, therefore, materialist] class position." Given, then, that the debate between idealism and materialism comes to be seen as a reflection of the class struggle in the domain of theory, it is, therefore, in theory that the class struggle can also play itself out. By tracing a " 'dividing line' inside the theoretical domain" between philosophical idealism and a more profoundly "scientific" but anti-empiricist materialism, Lenin's new practice of philosophy would, according to Althusser, be able to repel "the assaults of idealist philosophy" and adopt a materialist "proletarian class position." In this sense, Lenin's transformation of Marxist philosophy into a revolutionary, materialist practice constitutes a form of political intervention, one that transforms philosophy and, in Althusser's words, "can to some extent *assist* in the transformation of the world."[22]

Despite this last rather tepid endorsement, on a practical level at least, of the revolutionary capabilities of Marxist-Leninist theory, Althusser's accentuation of the materialist dimensions of Marxism and his effort to contest bourgeois ideology by theoretical means elicited the enthusiastic approval of *Tel Quel*: "[Althusser's] articulation of Marx and Lenin with Freud . . . ," Sollers wrote in the summer 1969 issue of *Tel Quel*, "has profoundly transformed the field of knowledge. . . . [B]y reactivating the line of demarcation between *idealism* and *materialism*, [he] has signaled . . . an essential, ideological moment of the present period, a moment in which bourgeois or petty-bourgeois ideology *must* unmask itself."[23] With regard to the specific concept of ideology, however, Althusser's views were only partially embraced by *Tel Quel*, primarily and

paradoxically because of his insistence on the materiality of ideol-
ogy itself. Rather than envisioning a practice that is structured, like
all practices, by a multiplicity of contradictory forces, including
the unstable relationship between idealism and materialism, be-
tween subject and object, Althusser in *Tel Quel*'s view undermined
his concept of ideological practice by a curious denial of the subject.
In his eagerness, as an antihumanist Marxist, to counter the subjec-
tivist notion that ideology is the product of a human consciousness
that uses it as an instrument of manipulation and domination,
Althusser claimed instead that ideology is a "profoundly uncon-
scious" structure, one that imposes itself "on the vast majority of
men not via their 'consciousness' " but by "act[ing] functionally on
men via a process that escapes them: Men 'live' their ideologies,"
Althusser wrote in *For Marx*. It is "in ideology . . . that men *become
conscious* of their place in the world and in history" (p. 233). Ideol-
ogy is not therefore simply determined by the human subject,
according to Althusser; the human subject also is determined in
and through ideology, constituted by the structure of ideas and
relations that brings him into being *as* a subject and that fosters his
illusions of subjective wholeness and self-sufficiency. This occurs
through what Althusser described in a subsequent essay as the act
of "hailing" or "interpellation," through which the individual is
singled out, addressed by others, and thus accorded his own sense of
identity:

> [I]deology "acts" or "functions" in such a way that it . . . "trans-
> forms" the individuals into subjects . . . by that very precise
> operation which I have called *interpellation* or hailing, and
> which can be imagined along the lines of the most commonplace
> everyday police (or other) hailing: "Hey, you there!" Assuming
> that the theoretical scene I have imagined takes place in the
> street, the hailed individual will turn round. By this mere one-
> hundred-and-eighty-degree physical conversion, he becomes a
> *subject*. Why? Because he has recognized that the hail was
> "really" addressed to him, and that "it was *really him* who was
> hailed" (and not someone else).[24]

For *Tel Quel*, however, this identification of ideology and lan-
guage (in the form of the "interpellated" subject) was laden with
problems insofar as it constituted a denial of the subject and of the

complexity of the subject's relation to language. As the following comments in a 1972 issue of the *Tel Quel* journal show, the group believed that both the subject *and* language were ultimately subsumed by Althusser under the overpowering, unconscious structure that he called "ideology":

> The subject in discourse is not the one "interpellated by ideology"; the unconscious is not identical with the position of class but they maintain among themselves complex relations . . . that must be studied scientifically. . . . [A] materialist science of ideologies will be able to articulate dialectically the *subject* of the signifying economy and the subject of ideology, as it articulates dialectically *language* and *ideology*. Do not make us take the dogmatism repressing language *under* ideology for a revolutionary theory (e.g., ideology "interpellates" the subject, etc.). A mechanism of this kind condemns those who engage in it to a fundamental misconception of both the subject *and* of ideology. . . . We know where all of this leads: to the restoration of capitalism, to ideological repression pure and simple in the name of "ideological apparatuses" where proletarians exist in name only [*qui n'ont plus de proletariens que le nom*].[25]

These remarks become particularly curious, however, when one considers that *Tel Quel*'s own emphasis upon the structuring role of language, through which the subject emerges as a conscious identity, functions in a way that is not unlike Althusser's notion of ideology insofar as language, like ideology, is not simply the product of a preconstituted consciousness but is the very structure through which that consciousness is constituted. Thus, one could argue that in both cases the subject is placed, using Kristeva's expression, "in process/on trial," inscribed within the linguistic and ideological practices that undermine as they form the subject's "integrated" identity. Indeed, if this amounts to a conflation of language and ideology and a concomitant reduction of complexity, it is perhaps, as I shall argue later, to be found in *Tel Quel*'s own theory, which ultimately overemphasized the repressive role of language as it serves the predominant ideology and underemphasized what they actually intended to accentuate, that is, those contradictions *within* language that would prevent it from performing its unifying function.

Suffice it to say for the moment, however, that *Tel Quel*'s remarks, which came after its break with the French Communist Party in 1971, reveal a marked change in attitude toward Althusserian Marxism, precipitated in part by Althusser's own unwillingness to part company with an organization that was, in *Tel Quel*'s mind, becoming more regressive. Thus, despite the many similarities in outlook, in the years following *Tel Quel*'s rejection of the PCF's "ossified Marxism," the members of the group became increasingly critical of the Althusserian perspective, which had, as far as they were concerned, ceased to be materialist. Althusser's analysis of ideology, his emphasis on the theoretical antihumanism he found in Marx's later work, *Capital*, with its notion of history as a "process without a subject," constituted a denial of "material process" in which the subject is also inscribed and thus erased the plurality of contradictions that reside within any social or signifying practice. As Sollers argued in reaction to Althusser's 1972 essay "Reply to John Lewis":

> Althusser repeats here his own personal arguments, for example, that of the "process without a subject," which, in my opinion, has nothing to do with Marxism. This argument avoids asking the real question: that of the dialectic between the subjective and the objective, between external and internal causality, and ultimately, all the questions relating to the *multiple* and *uneven* process of contradiction. The same applies to *practice*: it is impossible to underscore the importance of it in a "process without a subject." An immediate illustration: the political practice of Althusser himself. After having refused for years, he now lends his support to the political line of the French [Communist] Party.[26]

Echoing Sollers's remarks, Bernard Sichère, another contributor to the *Tel Quel* journal, took aim at Althusser's controversial distinction between science and ideology. Althusser's assumption that the dialectic—as a more profoundly scientific, anti-empiricist form of knowledge—can at some point free itself from its ideological moorings was seen by Sichère as accomplishing, once again, the "erasure of the category of contradiction and the category of material process": "Ideology is not the opposite of science because there is no Ideology or Science, only sciences and ideologies which are thought in the ensemble of material contradictions at a given moment of a given society."[27] Not only that, Althusser's actual formulation of the distinction was fraught with inconsistencies, according to Sichère, particularly when he claimed that there is no getting outside the realm of ideology while positing at the same time a radical rupture between Marx's new "scientific discovery" and the "prescientific theoretical ideologies" from which the Marxist dialectic was presumably able to disengage itself:

> It is because he lacks a proletarian theory of knowledge, because he lacks materialism, that Althusser remains caught in unresolvable difficulties and contradictions: on the one hand, he rigorously opposes ideology to science; on the other, he defines Marxism as an ideology "which is based this time on science— something that has never been seen before" (*Reading Capital*). But what does it mean to say that an ideology is "based this time on science," when [one claims at the same time that] "ideology is eternal, like the unconscious," when "only an ideological outlook could have imagined societies without ideology and accepted the utopian idea of a world in which ideology (not just one of its historical forms) would disappear without trace, to be replaced by science"? (*For Marx*)[28]

If, however, Sichère was right in pointing to those places in Althusser's writing where he articulates what appears to be a rather strict dichotomy between ideology and science, it should also be recognized that the dialectic for Althusser was not "a science like any other" but expressed an anti-empiricist, anti-positivist conception of knowledge, one that was in many respects quite similar to that of *Tel Quel*. Stressing the fundamentally ideological character of traditional empiricist forms of knowledge, which assume a perfect identity between a knowing subject and its object whose essence is simply uncovered by the cognitive process, Althusser sought to wedge an opening in this cognitive enclosure by examining the mechanisms involved in the cognitive process itself, mechanisms that ultimately undermine this correspondence theory of knowledge by showing that the act of cognition itself is not adequate to but involves the transformation of its object. Here once again the notion of practice comes into play—this time in the form of a scientific practice of theory that theorizes its own theoretical practice, that questions and analyzes its own continually evolving thought by focusing not so much on the product of knowledge but on the inner workings that allow that knowledge to be produced.

It is in this sense, then, that Althusser's materialist epistemology is considered to work in opposition to the closures of an empiricist ideology of knowledge. Conceived as an open-ended, inherently self-critical exercise, it examines those processes that had previously remained unreflected and, in so doing, engages in a critique of and a certain resistance to the empiricist, ideological notions of identity that are also part of its structure. Indeed, when Althusser claims in *For Marx* that "there is no *pure* theoretical practice, no perfectly transparent science which . . . will always be preserved . . . from the threats and taints . . . of the *ideologies* which besiege it" (p. 170), and when he suggests that dialectical materialism must engage in a continuous struggle against the ideology that occupies it, his notion of the dialectic is remarkably similar to *Tel Quel*'s own. By incorporating the materialist perspective and applying it to language and to the movement of the subject within the signifying economy, *Tel Quel*'s *pratique semiotique* is not based on the assumption that a dialectical analysis can be dissociated from ideology; it assumes instead that all forms of knowledge, dialectical or otherwise, are ideologically grounded and must be challenged from within the discourse of ideology itself.

Thus, in the course of investigating language and the laws at work in the production of the linguistic sign, the members of the *Tel Quel* group adopted in many respects Althusser's anti-empiricist stance. Although their "semiotic practice," as formulated primarily by Kristeva, incorporated the techniques and procedures of structural semiotics, its goal was to subvert scientific and theoretical discourse by attempting to reveal the basically ideological status of any scientific inquiry that remains uncritical of its own constructs, subsuming its object of study under a systematic body of concepts. While imitating in many instances the procedures of modern science and frequently borrowing from scientific and theoretical models (particularly those provided by structural linguistics and mathematics), the theory was to engage, in Kristeva's view, in a constant critique of its own preconceptions, always contesting and revising the models it used and produced, never allowing itself to adopt the fixed categories of the scientific or philosophical system. Thus, as a scientific method that was at the same time an antiscience, a critique of its own assumptions and methodology, Kristeva's revisionary semiotics claimed to move beyond the restrictive analytical models of the exact sciences and, in so doing, to challenge the objectifying and therefore reifying systems of discourse dominating all of our intellectual disciplines. In opposition, then, to what they came to view as Althusser's privileging of theory, with its controversial dichotomy between science and ideology, *Tel Quel* sought to articulate a space that lay at the intersection between the two, applying the principles of dialectical materialism to the literary text in an effort to uncover those mechanisms within language that cannot be simply equated with ideology, but that expose instead the limits of all ideologically structured practices, including those of science and theory and of literature as well.

'Tel Quel' 's Subversive Literary/Theoretical Practice

By moving Althusser's ideological struggle to the sphere of language and the literary text, the members of the *Tel Quel* group were not, however, attempting to replace Althusser's "theoreticism" with an exaggerated emphasis on literature. The distinction between the theoretical and the literary indeed collapses under *Tel Quel*'s notion of a revolutionary textual practice. Although the boundaries between the two were preserved on a superficial level (the group still used the categories of genre when discussing its "literary" activity—Sollers wrote what he called "novels," and the works of Pleynet and Roche were categorized as "poems"), the distinction was set up only to be torn down, undermined on a more fundamental level by a concept of the "text" which ultimately contested the conventions of genre and the traditional distinction between literary language and prose. What this means, then, is that any effort to examine the "literary" activity of the group would have to be done in conjunction with the theory. A reading of the poetic practice of Marcelin Pleynet would indeed be inadequate if it failed to account not only for *Tel Quel*'s theory of a revolutionary

poetic language, which at that time was given its most complete
formulation by Kristeva in *Séméiotiké*, but also for Pleynet's own
theoretical essays and most particularly his critical readings of
Lautréamont. Pleynet's *Lautréamont par lui-même* was one of the
first critical studies to consider Lautréamont's work as an open-
ended *pratique textuelle* and thus to oppose traditional biographi-
cal approaches with their notion of the author as creative subject by
calling attention to the writer's and reader's inscription into the
text's productive dynamics.[29] Although one would have to agree
that Pleynet's emphasis on *écriture* (writing) seems to support
those critics who stress *Tel Quel*'s formalism (and we shall see later
that the group did not succeed on a theoretical level in liberating
itself from certain formalist constraints), it should be remembered
that the group constructed a theory of the open text that was meant
to counter formalist principles.[30]

Indeed, for Kristeva the term "text," as elaborated in *Séméiotiké*
through her analysis of the writings of Barthes and Bakhtin, is not
confined to the purely linguistic, written body of literary or nonlit-
erary works but incorporates the unwritten, nonlinguistic signify-
ing practices also involved in the process of meaning formation.
Kristeva's notion of the poetic text, then, should not be viewed as a
simple linguistic entity; it is, rather, that which moves beyond the
boundaries imposed by language to become what Kristeva calls a
"pratique translinguistique," embracing through language those
elements that participate in the formation of the various operations
within the "literary" work while remaining in themselves irreduc-
ible to discourse. The structure of the text thus designates, accord-
ing to Kristeva in her still untranslated essay on Barthes, "what is
supplementary to the written, mute but always there, called to the
written surface by the textual variable . . . [which] makes the absent
texts (politics, the economy, myths) appear in the written text" (pp.
82–83). Emerging as an "open, transtextual infinity" that breaks
through the barrier imposed by the linguistic sign, the modern
"poetic" text brings into focus the whole complex range of non-
linguistic, productive practices or "texts" that participate in the
constitution of meaning. Although Kristeva claims that this princi-
ple is fundamental to the structure of any text, whether it be tradi-
tional or modern, she maintains that only in the modern "literary"

work is its intertextual function rendered explicit and actually becomes a governing principle: "For the poetic texts of modernity [this dialogue with other texts] is, we could say without exaggeration, a fundamental law: they produce themselves while absorbing and destroying at the same time the other texts of the intertextual space" (p. 257).

Revealing the influence of Kristeva's thinking on the other members of the *Tel Quel* group, her notion of intertextuality was embraced not only by Sollers, who stressed in his own analysis of Lautréamont the intertextual, translinguistic character of Lautréamont's texts; it shaped Pleynet's analysis as well, leading him to produce a second essay on Lautréamont in which he attempted to modify his earlier more formalist approach. Here, in response to a critique of his initial study that was offered, interestingly enough, by Sollers, Pleynet explains that an overzealous attempt to liberate Lautréamont criticism from a too strict adherence to biographical detail and literary sources, both of which are based on a much too traditional notion of mimetic representation, led him to overemphasize the formal, linguistic operations of the text and to neglect the plurality of nonlinguistic social, historical, and psychological forces that also shape the literary work. Drawing upon the analyses provided by Sollers and Kristeva, Pleynet thus expanded upon his earlier conclusions by focusing more specifically on the text's social and historical complexity, a complexity that emerges, according to Pleynet, not as an objectifiable reality that is mechanically reproduced within the linguistic confines of the text but as a multiplicity of often contradictory, productive forces that participate in the very process of textual production.[31]

Given, then, this constant exchange of ideas between the *Tel Quel* poets and theorists, the theoretical writings of the various members of the group should not be ignored in a consideration of *Tel Quel*'s poetic practice, a practice that, as we have seen, was to have aesthetic as well as important social and political ramifications. On the basis of their growing interest in Marxist theory, certain members of the group began to regard language and the literary text as a means to further the cause of social revolution and came to embrace a whole set of assumptions, some of which, as we shall see, should have been examined more critically, about the linguistic and cultural structures that their revolutionary project was meant to transform. Claiming that communicative language and the traditional notion of mimesis that underlies it are principal vehicles in the preservation of the ideological structures that dominate Western culture, the group, as I will attempt to demonstrate later, ended up overemphasizing the repressive function of mimetic representation (and of the social organization it supports) while neglecting the contradictions, which the group itself worked so diligently to uncover, implied in the representative function itself. Indeed, the considerable attention that *Tel Quel* paid to the literary tradition stemmed from the view that the Western concept of the text as a closed and basically meaningful literary object, whose representational language effectively safeguards the objective status of the reality it portrays, ultimately works to preserve the oppressive political structures that have dominated Western society from the feudal era to the bourgeois social system of the present day. Related to what Kristeva described as the traditionally "positivist" epistemology at the core of Western thought, the structure and function of the traditional literary text were seen to perpetuate an objectivist view of the world, one that had consistently refused to recognize that its belief in an ordered and objectifiable universe was not due to something inherent in the nature of things, but was a function of the predominant ideology that seeks to reduce the multifarious nature of the real to comprehensible and therefore controllable limits. Communicative, representational language, which assumes the possibility of an unproblematized replication of a preexistent social, psychological, or conceptual reality, and traditional aesthetics, whose logic of meaning and identity also posits a fixed and representable universe, are thus structured by the exclusionary and repressive mechanisms inhering in a very traditional notion of mimesis that suppresses the duplicities within the mimetic process itself by insisting, first of all, that language remain separate from the reality it imitates and then by engaging in the denial of that difference. Through this repression of the productive processes that interfere with the transmission of the author's intended meaning, the unified structure of the literary text and its communicative language thus serve the needs, according to the members of the *Tel Quel* group, of an essentially totalizing and oppressive social order, eliminating difference and heterogeneity in order to preserve the closed structures that a cohesive social system requires.

Consequently, by challenging this concept of the text as a perfectly controlled, communicative object, whose carefully regulated operations ensure the production and ultimate consumption of a fixed and unified sense, Kristeva and her associates sought to undermine the capitalist, objectivist precepts that, in their view, structured the totality of Western discourse and, in so doing, to shake the foundations of the prevailing social structure with its static and reified vision of the world. The literary text was to become the laboratory for a radically new discourse, one that would attempt to move beyond the traditional subject-object polarity by exploding the boundaries that separate the literary object from its reading and writing subjects, by revealing what Western culture has consistently denied—that the language of the text does not simply mirror from a position of exteriority a preexistent psychological or social reality, but is actually constitutive of the reality it purports to describe, and that the reader, in turn, does not merely lift out or extract the meaning implicit with the work itself, but in fact participates in the production of that meaning through his own interpretive activity. To question the objective status of the literary text and of the reality it portrays was thus to undermine, according to *Tel Quel*, a whole system of interpretive conventions. The text could no longer be reduced to or enclosed within a single and finite meaning, but would require instead a recognition of the processes that go into the production of that meaning, processes that serve in effect to open up the text, to break down the boundaries so necessary not only to the traditional concept of language and the literary text, but to what they perceived as the entire structure of Western positivist thought.

A concept of the open text, which breaks through the boundaries imposed by the mimetic enclosure by focusing on the *process* of textual production rather than on the finished product (that is, on the supposedly unique meaning that the text produces), is thus what emerged in the course of the *Tel Quel* critique. Although that concept raises a number of questions that need to be considered more critically, it would be useful to examine its practical applications and to ask how the notion of an open-ended textual praxis shaped the literary production of the two Tel Quel poets as it emerged during this collaborative period at Tel Quel. A good selection for the purpose of answering that question would be Marcelin Pleynet's Stanze, which, when it was first published in its entirety in 1973 as part of a yet to be completed more "global" project, gives us perhaps the clearest indication of what he and the other members of the Tel Quel group meant when they described the text as an open-ended pratique textuelle. Pleynet set out to break down the boundaries imposed not simply by a strictly representational enclosure but also by the repressive philosophical, social, and political structures that he saw dominating the Western metaphysical tradition as a whole.[32] This was to be accomplished, according to Pleynet, whose work embraces and at the same time restructures the Marxist and Freudian model, by bringing out into the open the various modes of production constituting Western civilization, by focusing on the productive forces that an objectivist, "capitalist" view of the world consistently represses, and thereby disrupting the cohesiveness of representational discourse as well as the myths and ideologies upon which traditional notions of culture depend.

The Practice of the "Open" Text: Marcelin Pleynet's 'Stanze'

The repressive power of a culture's ideological discourse is indeed evoked in Stanze's subtitle "Incantation dite au bandeau d'or" (An incantation recited to the golden headband). Referring to a Chinese legend in which an undisciplined, magic monkey, Souen le singe, is subdued by placing around his forehead a golden headband that tightens when his master recites an incantation, Pleynet uses it as a metaphor for the constitution of culture whose linguistic, representationalist structures, supported by what Pleynet has described as the dominant "bandeau économique," master the contradictory and unruly and ensure cultural homogeneity. By using Marxist theory to trace the various stages of economic development in constituting Western civilization, Pleynet does not, however, give a historically accurate description of the dominant modes of production but draws our attention to the plurality of historical forces that shape the sociopolitical community. He does this by pointing not only to linguistic, economic, and ideological factors but also to those destabilizing elements that, in the manner of the unruly *singe* of the legend, have the potential to challenge the prevailing social order through the disruption of the incantation's totalizing logic. This involves the disruption of certain totalizing aspects of Marxist theory as well, for although Pleynet clearly uses Marx's analysis of the relations of production and their different stages of development, his work also undermines its linear and developmental logic.

Thus, while each of the four cantos that comprise the text is devoted to one of the different modes of production—to the slave economy (canto III) or to the Asiatic mode of production (canto II)—certain stages are not only completely fictional but anachronistic as well. The first stage is characterized by its primitive, pre-Asiatic modes of production, but it is also what Pleynet calls "post-imperialist," with references to the rise in the price of gold in the 1970's. In an effort to call into question the schematization that the representation of a linear historical evolution would imply, Pleynet confronts the logic of that representation at every turn with what would normally be filtered out by communicative discourse. The reference to the thought of a Greek philosopher thus appears alongside nonsensical word games, homoerotic imagery, slang, and vulgarity, bringing into the text's so-called historical survey what Pleynet has described as our "histoire monstrueuse," those contradictory and marginalized elements that are normally excluded by traditional representations of history but that also make up the Western "cultural adventure."

Thus, in all four cantos, the pre-Oedipal, prelinguistic, pulsional forces that both constitute and undermine the cohesiveness of the individual subject and the discursiveness of his language are also clearly inscribed. As Pleynet writes, in a deliberately incoherent fashion:

> lait jaillissant de 60 000 seins
> iaiaiaiaiaiaiaiaiaiaiaiaiaiaiaiaiaia
>
> . . .

mère des dieux
écrite sifflement
. . .
uraetérus
ou division dans sa logique
. . .
musique renversée de la contradiction
(p. 67)

milk gushing from 60,000 breasts
iaiaiaiaiaiaiaiaiaiaiaiaiaiaiaiaiaia
. . .
mother of gods
written whistlingly
. . .
uraeterus
or division in its logic
. . .
inverted music of contradiction

The pages' pulsional, irregular rhythms, their infantile, often scato-
logical and nonsensical language call up Freudian images of the oral
and anal phases and point to that return of the repressed uncon-
scious so desired by *Tel Quel*. Although one could argue that a cer-
tain privileging of libidinal heterogeneity is evident in the cantos'
celebration of the transgressive capabilities of the semiotic (which
paradoxically determines the identity of a stage in which notions of
identity have not yet been constituted), the text's inscription of pre-
Oedipal instinctuality at the same time underscores the limita-
tions of a strictly linear interpretation of Marxist theory. In mark-
ing the presence of the unconscious as an otherness traversing the
different stages of cultural and economic development, the cantos
uncover a quality of sameness that undermines cultural unique-
ness, for none of the stages completely replaces the stages that
precede or follow. The first, pre-Asiatic stage, with its visions of the
"phallic mother" and its "dream of origins," reveals the movement
of history as a "monstrous force" whose infinitely repeated or re-
peatable beginnings contain traces not of an original plenitude but
of an always earlier, more ancient "degradation" (*pourrissement*):

la terre arrêtée de tout son poids et reconnue dans
la terre la forme empreintée
                          la trace la plus ancienne
le cadavre pétrifié la tête sur les genoux
                                    la plus vieille
histoire mourant
immobile à travers l'âge passé dans l'enfance

                                                    (p. 31)

the earth immobilized with all its weight and recognized in
the earth the imprinted form
                          the most ancient trace
the petrified cadaver its head in its lap
                                    the oldest
history dying
immobile through the age passed in childhood

In exposing this primitive "conditional" phase of cultural de-
velopment, the first canto sets into motion the processes that will
ultimately constitute the individual and collective subject. The
broken, pulsional rhythms structuring the canto's language, its dis-
membered bodies and unrepressed sexuality will not, however, be
left behind as a new, supposedly superior stage of economic de-
velopment emerges. Although each subsequent stage contains ref-
erences to those elements peculiar to it—to the cultivation of crops
and to the construction of systems of irrigation in Egypt, for exam-
ple, in canto II—each is also traversed by the archaic residues of its
conscious and unconscious past. Indeed, this "gliding" nonlinear
history exceeds the boundaries of representational language by
incorporating future time and space as well. Images of Egypt's past
collide with events of a later historical period. One encounters a
more recent newspaper clipping on the Palestinian resistance, a
radio announcement on China's admission to the United Nations,
a reference to the Aswân Dam in 1956, maps of India, Pakistan, and
China, all indicating that the historical moment is never self-con-
tained but must be seen in reference to other times and places. In
stressing the web of relations and forces in which a particular
culture (and the subject who observes it) is situated, *Stanze* thus
incorporates certain aspects of Marxist theory even while going

beyond it, for Marx, as François Bruzzo points out in his analysis of
Stanze, saw the evolution of his different modes of production in
relational terms. Interestingly enough, Marx used the anatomy of a
monkey or ape to explain the evolutionary process:

> Bourgeois society is the historical organization of the most devel-
> oped and most differentiated production that exists. The catego-
> ries that express its conditions and the understanding of its struc-
> tures allow at the same time for an understanding of the structure
> and the relations of production of all the types of society that have
> disappeared into the ruins and the elements from which it was
> constructed and of which certain vestiges, not yet obsolete, con-
> tinue to linger within it, and of which certain virtualities are fully
> opened out, etc. In the anatomy of man there is a key to the
> anatomy of the monkey. . . . Thus [in a similar manner] the
> bourgeois economy provides the key to the ancient economy.[33]

As an image of temporal and spatial otherness that traverses
individual and social identity, the monkey in Marx's evolutionary
tale, as in Pleynet's *Stanze*, marks the impossibility of cultural
closure. That it also undermines orthodox Marxism's teleological
narrative is a possibility, while overlooked by Marx, that is con-
fronted directly by Pleynet's *singe magique*, whose role, in com-
parison to the Marxist version, is considerably more radical. Not
only does the monkey come to be associated with the contradictory
forces of production that make up the social "unconscious," and
not only can it be linked to the "monstrous" libidinal impulses of
the individual unconscious, but, as a figure in a Chinese legend, it
inserts a different, nonteleological logic into the heart of the West-
ern "bourgeois" perspective:

> commencement   histoire
> dans sa force monstrueuse   prit-elle dialec-
> tiquement l'apparence du grand singe dont les mem-
> bres sont écrits
>
> aussi la matière dans sa force monstrueuse prit-elle
> dialectiquement l'apparence du grand singe dont les
> membres ont la fermeté de l'or
>
> . . .

légende sans commencement ni fin
commencée
accouplement sans commencement
ni fin et sans travail
ou encore ce qui change tout
près de lui sous lui le
singe savant couvert de sperme et éveillé sans autre
désir triant les femmes
ainsi   prit-elle   l'apparence
du grand singe force de combat
l'oreille en sang
mère armée
héros phallique

(pp. 16–18)

beginning   history
in its monstrous force   it took on dialec-
tically the appearance of the ape whose mem-
bers are written

also matter in its monstrous force took on
dialectically the appearance of an ape whose
members have the firmness of gold

. . .

legend without beginning or end
begun
coupling without beginning
or end and without work
or again what changes everything
near him under him the
learned ape covered with sperm and awakened without
any other desire selecting the women
thus it   took on   the appearance
of the ape force of combat
bloody ear
armed mother
phallic hero

Through the image of the *singe savant*, who provides us with no
master narrative or totalizing global vision, we thus come face to
face with an otherness that has not been excluded or repressed as we

pass from one stage to another but that is inscribed into the very dynamics of Pleynet's text as a process that both structures and inhabits cultural identity. Indeed, implicit in Pleynet's "cultural investigation" is the recognition that "culture" cannot be appropriated by a single, all-encompassing representation, for it emerges as an unobjectifiable locus of relations, a product not only of unconscious structuring forces that impel a subject toward an "other," thus providing the basis for the formation of the social organization, but of conscious ones as well. The concept of culture, according to Pleynet, is also an ideological construct and the product of a subject who is himself situated within the cultural history he investigates. As if to reinforce this notion, Pleynet draws attention to his own participation in the production of the text, outlining in almost excessive detail the organizational plan of what will eventually be nine cantos. As Pleynet tells it in the postface to his work, the cantos and the modes of production they represent are linked to a phrase, reconstructed by Pleynet, that appears in the work of a twelfth-century Chinese philosopher, Tshai Chhen. The phrase—"SI ON CONNAIT LES COMMENCEMENTS ON CONNAIT LES FINS" (IF ONE KNOWS THE BEGINNING ONE KNOWS THE END)—provides the grid, according to Pleynet, around which each of the cantos is organized, with each stage of economic development corresponding to one of the phrase's elements. As an example, "SI" is associated with the first canto's pre-Asiatic, post-imperialist period; "ON" is linked to the Asiatic mode, and so on. In addition, the phrase is incorporated into the spatial configuration of the "magic square" (carré magique), which, in accordance with the principles of what Pleynet calls "Chinese cosmogonic representation" (la représentation cosmogonique chinoise), is to be distributed as in the accompanying diagram.

```
  •   •  S  •   •                          •       •        •       •
    4     9     2                        LES     FINS      ON
  •   •   •   •                            •       •        •       •
E   3   5   7   W                  CONNAIT  COMMEN-   CONNAIT
                                             CEMENTS
  •   •   •   •                            •       •        •       •
    8     1     6                        LES      SI       ON
  •   •  N  •   •                          •       •        •       •
```

In giving Tshai Chhen's sentence the form of a square that remains indissociable from its circular "other," Pleynet aims to incorporate into his text all the contradictory aspects of the *carré magique*, whose finite angular lines and infinite circularity cannot be subsumed under a single interpretive category that would determine it as either "open" or "closed"; its form contains both possibilities simultaneously and therefore, as the text's epigraph suggests, remains indeterminate: "Regardée, elle ["*la grande image*," which is also "the magic square"] ne vaut pas qu'on la voie; écoutée, elle ne vaut pas qu'on l'entende. Mais employée, elle ne peut être épuisée" (p. 152) (Apprehended visually, [the magic square] is not worth seeing; apprehended audibly, it is not worth hearing. But when it is put to use, it cannot be worn out). Thus, although the structuring intentions and the precise guidelines for reading that Pleynet reveals in the text's postface appear to be in contradistinction to his emphasis on textual and cultural indeterminacy, it must be recognized that certain aspects of the spatial configuration outlined by Pleynet retain their enigmatic dimension and provide no overall comprehension of the text. As Pleynet writes: "Everything [is] arranged in a distributive grid which gives to each element its 'meaning' without for all that reducing it to its place on the extended line but, quite the contrary, drawing it into new relationships, into new conflicts from which it will not stop springing forth in new forms and [then] losing itself [*s'abîmer*]" (p. 159).

The meaninglessness usually associated with what Kristeva refers to as the "semiotic" is thus inscribed in what could be called the most "symbolic" section of the text, the postface, just as the "symbolic" operations of the postface are at work in the less discursive cantos that the postface supposedly explains. The entire structure of *Stanze*, like the square wheel it incorporates, is traversed by a multiplicity of contradictory elements. It functions as a complex cultural tapestry in which the interpretative, transformational activity of the writer and the constitutive operations of language are also inscribed. Not only have Marx's five stages of economic development been transformed by a writer who is historically situated and whose own approach has been determined by, among other things, his reading of a prior body of Chinese texts, but they have been subjected to the ordering law of language as well, to the phrase of a Chinese philosopher whose circular meaning redistributes the stages non-teleologically and inserts a more "primitive," Asiatic, non-Occidental logic into the supposedly more "advanced," Western stages of economic development.

In the course of that redistribution, however, the authority of language is undermined as well. The text's exposure of differentiality, of the relation to an other that has traditionally been effaced by the dominant ideology with its visions of cultural homogeneity, recalls Pleynet's Chinese legend and destabilizes its relations of power. The ordering representations of the master's incantations cannot control the magic monkey's shenanigans not because the monkey remains radically other and therefore untouchable, but because otherness is inscribed within the incantation itself, which functions as the discourse of ideology and, in Pleynet's words, as an "invocatory pulsion" (*pulsion invocante*), as a rhythmical *parole magique* that exceeds the bounds of representational discourse. Alterity is thus shown to be inscribed not only within the social and economic structures of a particular culture, not only within the speaking subject, but at the very heart of the language that constitutes them and that has now lost its constraining power.

The fact that the last post-imperialist canto constitutes a return to its pre-Asiatic, post-imperialist origins should not, then, be taken to indicate closure, for the text shows that the subject, whether it be collective or individual, is not a self-contained entity but is differentiated and multiple, always connected to an other, and incapable of closing in on itself. Indeed, the text's very title incorporates this multiplicity. Signifying, according to Pleynet, a "place of residence" or "dwelling" in Italian, a physical (and, one could add, political) "position" in English, and a poetic "stanza" in French, the title *Stanze* calls attention to the hybrid nature of the text as a practice that is both textual and worldly, literary and theoretical, poetic and political. Given that none of these meanings attains dominance, the text resists the theoretical dogmatism that insists upon a single point of view. The text does this not by remaining outside the closure that theory institutes but by incorporating theory and undermining its restrictive and reifying distinctions. For if Pleynet's textual practice is not simply theoretical, neither is it purely literary. Like the square wheel, the one is implied in the other, making it impossible to determine where literature or poetry ends and theory or the political begins and thus countering the integrated status and authority of each.

To assert, then, as did the members of the *Tel Quel* group, that the literary text is to be read in terms of the theory is to imply that the act of reading itself is to be performed differently, for the revolutionary text overturns not only its own literary and theoretical constructs but the conventions of reading as well. This is indeed the point of Pleynet's contribution to *Théorie d'ensemble*, "La Poésie doit avoir pour but . . ." (Poetry must have as a goal . . .), in which he analyzes the problem of reading in the "poetry" of his collaborator, Denis Roche. Here, he claims that the text cannot be viewed as a fixed object of analysis with specifiable properties and determinable boundaries; its open-ended structure resolutely resists all attempts at total comprehension and thus forces the reader, in the course of trying to establish patterns and logical consistencies, to become part of the process of textual production and alienated at the same time, made not only to recognize the inadequacies of his interpretive conclusions but also to become conscious of his own projections, to see that meaning and structure are not properties of the work itself, but are functions of the reader's interpretive strategies and constructs. The operations of the text thus bring to the surface the assumptions that govern all acts of comprehension and force the reader not only to challenge the authority of the constructs he imposes, but ultimately to question the entirety of his relations with the outside world. The reader of the *Tel Quel* text, then, comes to resemble Kristeva's semiotician. By constantly questioning the validity of his own interpretive assumptions, he becomes critical of his tendency to systematize, to reduce the complexity of the text to a simple and comprehensible structure.

The problem of reading was thus central to *Tel Quel*'s concept of an open-ended theoretical practice, and it raises one of the most fundamental questions of the entire enterprise, that of finding a way to read the revolutionary text in terms of the theory, in terms of its opposition to the concept of the closed literary object, without establishing the kinds of distinctions that in effect restore many of the objectivist assumptions that the group so vigorously attacked. It can be argued that *Tel Quel* theory did not succeed entirely in finding a satisfactory solution to the problem. As we shall see, their notion of the text as a revolutionary praxis did not always remain as unsystematic and as free of philosophical and ideological implications as the *Tel Quel* group would have liked to assume. That notion often depended on certain assumptions about the nature of the text and the act of reading that reinstated many of the positivist premises it meant to oppose. Indeed, as a result of their effort to construct and put into practice a theory of the "open" text intended to break down the boundaries imposed by Western positivist thought and by what they saw as an essentially repressive social order, *Tel Quel* was caught up in a situation that was, to say the least, self-contradictory. The group was involved in a collective effort to undermine traditional notions of the collective; it formulated a revolutionary program against the precepts of the traditionally programmed text. Although the group later came to question the revolutionary possibilities of the *Tel Quel* enterprise, its activity revealed an increasingly pronounced discrepancy between the group's revolutionary politics and its supposedly open-ended *travail textuel*.

Scissions, Ruptures, and the Marginalization of 'Tel Quel'

Unfortunately, Pleynet's "transhistorical adventure" bears little resemblance to the political pronouncements that proliferated at *Tel Quel* at the time of its publication and thus underscores the paradoxical nature of *Tel Quel*'s collective activity at that particular period in the journal's history, for his work points to a concept of community that the group itself seemed unable or unwilling to incorporate into its own politically motivated collective practice. The journal's endless "prises de position" that began as early as Sollers's "Programme" in 1967 and continued until its renunciation of Maoism in 1976 seemed only to undermine their struggle against repression and the strictures of "Western capitalist ideology" by contributing to the constitution of a collective that became itself increasingly restrictive. Through its insistence upon conformity, upon a common identification with its revolutionary ideal, it came to embrace, both in its discourse and in its very structure, the exclusionary mimetic logic it sought to oppose. Instead of the spirit of openness and exploration that seemed to prevail during the early days at *Tel Quel* when the journal and its collaborators were receptive to a wide range of divergent views, there now seemed to be one theme that came to dominate, at least in the *Tel Quel* editorials, throughout this highly politicized period. That was their adherence to a revolutionary Marxism as it intersected with Freudian theory. It led first of all to a rapprochement with the French Communist Party, which precipitated a bitter feud with a former member of the editorial board, Jean-Pierre Faye, who left the group in 1967 to found his own journal, *Change.* The series of attacks and counterattacks in which the members of the *Tel Quel* group were engaged were directed to a large extent at *Change*'s refusal to take a stronger position with regard to Marxist-Leninist theory. They attacked *Change* for its "eclecticism" (a curious charge, in light of their early affirmation of the eclectic) and for placing too great an emphasis on Chomskyan linguistics at the expense of dialectical materialism and the class struggle. Such attacks were not confined to *Change* alone but were aimed at other groups of intellectuals as well. The Union of Writers (L'Union des Ecrivains), which was organized during the politically volatile events of May 1968 and in which Faye and many other artists and writers became involved, was berated for its "confusionist positions," for becoming an "amorphous crowd" (*foule vaque*) governed by no overriding principle. "What can 'unite,' " Sollers asked on behalf of *Tel Quel*, "Françoise Mallet-Joris, Guillevic and Michel Butor? Bernard Pingaud and Maurice Roche? Mathieu Galey and Alain Jouffroy? Maurice Nadeau and André Gisselbrecht? Jeanine Worms and Jean-Paul Sartre? Daniel Guérin and Pierre Guyotat? . . . [W]ould it be the fact that they are 'writers'? But what they write is irreconcilable. . . . *In the name of what practice are they united* [*Au nom de quelle pratique s'unifie-t-on*]?"[34]

In rejecting those groups who refused to adopt a common practice and whose "discourses" were "contrary to the Marxist-Leninist line," *Tel Quel* revealed a rigid adherence to a political program that appears rather strange in the context of its presumably "open-ended" theory. It becomes all the more curious when one considers that the group, in the name of *Tel Quel's* open-ended theoretical practice, refused to become directly involved in the student uprisings of May 1968. To do so would be to reinforce the "subjectivist, idealist" model of "revolutionary" struggle by attempting merely to reverse traditional relations of power without examining the ideological foundations upon which all such power struggles are based. The student revolt and other such "voluntarist" forms of political action were thus, according to *Tel Quel*, nothing more than "pseudo-revolutions," giving, in Pleynet's words, "a revolutionary appearance to what could only be a petit-bourgeois and leftist ideological infiltration."[35] *Tel Quel*'s belief that the student revolt was a poor substitute for a genuine Marxist-Leninist understanding of the class struggle does not mean, however, that the group was ready to take up the cause, in a direct way at least, of the working class. A statement issued several years later by the journal, on the relationship between the avant-garde and "the struggle of the masses," makes this point exceedingly clear: "It would be comical to imagine oneself as the spokesperson for the proletariat, to claim to impose oneself as its political leader and the center of a veritable revolutionary party: although we will assist by every means possible in the constitution of the latter, this will be the job of the working class itself [celui-ci, dont nous aiderons de tous nos moyens la constitution, sera le propre de la classe ouvrière elle-même]."[36] Such "paternalist-intellectualist" notions of political engagement were rejected by *Tel Quel* not only because they ultimately reinstated a traditional concept of the subject in the form of the proletariat but also because they failed to recognize that change could not be realized through sloganeering or even through the engaged discourse of the Sartrean variety with its bourgeois instrumentalist view of language, for it was believed that the struggle against bourgeois ideology must take place on a more fundamental level, on the level of language itself.

In this sense, then, through its rejection of dogma, through its refusal to produce literature "in the style of slogans and posters," *Tel Quel* saw itself serving "the popular masses": "We say this: in producing a new practice (a new relationship of the subject to meaning and to ideological norms) and a new understanding of this practice, the specific struggle of the avant-garde on the ideological and political front serves *objectively* the struggle of the masses. In this sense, it will join in the struggle [*elle la rejoindra*]."[37] It was not a question, therefore, of formulating a militant literary or theoretical discourse; the crisis of May 1968 required a different form of writing, one that would not be subordinated to simplistically mimetic expressions of a political idea or cause. This meant that on a practical level the members of the *Tel Quel* group would remain, in some respects, on the periphery of those tumultuous events. What is curious, however, is that *Tel Quel's* refusal on theoretical grounds to express solidarity with the students did not prevent it from establishing a political alliance with the French Communist Party, and the Party's position with regard to the student movement was, in the early days of the riots at least, identical to that of *Tel Quel*. The PCF also saw the students as "bourgeois adventurists" whose activity reflected the interests not of the proletariat but of the ruling class. Indeed, on many occasions *Tel Quel's* editorials expressed the journal's solidarity with the PCF, with the last one appearing, interestingly enough, in the issue directly preceding their final break with the Communists: "*Tel Quel*, even and especially during the most difficult times, never fueled anticommunism, [but] declared itself clearly in favor of the union of the entire left, *that is to say*, firstly, with the Communist Party."[38] *Tel Quel* thus became what Patrick Combes described as "the secular arm [of the PCF] in the realm of literature." By affirming the Party's objectives, the journal "[gave] it a voice that it refus[ed] to give to the [student] movement" (p. 232).

Although *Tel Quel's* position in this regard seems utterly contradictory, it might seem less so in view of the highly charged political climate surrounding the events of May 1968, when position papers proliferated among writers and intellectuals who felt compelled to take a stand on the issues. With the divisions not only between the left and the right but also among those within the leftist camp itself along communist and anticommunist lines, it is not surprising that *Tel Quel* would also feel compelled to take a stand, especially in light of some of the vitriolic attacks directed at the journal itself. Indeed, the publication of Faye's article "Le Camarade 'Mallarmé' " in 1969 by *L'Humanité*, the PCF's daily newspaper, fueled a polemic between Faye and *Tel Quel* that would occupy the journal for a number of years and stemmed from Faye's not so subtle attempt to link Derridean theory, and indirectly *Tel Quel*, to Nazi ideology.[39] Although Derrida's name is never mentioned, he is clearly implicated when Faye takes Heidegger's "regressive" notion of the decline or the "fallenness of Being" and applies it, in a curious distortion of Derrida's theory (which has nothing to do with the concept of a "decline"), to "the idea that the spoken word [*la parole*] 'debases' writing." If Faye's critique has a strangely familiar ring to it for those acquainted with the attempt in recent years to establish some kind of link between deconstruction and Heidegger's Nazism, it is because he employs a similar strategy, collapsing Heideggerian and Derridean theory in order to make the following claim:

> We know that for Heidegger, all of Western history is reduced . . . to a fall of "Being" into being. . . . [T]his schema of a regressive history is drawn, word for word, from Krieck, a pathetic Nazi ideologue. For Krieck, history—until Hitler—was only a decline, a fall from Myth into *Logos*, into Western rationality. But now there is one last ideology that readopts such a schema. All history, according to [this ideology], would, in the West, be nothing more than a forgetting, or worse yet, a "debasement" of writing, its repression by the spoken word [*la parole*]. . . . Thus, history in the West would not cease moving backwards, "debasing" writing even further. . . . Revolution in reverse . . . regressive or retrograde revolution, as Thomas Mann described it when referring to this type of ideology in pre-Nazi Germany.[40]

Faye later denied making any allusions to either Derrida or *Tel Quel*, claiming that he merely wanted to show in what way "a language of the German extreme right was able to . . . insinuate itself into [that of] the Parisian left,"[41] but *Tel Quel* understood his comments as an indirect attack not only on Derrida but on its own textual practice. If *Tel Quel* thus engaged in a lengthy polemic with Faye, it was because the group believed that Faye's veiled insinuations of *Tel Quel*'s fascist and then Stalinist connections and his reference to a possible collusion in the early years of the journal between *Tel Quel* and the right-wing pro-Algeria forces needed to be addressed and indeed elicited a number of letters from outsiders and former collaborators who spoke in *Tel Quel*'s defense. Claude Prevost, an editor of the PCF's cultural journal, *La Nouvelle Critique*, offered the following response in a subsequent issue of *L'Humanité*:

Now, if one refers to the context of the polemics that Faye engaged in for almost two years against the *Tel Quel* group, there is no doubt: it is Philippe Sollers and his friends who are the objects of his attacks. . . . One need only be somewhat aware of the present literary debates to identify here the classical carica-ture of *Tel Quel* by its adversaries. That this caricature is crude to the point where one no longer recognizes the original is my profound conviction, buttressed by an assiduous reading of what is written there.[42]

As the debate became more heated, however, Faye's accusations became more direct, ultimately dispelling any doubts one might have had about his earlier more hidden references: "There is in Derrida's thinking [*démarche*]," Faye states in an interview with *La Gazette de Lausanne* in 1970, "a weak spot, a kind of blind spot marked by the influence of the philosophy of Heidegger, . . . an ideological *stain* deriving from what is the most regressive in Ger-man ideology during the period between the two wars." And refer-ring to the "neo-Jdanovians of *Tel Quel*," he adds: "At no moment was there [at *Tel Quel*] a genuine realization [*une prise de con-science*] of what occurred during the Algerian war, nor [of what occurred] in the course of the Stalinist tragedy, or of the Hitlerian counterrevolution."[43] Once again, former collaborators and associ-ates jumped to *Tel Quel*'s defense:

I am indignant at the way Jean-Pierre Faye judges *Tel Quel* and sings his own praises. If I had thought for one instant that you were "on the side of the colonels [*avec les colonels*]," I would never have collaborated. . . . And why did Jean-Pierre Faye agree to be on the committee of *Tel Quel* if he thought you were fascist? (Jean Cayrol; p. 96)

The foolish (and sordid!) campaign currently directed by the press against *Tel Quel* renders even more evident the "personal reasons" for which I resigned from *Change*. I want to make a point of offering you my sympathy, my *esteem*. (Maurice Roche; p. 96)

In spite of *Tel Quel*'s defenders, however, it was becoming clear that the journal's radical politics were contributing to its gradual marginalization, and in this respect Faye's remarks, though clearly exaggerated, are revealing, for they reflect a view that was gaining currency, particularly as the group moved further and further to the left. Jean Thibaudeau, a member of the PCF and a collaborator at *Tel Quel*, wrote in 1970: "From the moment that our work ... led us in a nonambiguous manner . . . to link our specific practice to Marxism-Leninism, the attacks against *Tel Quel* increased tenfold. This increase has as its principal cause anticommunism. In the reactionary outbursts that try in vain, week after week, to knock us down [*de nous abattre*], M. Faye is undoubtedly the most relentless [*le plus acharné*]."[44] Indeed, attacks similar to Faye's had been appearing in the press for some time. Claude Roy in his article for *Le Nouvel Observateur* (February 21, 1968) found in "neo-telquel-ism, in a more inoffensive form, the rigid mentality [*une structure mentale crispée*] that already characterized Jdanavo-Stalinism." Even the weekly entertainment guide *Pariscope* jumped into the fray with the claim that "the coterie of *Tel Quel* would no doubt have the fate of . . . the 'enfants terribles' of the fascist movement and . . . of the neo-Stalinist poets" (November 5, 1969).

Although epithets such as "fascist" and "Stalinist" were applied with considerable frequency by critics of *Tel Quel* and clearly showed an unwillingness on their part to grapple with some of the questions *Tel Quel* theoreticians raised, such attacks were un-doubtedly provoked by a certain hardening of the *Tel Quel* position, as evidenced in the endless flow of editorials and position papers that were increasingly polemical. *Tel Quel*'s strict adherence to its particular interpretation of Marxist-Leninist doctrine led to its re-jection of anyone who failed to follow the Party line, including finally the PCF itself. Indeed, despite frequent declarations of soli-darity with the Communist Party, signs of conflict between the two began to appear as early as 1968 and were related to what *Tel Quel* saw as a growing conservatism within the Party organization. The sequence of events leading up to the final break with the PCF is outlined rather clearly in *Tel Quel*'s "Chronology," published in the fall of 1971, giving a sense of the conflict and cleavages that re-sulted from *Tel Quel*'s political allegiances:

1967 At this time a crisis is emerging inside the committee of *Tel Quel* between those who want to follow a Marxist-Leninist line and the others (but *also* Freudians and the others). "The others" are the same ones who tried last year to repress information on the Chinese cultural, proletarian revolution. Scission.

1968 Beginning of the campaign by the bourgeois press against *Tel Quel*. . . . Refusal (justified) to adhere to the "Union of Writers," [a group] founded, at the time, on premises that we find confused and opportunistic; the first sign of a profound disagreement with the PCF, which is giving more and more recognition to the so-called Union.

1969 Redoubling of the bourgeois press's campaign against *Tel Quel*. . . . Tragicomical episode of the article entitled "Camarade Mallarmé" in *L'Humanité*. . . . It seems that the PCF is supporting more and more actively the opposition to the right of *Tel Quel*.

1970 . . . Slander and defamations on the part of *Tel Quel*'s opposition: the PCF isn't taking a position (in other words: it is taking a position). . . . What is becoming increasingly evident is the *organic* unity dogmatism-revisionism. (pp. 142–43)

Tel Quel's disenchantment with the Communist Party had clearly been building for some time. The Party's veering to the right while *Tel Quel* remained committed to the revolutionary aspects of Marxist-Leninist theory and to its restructuring of orthodox Marxism by incorporating the writings of Freud, Mao, and Mallarmé, among others, led inevitably to *Tel Quel*'s break with the Party in 1971. Provoked initially by the censorship at the Party's Fête de L'Humanité of an important work on China, Macciochi's *De la Chine*, which praised the accomplishments of the Cultural Revolution, *Tel Quel* published its "Movement of June 71" in opposition to the Party's "Stalinist" tactics. The Party's refusal to recognize the profoundly revolutionary implications of Maoist doctrine constituted a betrayal, in *Tel Quel*'s view, of Marx's revolutionary spirit and transformed the Communist Party in France into a conservative instrument of the French social system and its bourgeois ideology. The "Movement of June" and the preceding declaration thus issued what was nothing less than a call to arms to all those who sought to renounce the PCF's "dogmatico-revisionism" in favor of "the revolutionary line," and it concludes with a rhetorical flourish that stands in striking contrast to *Tel Quel*'s presumably open-ended, perpetually self-critical *pratique textuelle*.

Down with the corrupt bourgeoisie!
Down with rotten revisionism [*le révisionnisme pourri*]!
Down with their polarization of the superpowers [*leur binarisme de super-puissances*]!
Long live *De la Chine*!
Long live revolutionary China!
Long live the thought of Mao Tse-tung!

> Movement of June 71 against opportunism, dogmatism,
> empiricism, revisionism; for the thought of Mao Tse-tung.

It is difficult to imagine what logic could explain or justify such a marked discrepancy between *Tel Quel*'s politics and its notion of a nonrepresentational theoretical praxis, but this transformation of practice into dogma exposes and dismantles one of the fundamental illusions of the entire *Tel Quel* project, one that is derived not simply from *Tel Quel*'s utopian vision in all its *practical* manifestations but from a certain *theoretical* idealism that also structured the *Tel Quel* enterprise. The members of *Tel Quel* believed that their restructuring of Marxist theory would prevent the subordination of the theoretical to the Party's political agenda. Kristeva later outlined their thinking in her autobiographical essay, "My Memory's Hyperbole": "Dialectical materialism, which, in our view, represented Hegel overturned by Lucretius, Mallarmé and Freud (to cite only three parameters of a nonmechanistic materialism), gave us some hope, if not of modifying the bureaucratic defects of an oppressive machine—we didn't have the pragmatic soul of law-enforcers or founders of morally pure communities—at least of bracketing them" (p. 231). The group would, in this case, be able to "make use of the Communist Party" without being "used by it," to take advantage of an alliance on a cultural and intellectual level while maintaining *Tel Quel*'s theoretical "purity" as protection against the Party's and orthodox Marxism's doctrinaire logic. And indeed, in the early stages of their relationship, *Tel Quel*'s alliance with the PCF was quite successful, for through Party publications such as *Les Lettres françaises* and *La Nouvelle Critique*, in addition to two important colloquia, Cluny I and Cluny II, much of the work by *Tel Quel* and other avant-garde writers became known to the public. Yet as the Party's revisionism accelerated, so did its tendency to "recuperate and institutionalize" the aesthetically marginal, in *Tel Quel*'s view, leading to a revolt that stemmed not simply from the group's rejection of the Party's politics but also from a loss of faith in the subversive possibilities of political organizations in general: "[T]his shift to the outskirts of the P.C.F.," Kristeva explained, "gave us a clear view of the reality of a machine. . . . [T]his machine is the killer mechanism of individual difference" (p. 232). In turning toward Maoism as an "anti-organizational, anti-partisan antidote" or as "a utopia in pure form, which had nothing to do with sects of the left" (p. 232), *Tel Quel* was searching for a way to move beyond such restrictive political allegiances and, consequently, to preserve the integrity of a theoretical practice uncontaminated by the political dogmatism associated with orthodox Marxism.

This turn toward Maoism was not, however, as sudden as it might seem, given that the group had become acquainted with the theories of Mao through the writings of Althusser. In the mid-1960's, there were several *Tel Quel* associates, Sollers in particular, who became intrigued by the early stages of the Cultural Revolution, which, in their view, had set into motion a more authentically revolutionary practice of Marxist theory. Recalling his initial attraction to Maoism in a 1976 interview, Sollers explained:

> It was in 1966, precisely because of the Cultural Revolution, that I became interested in Marxism. I might not have been interested in it otherwise. Indeed, Mao, at the time, seemed to be reinventing the horizon, closed by Stalin, of the revolution. And, for me, the conjunction between Chinese culture, which had always attracted me both sensually and intellectually, and the promise of moving beyond the Stalinist cancer by means of another more open and inventive conception, of finding once again the practical intelligence of revolutionary action; this conjunction . . . gave me great hope: perhaps we would finally have a revolution that would surpass the revolution, which had become a counterrevolution, in the USSR. . . . In my view, Mao, during the last ten years, prolonged for us the life of what should be referred to today as the Marxist illusion.[45]

Despite this later rejection of Marxism in all its manifestations, the *Tel Quel* group, following its declaration of June 1971, saw in Mao a particularly efficacious means of countering the forces of revisionism within the PCF, whose belief in a peaceful transition from capitalism to socialism had led it to seek "common ground" with the capitalists and thus to abandon the revolution. Mao, on the contrary, held tenaciously, so the members of the *Tel Quel* group maintained, to the idea of the class struggle, a tenacity that stemmed from what Sollers described as Mao's radical appreciation of the complexity of the movement of history, whose contradictions could not be reconciled by the politics of revisionism. Contradiction, as Mao tells us, is "inherent in the very essence of things" and must therefore be seen as an integral part of any form of social change. Returning, then, to the theme that the group found so attractive in Althusser's restructuring of Marxist theory, Sollers insisted once again that Mao's theories on contradiction constituted a "considerable and completely original 'leap forward' for the theory of dialectical materialism," due in part to Mao's attempt to account for what Althusser had consistently neglected: the contradictory role of the subject.[46] Indeed, as Kristeva later argued in *Revolution in Poetic Language*, it was Mao, more than any other Marxist theorist, who viewed the "personal and direct experience" of a subject as "the essential materialist feature of practice." In this case, according to Kristeva, the subject is placed "in process," caught up in the contradictions shaping social history, while retaining at the same time, through its "personal participation in the practice that changes reality," its capacity to influence, to some degree, the course of human events: " 'Direct' and 'personal' experience," Kristeva wrote, "is perhaps stressed [in Mao's writings] more than anywhere else in Marxist theory and Mao's emphasis on it tends to bring to the fore a subjectivity that has become the place of the 'highest contradiction.' . . . Maoism, it would seem, summons and produces, above all this kind of subjectivity, one that it views as the driving force behind the practice of social change and revolution" (pp. 200–201).

What is more, and adding further to Mao's appeal, if social change cannot take place without the direct intervention of a subject, according to Mao, neither can it occur if it is confined solely to the sphere of the economic class struggle. Given the Marxist view that the economic substructure and the superstructure are mutually dependent, with each serving as the condition of the other's existence, Mao recognized that a proletarian revolution was not enough, that the struggle had to be played out on the cultural and ideological level as well. Needless to say, Mao's insistence upon the transformation of the superstructure as essential to the advancement of the revolutionary struggle provided the necessary justification for *Tel Quel*'s own revolutionary project. Indeed, in light of Kristeva's claim that Mao was "the only man in politics and the only communist leader since Lenin to have frequently insisted on the necessity of working upon language and writing in order to transform ideology," Maoist theory lent considerable support to *Tel Quel*'s effort to combat, by means of a radical transformation of language and the literary text, all forms of cultural and political institutionalization, including that of the French Communist Party.[47]

In the course, however, of its quest for a politicized practice uncorrupted by politics, *Tel Quel* fell victim to what Kristeva later described as "our exaggerated regard for theory." Its restructuring of Marxist-Leninist doctrine, through the writings of Mao and Freud, could not stave off corruption; it could not prevent the *Tel Quel* movement on either the practical or theoretical level from becoming tainted by the doctrinal formulas of party politics. Even after the break with the PCF, the journal persisted in producing editorials that were engaged in some form of political combat, displaying what one critic has described as *Tel Quel*'s "will to scission" that continued well into the 1970's. Former collaborators whose influence at *Tel Quel* was at one time considerable, such as Hallier (one of its founding members), Ponge, Thibaudeau, Derrida, and others, became the object of rather snide attacks. *Tel Quel*'s break with Derrida, for example, on grounds relating in part to Derrida's unwillingness to commit to Marxism, was never announced formally in the journal but appears evident when Derrida's theory of "writing," a notion *Tel Quel* once rigorously defended in its debates with Faye, is referred to in a 1975 editorial, no doubt inspired by the recent publication of Derrida's *Glas*, as "*le gla-gla précieux derridien*" (affected Derridean gobbledygook).[48]

The final rupture with Ponge was far more clear-cut and dramatic. Following Ponge's publication of a leaflet attacking Marcelin Pleynet's treatment of Braque in *Art Press*, Pleynet responded with a virulent editorial, "Sur la morale politique," in which he attempted to uncover the ideological underpinnings of Ponge's attack, linking it to Ponge's association with the Communist Party and its "anti-Semitic," "terrorist" politics.[49] Although many of *Tel Quel*'s editorials were responses to attacks whose polemical character undoubtedly made it difficult for the group not to answer in an equally polemical fashion, their combative approach and the obvious relish with which they participated in the many verbal altercations produced an "us against them" mentality that found reinforcement in the journal's generally strident tones: "Who is the principal enemy?" *Tel Quel* asked. "Again, we say: the right and revisionism."[50] Indeed, the content of their editorials bears a curious resemblance to the assaults directed some years earlier at *Tel Quel*'s "fascism," for the term "fascist," now used frequently by the members of the group, seems to apply to anyone who opposes *Tel Quel*:

> The alliance, clearly evident today, of dogmatico-revisionism with the bourgeoisie . . . runs the risk, which is much less hypothetical than one thinks, of a slow and continuous fascization of this country as of so many others. In saying this, we do not mean that fascism will necessarily take the forms that we have known in the past, certainly not: postrevisionist, it will be at the same time less open [*avoué*] and more powerful, more diffuse and more secretly repressive than before.[51]

> The reactionary resistance of bourgeois intellectuals to psychoanalysis . . . reveals daily their collapse [*l'effondrement*], giving rise to a fascistic hardening of perspective [*une crispation de type fasciste*].[52]

Clearly, the politics at *Tel Quel* and its polemics of "for and against" clash dramatically with its notion of a nonrepresentational theoretical practice, leading to the paradoxical reinstatement of the very tactics, behavior patterns, and thought processes of the oppressive linguistic and socioeconomic systems the group had initially hoped to contest and also to the constitution of a binary vision of reality that could not but insinuate itself into *Tel Quel* theory. The oppositional, objectifying, and therefore capitalist logic that grounds *Tel Quel*'s polemics also structures its notion of the revolutionary text. It requires that the closed, essentially readable product of the literary tradition be seen as diametrically opposed to the open, unreadable process of textual production. Indeed, the challenge to what Kristeva has called the traditional "monological" novel, with its subordination to the "Law of One" (one author, one meaning, and one legitimate interpretation), does not come, as we shall see, from within the structure of the novel itself. It comes instead from a radically different text, from the "polyphonic" novels of Kafka or Joyce or from works following the example of Mallarmé and Lautréamont, "which are conceived in their very structure as a production irreducible to representation."[53] *Tel Quel's* politicization of the literary text, which stems from the unquestioned belief in its revolutionary capacities, thus raises a number of difficulties for *Tel Quel* theory, not the least of which is the assignment of a certain essence or specificity to the structures it is working against, assuming a quality of cohesiveness that is taken to be intrinsic to both the social system and the traditional literary text.

CHAPTER 2

Textual and Cultural Enclosures

Kristeva constructed a particularly forceful argument in support of the inherently cohesive character of traditional literature in her essay "Le Texte clos," parts of which appeared first in *Théorie d'ensemble* and were developed more fully a year later in *Séméiotiké*.[1] Here, she used Antoine de La Sale's fifteenth-century novel *Jehan de Saintré* to demonstrate the "structural closure" that she claimed characterized not only the traditional novel but all of Western literature before the "epistemological break" of the late nineteenth century, when writers like Mallarmé and Lautréamont attempted to challenge traditional aesthetics. She argued that the entire trajectory of La Sale's text is controlled and directed by what is announced at the outset: "The text opens with an introduction that shapes (shows) the entire itinerary of the novel. . . . We thus *already* know how the story will end: the end of the narration is given before the narrative itself even begins."[2] This means, however, that "all anecdotal interest within the novel is eliminated," in Kristeva's view, and although the multiple twists and turns of the narration do contribute to the development of the plot, they do not, according to Kristeva, alter the outcome in any significant way. The text merely plays itself out by alternating between the various thematic oppositions (love and hate, life and death, vice and virtue, for example), and despite the deviations and sudden reversals (which also contribute to the illusion of openness, according to Kristeva), the final result remains unchanged; nothing interferes with the inevitable choice of one side of the opposition or the other. The disjunction that opens the novel and sets into motion the interplay between opposites that carries the novel along are always absorbed by the "non-disjunctive" operations of the text's discursive language, which resolves all conflict and contradiction and assures the production of a unified and immediately appropriable meaning.

The traditional text, then, according to Kristeva, is structured by a number of closural devices. Its completely programmed trajectory, the simple binary relationship between its various thematic elements, and the progression toward the inevitable "agreement of deviations" all serve to close the text by rendering every deviation and permutation completely ineffectual. The operations of the text remain at all times subservient to the preliminary message with each element acquiring significance only as it relates to that message, as it repeats what was programmed into the text from the beginning. Consequently, far from contributing to the complexity of the text by constituting a plurality of meanings, each successive image becomes a mere variation of the same immutable identity, and the totality of the text comes to be perceived as a single unit of meaning where nothing interferes with the transmission of the initial authorial intention.

Within the traditional framework, then, the operation of both the text and the reader are carefully regulated. Related to the author in one way only as transmitter and receiver of the author's message, both are subordinate and never function themselves as producers of new meaning. This conception of the text as a perfectly controlled communicative object is one that Kristeva strongly criticized, for it refuses to recognize that the operations within language as well as the interpretive strategies that the reader employs also structure the work and lead ultimately to the pluralization of the text's meaning. She pointed out, however, that this suppression of the independently productive operations of both the reader and the text is essential if the imposition of a fixed meaning is to be assured. The literary tradition cannot admit that the movement of differentiation within language actually diffuses the author's intentions by producing a multiplicity of possible combinations and relations between words, or that the assumption of objectivity upon which the communicative model of interpretation is based is itself an ideological construct, one grounded in a whole system of scientific, philosophical, and literary conventions that shape and determine the analyst's point of view: "Such an ideology, which proceeds from a society of exchange and its 'communicative' structure, imposes *one* possible interpretation of semiotic practices ('semiotic practices are forms of communication') and conceals the very process involved in the elaboration of those practices."[3] For Kristeva, then, any conception of the object, whether it be literary or otherwise, is a function of a perceiving subject: "The object is, that is to say, is true, only to the extent that the subject gives it meaning (*predicari est intentio*) through judgment."[4]

To make a claim such as this, however, is to imply, rightly enough, that the classical conception of the text results from a particular kind of reading, one that excludes or suppresses the multiple productive practices in order to focus on the predetermined sense. In this instance, Kristeva appears to indicate that the concept of textual closure is not a function of the text's operations, but is the result of the interpretive strategies that the reader imposes, that the reader and not the text or the author produces a closed, autonomous artifact "while refusing to *read* the process of its productivity."[5] Kristeva's conclusion, however, that the determination of the literary text as "object" is ultimately grounded in the ideological projections of the reading or writing subjects does not lead her to question her own assumptions about the closed character of the traditional novel form. Although she sees her analysis as differing from the classical interpretive model because it focuses on the various "functions" within the text rather than on the meaning it produces, many of her conclusions are based on an apparent acceptance of the classical view. Her description in "The Bounded Text" of the various closural effects within the literary work reveals that for Kristeva the idea of "closure" is not a problem of reading; it is not some ideological construct imposed upon the work, but is an integral part of the traditional novel form, the result of the text's and not the reader's own restrictive activity:

[A] suprasegmental analysis of the utterances contained within the novel's framework will reveal it as a bounded text [*un texte clos*]. (p. 38)

The initial programming of the book is already its structural finitude. . . . [T]he trajectories close upon themselves, return to their point of departure or are confirmed by a censoring element in such a way as to outline the limits of a closed discourse. (p. 55)

The . . . social text eliminates all notions of production from its scene in order to substitute a product (effect, value): the reign of *literature* is the reign of *market value* occulting . . . the discursive origins of the literary event. (pp. 57–58)

Apparently, then, for Kristeva the operations of the traditional novel *do* remain perfectly controlled, for she argues that *because* its teleological structure completely represses the complex processes involved in the reading and the writing of the text, the traditional form must be undermined. Consequently, rather than shattering the assumption of closure by showing how the multiple operations within the text tend to pluralize and fragment the presumed unity of meaning and work against the rigid binary relationship between the novel's "exclusive" and "non-alternating" oppositions, her conclusion that the activity of the text succeeds in repressing all that detracts from the initial intention serves to support that assumption and reinforces the tradition of total authorial control and of textual unity. Thus, although Kristeva claims that the work of the literary avant-garde has made it possible for us to read "various texts of the past in a different way, as something other than 'literature,'"[6] her own reading of the novel does not challenge the interpretive norm as much as she would like. The traditional definition becomes Kristeva's definition; the closed structure she uncovers is a property of the text itself and not the result of her projections: "[T]he novel is already 'literature'; that is, a product of speech, a (discursive) object of exchange with an owner (author), value, and consumer (the public, addressee)."[7]

This criticism can apply not only to Kristeva's analysis of the traditional novel form but to the other signifying practices within the social system as well. Indeed, by defining Western society as a system of self-contained "isomorphic" structures, as a "collection" or series of "finite systems" that must be broken down, Kristeva runs into some of the same difficulties she encountered in her analysis of the traditional novel. She seems to be assuming not so much that the establishment of a closed society is the ultimate *aim* of Western sociopolitical systems and their ideologies, as that they succeed in creating and maintaining the closed structures that the oppressive social order requires. Implicit in her notion of the contemporary crisis in social and religious institutions, the first signs of which appeared at the end of the nineteenth century when the writings of Freud, Marx, Mallarmé, and Lautréamont testified to a profound rupture with the tradition that was to have repercussions within the social system as well, is the view that posits the pre-crisis triumph of the unifying function:

> From the time of this rupture [*cet éclatement*], which has continued to grow deeper and broader in scope since the end of the nineteenth century, . . . from the time of this rupture of sociosymbolic finitude (sign, family, State, religion), [we affirm] that it is possible to pose the alterity of these other practices and signifying systems: the fact that they are irreducible to ours, but obey another distribution of the relation unity/process, symbolic system/semiotic drives. . . . The signifying practices and the mode of production in question enter henceforth into a process of the dissolution of unity: logical, linguistic, familial, statist, subjective. For the first time in history, conditions are right not for a sweeping away of unity, for that would amount to the dissolution of sociality itself, but for analyzing it. . . . For the first time in history, conditions are right for the relativization of the statist, familial, religious function.[8]

According to Kristeva, whose analysis here and in both *Séméiotiké* and *Revolution in Poetic Language* provides the theoretical basis for *Tel Quel*'s revolutionary project, the "Law of One" rules Western society, and more particularly the modern social system dominated by the bourgeoisie. This dictates that all diversity, all that deviates from the norm and poses a threat to the cohesiveness of the total social organization, be either repressed or enclosed within the system. The structures in society, including the family, the state, language, and religion, are to remain at all times internally homogeneous and homologous, working in complicity with

one another to preserve the social order and to guarantee its repro-
duction. The family unit, for example, suppresses the potentially
unproductive sexual impulses and pleasures associated with its
generative function in order to assure the propagation of the species
and to meet the needs of the capitalist system of commodity ex-
change where "procreation," Kristeva wrote, "is the determining
factor in the production of goods."[9] Indeed, the whole of Western
society, which according to Kristeva is founded on "the production
of goods," is governed by capitalist laws of exchange, and her anal-
ysis of its various structures, including language with its emphasis
upon communication and the exchange of messages, tends to be
determined by this overall view. The social organization forms a
system of production whose controlled operations contribute to
the productive and reproductive capacities of the bourgeois state
and assure its cohesiveness and stability by emphasizing not only
their own structural coherence but the self-contained and unified
identity of what they produce:

> The regulation of the relations of production by the *State* and the
> law, like the regulation of the relations of reproduction by the
> *family*, sustains a certain type of relationship between *unity* and
> *process*. . . . This type of relationship consists of privileging the
> unifying function—that which constitutes the coherence of the
> sign, of the system and of sociality—to the detriment of process,
> which is relegated to the margins under the name of madness,
> the sacred or poetry. The State represents this unifying instance
> with regard to the process of contradiction that traverses the
> productive forces and the relations of production. The family
> assures unity with regard to pulsions and "jouissance." That this
> unity of the state and of the family is constituted as a result of a
> murder or sacrifice—that of the soma, of the drives, of process—
> this is what religion tells us while claiming for itself the privilege
> of representing, that is to say, of unifying that which is hetero-
> geneous to sociosymbolic unity.[10]

The suppression of the heterogeneous processes that precede or
exceed the constitution of unity is thus the goal of the various
signifying practices that structure Western society. The problem,
however, is that in Kristeva's effort to problematize the *objectives*
of an essentially repressive socioeconomic system, she ends up

embracing its "unifying logic" by defining the social order in the very terms that she sets out to contest. Indeed, that definition provides the basis for her assumptions about the homologous relationship between the different practices within the social system whose uniformity and cohesiveness are placed in direct opposition to the marginal, heterogeneous elements that these practices successfully repress. As Kristeva wrote: "[The] logic of control and of production" that has dominated the bourgeois sociopolitical system "organizes autonomous structures, which, ultimately, are subordinated to the law."[11] Although there were, according to Kristeva, moments in the history of Western culture that brought a provisional disruption of the social order, as in the case of the French Revolution, for example, such periods were followed by a tightening of social constraints, leading in the nineteenth century to an even more repressive society in the form of the bourgeois state. Citing Arthur de Gobineau's study of France in the 1870's, which, in Kristeva's words, "clearly describes the oppressive structure of the bourgeois system," Kristeva concurred with his view that the bourgeois state represents "the fulfillment of all the despotisms that history has known, their perfection and their apogee. . . . The power of the One in the form of the Prince or the King, replaced by the power of All represented by the State, only broadens its influence over the masses and therefore consolidates the principle of power."[12]

In accepting these conclusions, however, Kristeva presents the idea of structural unity not as the *desire* of a culture whose cohesiveness is possibly undermined by those marginal elements Kristeva so effectively describes, but as a fact that has come to define not only Western literature—"all 'literature' before the epistemological break of the nineteenth/twentieth centuries . . . is . . . as ideologeme, closed and terminated in its very beginnings"—but the social structure as a whole.[13] Indeed, Kristeva and the *Tel Quel* group in general remained uncritical of their own assumptions about the uniformly cohesive character of all Western social structures, and their apparent reduction of social complexity runs counter to the very theories of contradiction, developed by Althusser through his readings of Mao, that they had so readily embraced. Althusser's emphasis on the permutations and contradictions that are inherent in the social system itself, with social change occurring as a result of a plurality of both external and internal causes, has been replaced by a more conservative application of the dialectic, which in this case reduces heterogeneity by inscribing it into a simple oppositional logic and thus denies the permutations and interdependencies of the relation between the two opposing terms, that is, between unstructured heterogeneity and a structured, cohesive sociosymbolic unity. Moreover, the effort to move beyond those structures to reactivate this "heterogeneous reality" carries with it a certain conception about the specificity of that reality that is in many ways as reductive as the subjectivist perspective they oppose, for it is not to be found in the sign, in the social structure or its systems, nor is it located in the judgment of the omniscient subject; it resides in the unstructured, heterogeneous process that precedes and participates in the constitution of these entities with its boundaries determined by its opposition to all uniform structures within Western society.

Kristeva's Revolutionary Poetic Language: The Semiotic and the Symbolic as a Political Distinction

The opposition between heterogeneous reality and the uniform structures within the Western social system is central to Kristeva's well-known and much debated distinction between the "semiotic" and the "symbolic," which has grounded Kristeva's theory from *Séméiotiké*, where the discussion was more in terms of the "geno-text" and the "phenotext," to her work in the 1980's, when it was modified to some extent and so rendered the opposition itself somewhat more complex (I shall return to this). In her earlier work, however, and despite her claim that the two modalities are interdependent and therefore inseparable, the semiotic and the symbolic are often separated by rather clear lines of demarcation. Indeed, a number of Kristeva's critics have challenged in rather strong terms her tendency to view the semiotic as the "outside" of language, as an "archaic, instinctual and maternal territory" that has none of the elements that make up the symbolic order of signification and must be "repressed" or "sealed off" if the symbolic order of identity is to function.[14]

A brief review of Kristeva's familiar distinction indeed confirms the critics' argument, for the symbolic, as Kristeva describes it, always refers to the logical and syntactical function of language. It includes the order of the sign, of nomination, signification, and denotation and at all times presupposes an integrated, speaking subject. The semiotic, on the other hand, is a prelinguistic state resembling, in Kristeva's words, "the first echolalias of infants as rhythms and intonations anterior to the first phonemes, morphemes, lexemes, and sentences."[15] In this case, sounds, rhythms, and intonations are articulated according to the needs of "the body's drives," but they convey no meaning: "no sign, no predication, no signified object and therefore no operating consciousness of a transcendental ego" (p. 133). The semiotic is thus chronologically prior to the constitution of the linguistic sign and the subject, and although Kristeva maintains that it is also necessary for the acquisition of language itself in that it provides the foundation out of which language and the subject develop, the integral identities of both can only be constituted after cutting themselves off from this anteriority, by repressing these prelinguistic "heterogeneous pulsions." The task, then, of the revolutionary text is to reactivate these "repressed drives," to introduce the semiotic in the form of rhythm, intonation, and the repetition of sounds and rhyme, which becomes the genotext, into the phenotext (the symbolic), so that the unity of the sign-subject will ultimately be undermined and the differential process of generation itself will be allowed to emerge uncontaminated by its precepts.

What occurs, however, as a result of this distinction is that Kristeva must uphold the very concept of language, with its premises of unity and meaning, that she set out to undermine. This problem is particularly evident, I would argue, in her distinguishing the discourses of poetry, which render explicit the ungrammaticalities of semiotic rhythms and intonations, and the discursive operations of normative language, which "tend to reduce as much as possible the semiotic component" (p. 134). The problem is not so much her claim that poetic language brings to the foreground the "undecidable character of any so-called natural language . . . [which] univocal, rational, scientific discourse tends to hide" (p. 135), as her tendency to forget the undecidability inhering in all forms of discourse when she stresses the unsettling, disruptive, indeed revolutionary potential of the "poetic" and of the semiotic processes with which it is linked. For normative discourse, especially when it is tied to the formation and socialization of the speaking subject, acquires a coherence and a uniformity that allow it to perform a strictly repressive role:

> The semiotic activity, which introduces wandering or fuzziness into language and, *a fortiori*, into poetic language is, from a synchronic point of view, a mark of the workings of drive . . . and, from a diachronic point of view, stems from the archaisms of the semiotic body. Before recognizing itself as identical in a mirror and, consequently, as signifying, this body is dependent vis-à-vis the mother. At the same time instinctual and maternal, semiotic processes prepare the future speaker for entrance into meaning and signification (the symbolic). But the symbolic (i.e., language as nomination, sign, and syntax) constitutes itself only by breaking with this anteriority, which is retrieved as "signifier," "primary processes" . . . but which always remains subordinate—subjacent to the principal function of naming-predicating. Language as symbolic function constitutes itself at the cost of repressing instinctual drive and continuous relation to the mother. On the contrary, the unsettled and questionable subject of poetic language (for whom the word is never uniquely sign) maintains itself at the cost of reactivating this repressed instinctual, maternal element. If it is true that the prohibition of incest constitutes, at the same time, language as communicative code and women as exchange objects in order for a society to be established, *poetic language would be* for its questionable subject-in-process the *equivalent of incest*: it is within the economy of signification itself that the questionable subject-in-process appropriates to itself this archaic, instinctual and maternal territory; thus it simultaneously prevents the work from becoming mere sign and the mother from becoming an object like any other—forbidden. (p. 136)

If this introduction of the unconscious, generative processes of the semiotic into the economy of signification prevents language from becoming a "finished product" with a precise and communicable meaning, then the symbolic itself must be assumed to have a unified structure; it cannot be considered to have heterogeneous or contradictory elements within it. We shall see, however, that Kristeva herself shows that the sign is not always unified. She points out that the Saussurian theory of the differential nature of language demonstrates that an opening already exists within the sign, that the movement within language toward the production of meaning, which creates a constantly shifting interplay between those elements that constitute the linguistic sign, serves to complicate the simple one-to-one relationship between signifier and signified. The signified, in this context, always finds itself multiplied and produces as a consequence a "surplus of value" in which the "acoustic image" (the signifier) becomes linked to several concepts rather than to one alone. In addition, Saussure's *Anagrammes* furnishes the proof, according to Kristeva, that the sign is not a unified entity. The search for words hidden in other words is an indication that once again the signified acquires "a value added [*surajoutée*] to the explicit, linear value of the signified."[16] One must conclude, then, contrary to Kristeva's theory of the symbolic, that heterogeneous elements are already at work within language, that a certain "fuzziness" has already wedged an opening in the sign, with the obvious result that Kristeva's opposition between poetic and discursive language becomes exceedingly difficult to maintain.

Although Kristeva modified her view in her work of the 1980's, first in *Tales of Love* and then six years later in *Strangers to Ourselves*, where, as we shall see, she raised questions that ultimately complicate the very terms of the opposition between the semiotic and the symbolic, Kristeva's earlier tendency to formulate her distinctions in rather categorical terms can undoubtedly be attributed to the revolutionary politics that structured her writing during the period of militancy at *Tel Quel*, when the politicization of the semiotic, the affirmation of its revolutionary potential, often led her to view it as an absolute category, distinct from the symbolic and unrestricted by its logic. Indeed, it seems incontrovertible that the process of politicization informed Kristeva's reading of the literary text as well: she did not radically interrogate the representational assumptions structuring all traditional notions of language and literature, and consequently recognize that the resistance to closure can be found within mimetic representation itself; rather, she placed the presumably unified structure of representational discourse in opposition to its more aberrational, unstructured, poetic manifestations. Kristeva believed, at the time, that the modern, "polyphonic" literary text, whether in the form of Céline's scatological narrative and its "vision of the abject" or the "poetic language" of Sollers's *Nombres* with its meaningless repetition of sounds and rhyme, could restore to discourse the repressed heterogeneity often associated with the maternal phase, and thus break out of the closures constituted by the literary and philosophical tradition. Needless to say, the oppressive laws of an essentially patriarchal social system could be undermined as well.

Although Kristeva later found examples of the polyphonic in the structure of the traditional text itself, thus abandoning her tendency to pit one against the other, her earlier work not only furnished the theoretical ground for *Tel Quel*'s struggle against what one of its editorials referred to as the "continuous 'fascization' of the bourgeois state and its police,"[17] by pointing to the possibility of a reactivation within discourse of repressed heterogeneity, but it also, as I indicated, provided the framework for the literary activity of the poets who belonged to the *Tel Quel* circle when the idea of a "collective practice of writing" was emerging. Indeed, much of Denis Roche's later poetry, and Marcelin Pleynet's as well, can be viewed as an outgrowth of the theoretical investigations of language Kristeva and other *Tel Quel* theorists then conducted. Discussing his association with *Tel Quel* in an interview that appears in Serge Gavronsky's *Poems & Texts*, Roche saw himself (until 1973, at least—when he resigned from the editorial board of *Tel Quel*) participating in a "community of experience" in which new developments in poetry would occur in conjunction with certain advances in critical theory. His "revolution" in poetic language, which began as an attack on traditional poetic conventions in the early 1960's and gained greater political force during his association with *Tel Quel*, culminated in the publication of his last and most provocative work of poetry, "Le Mécrit," in the fall 1971 issue of *Tel Quel*. Reprinted a year later as part of the Collection *Tel Quel*, the work is more than a purely personal attack on linguistic and literary conventions. Roche's work, like that of Pleynet, incorporated the *Tel Quel* aims and objectives, attempting to bring about a radical transformation not only of the poetic text but of what Roche has called the "retrograde, obscurantist ideology" dominating Western culture and thought.[18]

To suggest, however, that Roche's and Pleynet's poetic texts are to be viewed as a praxis that incorporates the *Tel Quel* conception of the revolutionary text is once again to point to the numerous difficulties inherent in the *Tel Quel* project. If one is to assume that their *pratique scripturale* remained free of the theoretical and political dogmatism that the group itself seemed unable to resist, is that not to posit a purity of praxis that is itself a form of closure? Indeed, to construct a theory of the text on the basis of its revolutionary character is already to impose certain limits, to close off its supposedly open-ended structure by defining the text in terms of its difference from its more traditional counterpart. Not only that, but the reader must respond to the text in a particular way, which implies a structuring principle of some kind, a controlling force governing the operations of the literary work.

Tel Quel's conception of the revolutionary text thus accentuated the paradoxical nature of the *Tel Quel* position, for it involved the practice of a theory that was meant to undo theory's closural effects; it required an intentional strategy to contest the notion that a text is the unproblematized expression of a preexistent authorial intention. An examination of the practical implications of this conception of the text in terms of its effect on the formal configuration of the work and on the mechanics of reading will thus provide the basis for the following analysis of "Le Mécrit." It will become clear after a preliminary reading of the work as an "open" text that questions of intentionality and textual comprehensibility are raised by the work itself that are not ultimately raised by the theory. A closer look at the theory will indeed reveal that in certain respects it did not challenge the interpretive norm to the extent that the *Tel Quel* group would have liked. On the contrary, it permitted a very different reading of "Le Mécrit," one that restored many of the precepts of the closed, programmed literary work it was meant to oppose.

Denis Roche's "Le Mécrit"

Turning, then, to "Le Mécrit," a work made up of six texts and two inscriptions, one finds that the effort to exploit the unlimited possibilities of the open text, with its shattering of the linguistic, representationalist enclosure, is most immediately apparent in the poem's fractured poetic structure. Preceded by a discursive theoretical preface, which is enclosed in a well-defined, rectangular frame, the six texts that follow seem to be breaking through those structural boundaries, their margins eliminated, opened, or displaced, with the words often spilling over the edges, appearing unrestricted by the confines of the poetic text. This impression of openness and incompletion is accentuated by the lack of finality in the concluding lines. Often ending in midsentence (if it is possible to call this chaotic juxtaposition of words a "sentence") or with a dash instead of a period, the operations of each poem appear to progress interminably from one text to another, with each successive text transforming and ultimately bringing about the disintegration of the initial enclosure. It is almost as if the closed, discursive space of the preface is exploded into little fragments, with bits and pieces scattered throughout the work; as an example, "m'y enfoncer" (thrust myself into it) in the preface becomes "jl'enfonc" (Ithrus i) in text 2 and "J'enfonce" (I thrust) in text 5; "dans les limites très étroites" (within the very narrow limits) becomes "l&enflant étroit" (the &narrow swelling) in text 4, "dans l'&troit moi" (within the n&rrow me) in text 5, and "à l'étroit dans" (to the narrow within) in text 6. Although "meaning" as such has not been completely eliminated (for instance, the expression "forte tour" [fortified tower] appears repeatedly throughout the texts, carrying over semantically the idea of enclosed, limited space), the possibility of communication, the allegorical (that is, representational) function of the traditional poem, is essentially obstructed; the ordered discursivity of the preface becomes an anarchic jumble of words and typographical symbols.

The disruption of syntax and signification, then, can also be seen as an "anticlosural" strategy, one that works in conjunction with the structural derangement of the text to prevent the traditional, discursive progression toward a meaningful conclusion.[19] This attack upon the finality of meaning and the effort to undermine all closural effects occurs on the most fundamental level, that of the word itself, whose unity is broken by the omission of letters, by the splitting of a word in two so that it appears on two different lines within the poem, or by the appearance of an unnecessary and misplaced capital letter. The linguistic operations of the poem, then, become manifestly self-destructive, waging war on the prevailing rules of grammar and punctuation by "pulverizing" the very structure of the word, producing a system of shocks and tensions that upset the regular rhythms of the traditional poem.

Thus, in almost every possible instance, the traditional qualities of closure (that is, unified meaning and structure) are contested by "Le Mécrit," with the spatial configuration of each text all but obliterating the framed introduction and undermining, as a consequence, the teleological character of the traditional literary form. No longer following the pattern of the conventionally "programmed" text as defined by Kristeva, the trajectory of "Le Mécrit" does not just repeat, in accordance with a simplistic notion of the mimetic, the introductory preface; it engages that preface in a series of transformations and permutations that proceed toward no point of culmination but are inscribed in an ultimately unresolvable, open-ended process. Not even the margins of the pages succeed in imposing limits. The texts flow into one another, each one repeating and transforming the various components of the preceding structure: "la ferme" (the farm) in text 1 is either repeated in text 2 or reemerges as "la fermieR" (the femaL farmer) in text 3 or "le fermier" (the farmer) in text 6; "2 pourceaux" (2 swine) in text 2, which reappears in text 3, becomes "Pour ces 2-ci" (For these 2 swine here) in text 5 or "2 doux pourceaux" (2 sweet swine) in text 6. All of this is, of course, not to evoke some idyllic, pastoral vision but rather to accentuate the movement from text to text, with the semantic and typographical variations of the preface also appearing to reverberate throughout.

This emphasis on the mutual interaction between texts whereby each is constructed on the basis of its relationship to other textual surfaces once again serves to open the text. The individual poems are permutations of texts within "Le Mécrit" itself as well as expressions and contradictions of an entire body of literature whose traditional aspects are called to mind even as they are being transformed. As Roche states in the preface to *Eros énergumène*: "To defigure the convention of writing is to bear constant witness that poetry is a convention (*of genre*) within a convention (*of communication*)."[20] Moreover, in conjuring up the literary conventions it sets out to negate, the work inevitably implicates the cultural beliefs and presuppositions with which it remains inextricably intertwined. Consequently, the operations of "Le Mécrit" do not simply attempt to negate the rigid stanza arrangements and the closed communicative patterns of the traditional poem but are directed at an entire culture; the poem's antipoetic, antidiscursive writing ("mécriture") is to lead, as the words of the preface to "Le Mécrit" seem to indicate, "poetic production toward its most extreme 'miscultural' point [*méculture*], the zero point, clearly of poeticity."[21]

Underscoring this effort to move beyond cultural constraints are the Etruscan and Mongolian inscriptions, which, from the point of view of *Tel Quel* theorists, provide a means of breaking out of the bounds of Western ethnocentrism by introducing other civilizations and other forms of language, particularly the languages of the Orient, with their emphasis on tonality and rhythm disrupting the ordered and logical system of Western discourse and thus contesting the rigid constraints imposed by Western rationalist thought. In addition, the basic incomprehensibility of the inscriptions (to the average Western reader, at least) serves to counter to the most extreme degree traditional interpretive approaches by confounding the reader's search for meaning, leaving him with little more than the formal arrangement of the symbols on the page. The inscriptions, then, whose "system of functioning," Roche writes at the end of the work, is closely related to that of his own poetic texts, become in certain respects "models" for the other texts within "Le Mécrit," where the attempt to emphasize the mechanisms of language and textual formation is intended to dissolve all totalizing meaning. Thus, just as the theoretical preface participates in the structuring of "Le Mécrit" through the negation of its closed discursivity, so too do the inscriptions, which must be confronted as a complex system of writing and not simply in terms of their content, influence the formation of each text.

This emphasis, however, upon the materiality of language should not, according to *Tel Quel* theory, be interpreted as a purely formalist position, as an attempt to constitute an exclusively verbal universe separated from all social, historical, or even psychological considerations. As we have seen in the context of Kristeva's notion of intertextuality, it is precisely this exclusivity, the limitations imposed by those who consider language as a strictly formal and basically analyzable system, that the revolutionary text is to counter. Although we shall see that the *Tel Quel* theory of the text remained in some respects within the formalist enclosure, the group considered formalism to be as closed and repressive as the aesthetic idealism it was meant to replace. The operations of "Le Mécrit," then, are to be viewed as more than a simple verbal exercise. Structured by a multiplicity of written and unwritten influences (namely, the literary conventions and the philosophical assumptions of the tradition it attempts to negate, the rhythmical antidiscursive practices of the extra-European cultures it seeks to affirm, the interweaving of the texts within "Le Mécrit" itself, the intentions of its author, and, as we shall see, the interpretive activity of the reader), the text emerges as an open, dynamic interweaving of linguistic and nonlinguistic practices which complicates the formalist model by moving beyond the confines of a static linguistic system and frustrates the reader's attempt to analyze the text, to reduce it to a monolithic structure.

The reader, then, is also caught up in the dynamics of the open text; his effort to establish consistent patterns is both stimulated and frustrated by its complex operations.[22] The various gaps that appear within its structure, the broken words and the omitted letters play upon the reader's tendency to link things together, to marshal all elements into a single and finite meaning, by inviting him to participate actively in the reconstitution of the text. The reader finds, however, that his attempts at reconstruction fail abominably. The rejoined words convey no unified image; the various patterns offer no point of convergence. This is particularly evident in the substitution of "&" for what the reader assumes could be either "e" or "u" (as in "dans l'&troit moi" or in "&n"), and yet the reader immediately finds that his process of decoding uncovers no underlying system, for his conclusions are countered by the appearance of the symbol in other contexts where it has no apparent justification (for example, in "&u&cs").[23]

The text, then, continually provokes the reader into establishing his own connections and at the same time interferes with his ability to do so. The reader discovers that for every meaning he attempts to impose upon the work there is a conflicting possibility. Turning to the preface in his search for consistency where, on the basis of his experience with traditional textual analysis, he expects to read certain directives that will guide his interpretation, he finds that the preface only adds to his uncertainty, first heightening his expectations and then preventing their complete fulfillment. Each succeeding text within "Le Mécrit," whose operations challenge the conventions of genre and communication by undermining referentiality and poetic principles of structure and versification, appear initially to be working in conformity with the stated aims of the preface: "As for what they call *poetry*, as far as I am concerned I must always try to thrust myself into it more deeply, carrying into it the poetic material in order to bring it to the point where it figures only *reductively* [afin de l'amener à ne plus figurer *qu'en moins*] and that within the very narrow limits of the only landscape in which I still move about." The traditional poem is transformed into a multiplicity of "texts" whose chaotic juxtaposition of words and pulsional rhythms counters the traditional conceptions of poetic structure and meaning. Thus, in response to the indications set forth in the preface (and rendered all the more authentic, the reader assumes, by the dated signature that closes the statement), the reader abandons his habitual search for the thematic or symbolic content of the work and looks for consistency on the formal level alone where the preface again provides certain guidelines: "So it is necessary, in order to better dispose of the spectacle of writing, through the expedients that enable our signs to carry on, to bring poetic production toward its most extreme 'miscultural' point, the zero point, clearly of poeticity." The reader is thus led to assume that the visible play with form and language becomes the unifying force within the work, a view that is initially and briefly reinforced by the spatial configuration of each text—the heavy concentration of words at the center of the page gives the poems a closed, hermetic appearance that encourages a purely visual appropriation.

Once the reader decides, however, that the formal unity of writing as "spectacle" replaces the semantic unity of the traditional poem, he finds that certain discrepancies arise. He discovers that the succeeding texts also appear to be working against the notion of spectacle by dissolving the borders of the frame and by bringing the reader *into* the text, forcing him to become involved in the process of textual construction rather than remain outside in a mere spectator's role. The reader at this point becomes uneasy about his interpretation of the text as a purely formal construct, for he realizes, on the one hand, that the work could not be completely devoid of "message" or content (for the content becomes the form itself) and, on the other hand, that his enclosure of the work within the bounds of a single and determinate "meaning" is exactly what the succeeding texts appear to be contesting. The closed configuration of the preface, with its well-defined frame, the finality and conclusiveness that the author's signature implies, the rigid discursivity, and the idea of closure and limitation that its language conveys ("within the very narrow limits"), is fractured by the work's open-ended intertextual structure. In this regard, even semantics has a role to play: throughout the texts, words or images appear that evoke open, unlimited space ("une portE/*ouve*/r te" [an *op*/en/dooR], "la mer" [the sea], "le vent" [the wind], "les nuages" [the clouds]) or indicate an attempt to break through or to expand all boundaries either in the form of erotic or obscene images or expressions such as "me voletant autoU/r *de*. cette forte tour" (fluttering aroU/*nd*. this fortified tower), "cette forte tour gonfle poUr/r rire" (this tower blows tO/o laugh), "J'enfonce le/s 2. qui sortent tous—Les fortes tours" (I thrust th/e 2. who all leave—The fortified towers).

Given the text's contradiction of the preface in all other areas, the reader begins to assume that the unifying principle resides in this deliberate negation of the prefatory statement and that the author actually planned a reversal not only of its well-defined structure but also of its explicitly formulated intentions. Yet the reader sees that his attempt to find a consistent pattern of negation is also undermined, for the texts, as we have seen, often attempt to carry out the dictates of the initial statement and actually repeat, or so he assumes, many of its elements. Images of closure appear that contradict those signifying openness, and the idea of the solitary voyage in the last two lines in the preface is expressed in texts 2, 4, and 5—although, here again, he can never be sure whether the coarse language in the last two lines in text 4 is meant to confirm that idea or to disparage it, or even, taking it one step further, whether he can state with certainty that the two lines are related to the preface at all. The language of the text, then, and its structure as well do not permit the reader to find consistency either in the affirmation of the preface or in its negation. The texts appear to accentuate the visible manifestation of form and to contest it at the same time, not only structurally, but semantically as well; the eye sees ("leurs cils errant son R" [their eyelashes wandering its (his/her R)]) and it does not see ("sans avoir vu écrit" [without having seen written], "pas rien qui confie qui voit" [not nothing that entrusts that sees]). The reader's attempt to focus on content is thus countered by the prominently formal aspects of the work, and yet his accentuation of form only makes him more acutely aware of the content.

The text thus arouses continual conflicts within the reader, making him increasingly uncertain about interpreting it in accordance with the preface as a pure spectacle of writing and yet preventing him from declaring with certainty that the texts are engaged in a deliberate reversal of the "author's" introductory statement. The reader thus comes to realize that the preface provides no real guidelines for his interpretation of the work and that its insertion raises more questions than it answers. Finding that the succeeding texts represent not just a simple confirmation but also a denial of the prefatory "intentions" and yet never certain that a complete reversal of the preface was "intended" by the author of the text, the reader begins to reexamine the problem of intentionality itself, to question not only his preconceptions about the role of the preface in programming both the text and the reader's response to it, but his assumption that the prefatory statement expresses the actual intentions of an empirical author and, more important, that those intentions could ever truly be ascertained. Thus, in this case as in all others, the text resists appropriation and subverts the teleological operations of traditional literary form by offering a multiplicity of conflicting perspectives over which the author, his preface, and the reader do not have total control.

The process of reading, then, no longer guided by the traditionally programmed text, requires a continual change of viewpoint, a constant modification of the reader's preconceptions. Deprived of a specific frame of reference, which in the traditional text the preface might provide, and supplied with no precise indications within the texts themselves for interpreting them, the reader becomes increasingly disoriented, entangled in the operations of the text in his effort to piece things together and alienated at the same time, compelled either to reject or to question the meanings he himself proposes. This discovery of the basically provisional nature of any and all projections of meaning heightens the reader's awareness of his own interpretive activity, an awareness elicited the moment he approaches one of the texts. Finding the margins in some instances *within* the texts rather than outside, the reader immediately becomes concerned about the appropriate method of reading, asking himself whether the divided parts should be read vertically, as separate columns, or from left to right in the traditional horizontal fashion. The process of reading itself, then, becomes a prominent feature within the work. The reader "reads" his own activity, his attempts at reconstruction, and comes to recognize that he is himself a productive force within the text, that the meaning he uncovers is not necessarily due to something inherent in the work itself but is the result of his own interpretive projections. The reader, as a consequence, becomes increasingly self-critical, constantly scrutinizing or revising the expectations underlying his search for textual comprehensibility and ultimately realizing that his own interpretive capacities are limited, that he can never fully dominate the operations of the text.

Here, then, within the reader through the modification of his usual modes of perceiving and interpreting the work, according to *Tel Quel* theory, lie the revolutionary possibilities of the open text. By presenting itself as a constantly changing object that involves the reader in the endless production and cancellation of meaning, the revolutionary text deprives the reader of a central focus, prevents him from attaining the distance he needs to formulate an all-encompassing perspective. The text comes to be viewed not as a product to be consumed, analyzed, or dissected from a position outside its perimeters but as an open process of textual production which the reader apprehends not by means of a purely visual appropriation but "dynamically," by becoming directly involved in the dynamics of the open text. The operations of the revolutionary text thus constitute, according to *Tel Quel* theory, a radical transformation of the conventions of reading. As Sollers wrote in the *Tel Quel*

"Programme" of 1967: "This textual rupture . . . is the crisis itself, the violent revolution, the leap, of readability."[24]

Theoretical Closure

That this rather categorical opposition between the closed and essentially readable literary product and the open, "unreadable" process of textual production might in itself undermine the theory of the open text is a possibility the members of the *Tel Quel* group never seriously considered. As we shall see, implicit in the concept of the text as a revolutionary praxis is the idea of a certain complicity between the reader and the written text that in a number of ways reinstates the communicative model of interpretation by restoring many of the assumptions governing the traditional relationship between author, reader, and text. If the practice of writing is to be a revolutionary weapon, a means of fulfilling certain goals and objectives, then the operations of the modern literary work must be strictly controlled in order to produce the desired "effect" on both the reader and the society of which he is a part. And the reader in turn must be carefully programmed as well, guided toward the "correct" and appropriate response.

In this context, a second reading of "Le Mécrit" produces quite different conclusions. Referring to the author's theoretical pronouncements in an effort to interpret the work, the reader discovers that explicitly stated intentions underlie the structure of the text itself and are to inform the reading of it as well. Outlining his position in the notice on the back cover of *Le Mécrit*, Roche writes: "*Le Mécrit* marks the end of a search . . . that wants to be, through the *denatured, materialized* utilization of every aspect of the poetic process whether it be traditional or not, a progressive annulment of both the retrograde, obscurantist, in a word, inane ideology, which is embraced by those who 'write poetry,' and of the practices in which they habitually engage." Responding to a question in his later "novel," *Louve basse*, about his apparent renunciation of poetry after writing *Le Mécrit*, he states: "I never used the word 'renounce.' In fact, *Le Mécrit* is only the result of an enterprise, of a demonstration inaugurated at the time of the publication of *The Centesimal Ideas of Miss Elanize*. When I gave *Le Mécrit* to my editor, I had the impression that I had arrived at the end of this demonstration, that it was closed."[25] That this demonstration itself depends upon the existence of certain structuring principles and controls does not seem to concern Roche, and yet his apparent indication of the ultimate success of his venture confirms rather than subverts the closed teleological structure of the traditional text by positing the fulfillment of certain goals and objectives and indicating, as a consequence, that specific principles and intentions continue to program the operations of the text.

The problems inherent in Roche's comments above thus bring into sharp focus the difficulties that plagued the *Tel Quel* theory as a whole. To view the text as a demonstration or an application of a revolutionary theory of textual practice, one that is to undermine the sovereignty of a preexistent authorial intention as the principal determining factor, is not to do away with the problem of intentionality. Rather, the problem moves to another level, where the intentions of an individual author become those of the revolutionary group whose precepts serve as the primary motivating force behind the literary work. Roche's identification with the *Tel Quel* project thus leads him, as we shall see, to counter his own position in certain respects. While attacking the traditional concept of the poem as a perfectly controlled, communicative object whose signification emanates from a single structuring source, he at the same time, by virtue of his endorsement of a revolutionary theory or program, posits a capacity to control the operations of the text. In his interview with Serge Gavronsky, where he discussed his association with *Tel Quel*, Roche's comments revealed the deliberateness and sense of purpose that underlie his own and the *Tel Quel* position.

> This poetry of *Tel Quel* . . . can be characterized by a desire, a very determined desire, to negate or deny completely everything that could be said to belong, strictly speaking, to poetry. . . . Let us say that we are moving further and further away from the metaphor, or from a well-turned poetry. . . . We are trying to do something being fully conscious of it, and doing it voluntarily and naturally in order to succeed at it.[26]

This presumably deliberate effort to contest prevailing poetic conventions thus provides the organizational principle that programs both the language of the text and, as Roche's comments clearly indicate, the reader's reactions as well. Discussing his own works of poetry and their role in shaping the reader's response, Roche stated: "[A]ll of my poems are always of the same length in order not to distract the reader by extensions or retractions or things like that. They are always of the same form, the speed of narration, so that the reader will be solely preoccupied about what is going on inside the poem itself and with the language itself, continuously folding back upon itself" (pp. 178–79). The capacity of the text to control the reader's reactions is also what Kristeva implies in her discussion of various modern texts, most particularly those of Mallarmé, Lautréamont, and Sollers, where she often indicates that the structure of the work itself induces the reader, by directing his attention away from the "meaning" of the text (the phenotext), to focus on the process of textual production (the genotext). Indeed, despite Kristeva's claims that the modern literary work operates "constantly on the line that swings from the phenotext to the genotext and vice versa" and that this "joining of the two" prevents the reader from finding a central focus, she maintains that it is the genotext, and not the linguistic operations of the phenotext, that must be perceived by the reader:

> Confronted with the formulas [that is, formulas of meaning—an expression Kristeva uses to stress the complex relationship between the process of meaning formation and the text as a visible, readable phenomenon] projected and as if *ejected* by the generative process, the reader is invited to make a leap in the opposite direction: from the narrative [*récit*] to the numbering infinity [*l'infinité nombrante*], from representation to transformation, from waste to *jouissance*. Without mediation, we are led through the zone of representation to the place where the mirror is liquefied.[27]

> [W]e must . . . break through the sign, dissolve it, and analyze it in a semanalysis, tearing the veil of representation to find the material signifying process. The drive process cannot be released and carried out in narrative, much less in metalanguage or theoretical drifting. It needs a text: *a destruction of the sign and representation*, and hence of narrative and metalanguage, with all their lock-step, univocal seriousness.[28]

The sign, in this case, must either be dissolved or bypassed in order for the genotext to be perceived. This means, however, that the text ceases to function as "a double punctuation," whose operations are to be read in a multiplicity of ways, and that the reader possesses the capacity to disengage himself from its operations, to be freed of all linguistic constraints in order to focus on productivity to the exclusion of the product: "We must leave the enclosure of language to seize what operates in a genetic and logical time before the constitution of the symbolic function."[29]

This exclusion of the symbolic, the linguistic operations of the phenotext, is, of course, essential if the unlimited movement of textual productivity is to be preserved "as such," if its operations are to be inscribed within the surface structure of the text without being absorbed by that structure, without textual productivity itself becoming a concrete and appropriable phenomenon. Yet this very separation of the productive process from its product already limits the movement of the genotext by imposing certain boundary lines that play a part in defining and determining its structure. To establish productivity as the most significant property of the literary work, as that which is most worthy of the reader's attention, is to reinstate the notion of product by assigning a particular meaning to the text, one that is taken to be implicit in the structure of the text itself and actually determines its specificity.

Kristeva's formulation of the distinction genotext/phenotext thus turns out to be rather problematical. In presupposing the existence of certain characteristics peculiar to each category, it reinforces the phenomenalism it was set up to undermine and, in so doing, places the modern literary work in a position not dramatically different from its more traditional counterpart. Not only does the text convey a single message to a supposedly neutral reader, but its binary structure, which incorporates both the process and its product, curiously resembles that of the traditional novel form, where, according to Kristeva, the interplay between opposites always leads to the inevitable "agreement of deviations" and thus assures the production and ultimate consumption of a single and finite sense. In this case, and despite Kristeva's insistence that there is no possibility for resolution in the modern text, that one side of the opposition cannot be subsumed under the other ("The text will never leave this double position, but will occur constantly at the site of the cut which separates the two spaces, that of the generative process and that of the phenomenon"),[30] she argues, at the same time, that the productive process, or genotext, ultimately prevails; its very inscription within the phenotext destroys all unity of meaning: "[T]he massive arrival of the genotext in the formula erases all the surface meaning [*sens facial*] that is able to *present itself* and . . . provokes as an immediate and indispensable effect, the disappearance [*l'évanouissement*] of present Meaning."[31] It appears, then, that within the structure of the modern text, the opposition is resolved by a simple reversal of the traditional format. Here, it is not the sign but the process that gathers all elements into a complex unity, thus revealing that far from eliminating the principles of unified structure and meaning in the traditional novel form, the modern text is actually dependent upon the same principles of construction, duplicating by means of an inversion the nondisjunctive operations of the traditional text.

Thus, despite Kristeva's attempts to avoid the pitfalls of what she calls "le rationalisme positiviste" that characterizes Western thought, a concept of productivity as object emerges from her analysis of the modern text, a concept paradoxically reinforced by her effort to preserve the unappropriable character of the text's "poetic language." In viewing the text as a revolutionary literary practice whose operations cannot be recuperated by the linguistic sign—"a new semiotics" sees literature "as irreducible to the level of an object for normative linguistics (which deals with the codified and denotative word [*parole*])"—Kristeva determines its specificity by establishing it as different from other modes of discourse and ultimately reinstates a distinction between the literary and the nonliterary that has always been fundamental to the "Western" concept of the text.[32] This distinction is reinforced by Kristeva's assertion that literature, and most particularly poetry, possesses the power to work against the social order. Claiming that its rhythmical patterns, rhyme schemes, and intonations have already wedged an opening in the linguistic sign (and thus perpetuating the view that normative discourse, when uncontaminated by poetry, preserves its unitary structure), Kristeva sees poetic language as the means by which the ideological notions of subject, structure, and meaning can most readily be undermined:

> So within this saturated if not already closed socio-symbolic order, poetry—more precisely, poetic language—reminds us of its eternal function: to introduce through the symbolic that which works on, moves through and threatens it. The theory of the unconscious seeks the very thing that poetic language practices within and against the social order: the ultimate means of transformation or subversion, the precondition for its survival and revolution. . . . Literature has always been the most explicit realization of the signifying subject's condition. Indeed it was in literature starting in the second half of the nineteenth century, that the dialectical condition of the subject was made explicit, beginning in France with the work of Nerval, but particularly with Lautréamont et Mallarmé.[33]

The problem here, of course, is that the text acquires an essentially "literary" identity by virtue of its difference from ordinary, communicative language, and it assumes a position of privilege with regard to all other signifying practices within the social system. Although Kristeva insists that "[l]iterature does not exist for semiotics," that it is merely one productive practice among many with no particularly privileged status, she argues that the literary text has the "advantage" of "making more accessible than others the problematics of the production of meaning."[34] And the modern text, written *after* the "epistemological break" in the late nineteenth century, is in her view most effective in this regard. In Lautréamont's *Poésies II*, for example, Kristeva finds that the accumulation of short, choppy sentences produces an "accelerated rhythm that engages the reader in a way that makes their meaning fade into the background; one doesn't stop there, the meanderings of reason escape, and music imposes itself once again."[35] Sollers's *Nombres*, with its disruption of syntax and the accentuation of the sonorous or visual properties of language, performs the same function. "[T]he text," Kristeva writes, "pulls you away from your vision of the surface and leads you to the edge of this frontier [where the generative process emerges]."[36] The emphasis in *Nombres* upon the phonic and graphic disposition of words or letters on the writ-

ten page, which is accomplished through the repetition of pho-
nemes and certain phonic groups, dissolves all unity of meaning
within the text and provides the reader with a concrete manifesta-
tion (and, therefore, *representation*) of the engendering process,
of words generating other words and of sounds generating other
sounds. Here, as Kristeva describes the process in *Séméiotiké*, the
vowel in particular ceases to remain subservient to the semantic
function of language by operating primarily as an engendering
agent and thus bringing into focus the productive mechanisms that
structure the text: "[I]t is the vowel that will be the bearer of the
modulation of the genotext" (p. 305); "The graphic or phonic ele-
ment, having become a signifying differential exemplified by the
vowel, permits the overturning [*renversement*] of representation
and communication ('emission,' 'projection') and opens toward the
infinite numbering-space of the genotext" (p. 306); "a *notation* of
vowels appears . . . exempt of meaning by dint of engendering it
infinitely: I-O-U-I-A-I" (p. 315).

In stressing the importance of the vowel in Sollers's text, Kris-
teva not only gives it once again a certain meaning or significance
by virtue of its participation in the productive process, but she
assigns to the modern literary work an ordered and purposeful
structure, one that adopts many of the restrictive procedures that
characterize the traditionally programmed text. Here, the irregular
rhythms, the gaps that appear within the structural and informa-
tional flow of its language (which serve initially to involve the
reader in its movement), and the text's continual negation of
the reader's interpretive constructs, all work together to prevent
the reader from reducing the text to some identifiable meaning so
that he will be left with no choice but to focus on the operations
of the text itself. As Kristeva writes: "Piercing the space and the
line of the comprehending subject ('you') . . . breaking through
temporal and signified representation, it is production (without
product) that is implanted" (p. 345). Consequently, because of this
alienation of the appropriating reader, an estrangement that re-
sults, paradoxically, from his actual involvement in the productive
process, the modern reader finds himself in a position much like
that of his predecessors, impelled by various textual controls to
come to a specific understanding of the literary work. Despite

Kristeva's claim that the reader is provided no single point of refer-
ence with which to validate his response, that "no verification . . . is
possible" within the modern text, the notion of a "correct" reading
emerges once again, one that requires that the reader, like the text
itself, engage in a certain "bracketing" of those elements that do
not correspond to the authorized view. Indeed, this kind of reading,
Kristeva asserts, which forces the reader to pierce "the phenomeno-
logical surface of the 'énoncé' (the phenotext)," is "entirely foreseen
by the text" where "it has become impossible [and here she is citing
Sollers] . . . to make of writing an object to be studied in terms other
than those of writing itself" (pp. 288–89).

Rereading "Le Mécrit"

An examination of "Le Mécrit," then, with these comments in
mind would produce a completely different conception of the work.
Confronted, first of all, by the preface, which outlines the revolu-
tionary principles and intentions that lie behind the work and
which, according to Roche himself, was inserted "as a prefatory
note to my friends," the reader comes to realize that his interpre-
tive effort is not to be countered and contested at every turn but is
to be carefully guided by its theoretical precepts.[37] By constantly
referring to the preface in his effort to make sense of the text's
distorted syntax, he discovers that a certain comprehension of the
work becomes once again possible, provided, of course, that he
abandon his search for meaning on a purely referential level and
attempt to view the text, in accordance with the preface, as a
"spectacle of writing," as an infinite process of poetic production
that, drawing both the author and reader into its unlimited move-
ment, is meant to undermine the conventional relationship be-
tween author, reader, and text.

What occurs, however, is that rather than undermining this
relationship between the "author," the text, and its reader, the
preface, which functions as a kind of revolutionary manifesto in
miniature, becomes the means by which that relationship is ul-
timately reinstated. A structuring intention or theoretical precept
is given command over the text and is presumed to organize the
subsequent operations in such a way as to assure total control over

the reader's reactions. The uncertainty that the reader felt upon first approaching the text, when he found himself continually invalidating his own interpretive constructs, gives way to the certainty that each succeeding text works in support of the prefatory intentions and, in fact, imposes certain constraints on the reader to ensure the appropriate response. The disruption of the normally referential or mimetic function of language within the individual poems becomes part of a deliberate effort to prevent the reader from thinking of the work as a simple representation so that he will be forced to look elsewhere for a common element or unifying principle. Turning to the preface to guide him in his search for consistency, he finds that unifying principle not in the relationship between the text and some concrete and well-defined image of reality but rather in the relationship of text to text, where the mechanism of language, the process of textual production, is the one interpretive construct facilitated by the guidelines and directives in the preface and by the emphasis within the text on primarily formal considerations.

The reader, in this case, perceiving certain structural similarities as he moves from text to text, ceases to direct his attention outside the perimeters of the work but becomes conscious of the inner workings of the text itself. Thus, reading the text on the most literal level, he sees the repetition of images such as "le champ" (the field), which first appears in the preface and is then repeated in text 6 or becomes "le pré" (the meadow) or "les prés" (the meadows) in texts 2 and 4. He notices the emphasis on the visual, which is accomplished semantically, with words such as "oeil" (eye), "vue" (sight), and "regard" (look) in various places throughout, and formally, through the graphic and phonic disposition of words or letters on the page. He finds himself caught up in the irregular rhythms of moving from word to word and sound to sound, and he becomes aware of the succession of the pages as well as the movement of his own reading as he passes from text to text. Thus, reading the text comparatively rather than referentially, he comes to the conclusion, with the aid of the preface, that this system of intertextual relationships is the single principle governing the organization of the work, that continuity can be found in the uninterrupted flow of the writing itself.

Read in accordance with the theory, then, the text becomes a purely formal construction. The network of intertextual relationships comes to be perceived not as a means of opening the text, of rendering it multidimensional and plural, but as a rule or law governing the system of textual production, a formal principle of generation that is to be rendered visible and apprehended by the reader at the expense of its content. And yet, as we have seen before, by providing a principle of ordering, a fixed center around which all else is organized, the content or sense of the work has not been eliminated but is in fact reinstated. The incompatibilities and contradictions that the reader finds on a simple referential level become, as Michael Riffaterre has pointed out in his analysis of various poetic texts, logical and comprehensible once the reader perceives them as part of another system of relationships. Consequently, by learning to read the text on a primarily structural level, by focusing on the mutual interaction between texts, the reader comes to a new understanding of the literary work, performing what Riffaterre has called a "semantic" or "semiotic transfer" whereby the "ungrammaticalities" that the reader finds with regard to the mimetic function of language are "eventually integrated into another system."[38] Here, the system of writing, the process of textual generation, determines the specificity, or what Riffaterre calls the "significance," of the literary work, replacing the semantic unity provided by referential meaning with a formal, intertextual unity that becomes in effect its "content."

In this context, the ungrammaticalities within "Le Mécrit" become once again "grammatical." The repetition of sounds, the various permutations of a particular word, of the verb "monter" (to climb), for example (which becomes at various points "montant," "montons," "monte," "remonte," and "remontant"), are viewed as part of the organizational plan or design of the text and are to expose the reader to the mechanisms generating the text, to the process by which one word or one sound generates another. Thus, everything within the text acquires meaning as it relates to the ideas expressed in the preface—that is, as it signifies the engendering process. Although the syntactical and grammatical distortion in text 5, for example, of the concluding lines of the preface may be a negation of the coherent and logical structure of its language, the idea of an endless and solitary voyage remains. The "nous nous dirigeons" (we make our way toward) in the preface becomes "nos 2 voix remontant" (our 2 voices climbing up again) in text 5; they both designate the involvement of reader and writer in the movement of language itself. The "nous" in this case is not to represent the traditional fusion of two unified subjects; it underscores, as Kristeva's analysis of Sollers's *Nombres* seems to indicate, the dissolution of the subject: "The inclusive 'We' . . . marks the impossible place—axial, sacrificial—of the non-person in the unidentified, a-personal multiplicity. Pronoun of the a-person, pronoun of engenderment."[39] The "we" designates "process," "production," and the absence of closure in the final line of text 5 following the reference to the Greek port Itea, which is both a destination and a point of departure, thus reinforces this sense of irresolution and open-endedness that characterizes the modern poem.

The conclusions one can draw from this particular reading of the text thus become rather obvious. The attempt to interpret the work in conformity with the dictates of the preface as an infinite "spectacle of writing," as a "formalism" of process, which is to be perceived at the expense of the product, does little to preserve the sense of openness and incompletion the texts are meant to convey but produces a conception of the work that is limiting and constrictive and actually reinstates the logic of mimetic representation it was meant to exclude. As that which represents the process of textual production in accordance with the dictates of a preexistent prefatory intention, the open and dispersed intertextual space of the modern literary work, which is meant to question traditional modes of interpretation, becomes enveloped in the closed theoretical space of the preface, where the notion of intertextuality, which is also the notion of process, the unlimited movement of writing itself, becomes a restrictive theoretical construct, that is, the only acceptable interpretation of the work.

This, then, is one of the major drawbacks of the *Tel Quel* theory of the revolutionary text. If the notion of intertextuality, or the process of textual production, is to become the single mode of interpretation, the only structuring principle at work within the text, then the concept of intertextuality may actually foster the kind of reading it was initially supposed to contest by giving the work an inner coherence and logic that merely repeat, by means of an inversion, the ordered uniformity and the representational logic of the traditionally programmed text. Structured by a theoretical intention, the implied author of the work, and interpreted by the reader in accordance with those intentions, the text becomes part of a meaningful circularity, forming a closed circuit of communication in which the "author" as producer and the reader as consumer come together and function as one: "That toward which we make our way, henceforth assured of our solitude, and without it being possible for anyone to follow us."[40] For Kristeva, the "we" designating process also belongs to "the revolutionary masses," designating communication, a fraternal solidarity between "author" and reader that may ultimately serve rather than contest the tradition by reinstating the "Law of One."

PART II

Rethinking the Collective
and the Political

CHAPTER 3

Dismantling the 'Tel Quel' Community

The Multiple Languages of Dissidence

Given the contradictory nature of the *Tel Quel* project, it is not surprising that Sollers, Kristeva, and others came ultimately to question the value of their politically motivated collective practice. As their disillusionment with the effects of the Cultural Revolution set in, following their visit to China in 1974, when they saw that Chinese Marxism differed very little from the Soviet model, they began to suspect their own "intellectual conformism," recognizing that their demand for ideological consensus suppressed the diversity of their practice by subsuming it under the homogenizing discourses of Marxist theory and its "totalizing rationality." For this reason, as Sollers recalled in his interview with Shuhsi Kao in 1981, they dismantled their "ideological collectivity":

> We have abandoned the notion that the group, the activity of each member and the review itself, has to be subordinate to an overall political view. . . . The activity on the theoretical level since 1975/76 . . . may appear less cohesive, less monolithic, but that is perhaps what makes it much more subversive, to the extent that it is dispersed, with bizarre points of singularity. *Tel Quel* changes its topology, perhaps because we have reached a point where to become definable is to be vulnerable. Hence *Tel Quel* called *Tel Quel* into question, an example of permanent revolution.[1]

Addressing specifically the question of *Tel Quel*'s relationship to Marxism, Sollers stated in a 1977 issue of *Tel Quel*:

> I thought . . . that Marxism was the positive alternative to all this fascist and colonialist muck [cette boue du fascisme et du colonialisme]. . . . And one of the most painful experiences was to discover little by little what Marxism was used for: for gaining an ever-increasing hold on power through concentration camps and psychiatric internments . . . , for the reinforcement, again and again, of the police, the army. . . . Thus, the 20th century is still that of fascism and Stalinism. They persist; they return; they are the wound and the shame of intellectuals.[2]

Having thus relinquished the all-encompassing discourse of a revolutionary Marxist ideology, *Tel Quel* turned toward the more "specific" and individualized discourses of Russian and Eastern Bloc "dissidents" whose personal and non-ideological struggle for individual rights came to replace the Marxist myth of the "good society," which for Kristeva and others now had totalitarian implications. Serving no political program and resolutely resisting the discourses of power and coercion by maintaining, in the words of Guy Scarpetta, "a position of listening, of nonmastery . . . [and] of dispersion,"[3] the singular practices of dissidence were seen as ultimately dissolving the "ideological community" that adherents of Marxism—and *Tel Quel*—had come to represent. As Kristeva wrote:

> It is the task of the intellectual, who has inherited those "unproductive" elements of our modern technocratic society which used to be called the "humanities," not just to produce this right to speak and behave in an individual way in our culture, but to assert its *political value*. Failing this, the function of the intellectual strangely enough turns into one of coercion. In the wake of the priest, it is the Marxist and the Freudian who today have become these manufacturers of an all-embracing [*totalisante*] rationality. When taken out of their own time and space . . . Marxism and Freudianism . . . often become the magic password that closes the door and reinforces the belief in a society shaped by constraint, thus justifying the obsessional dialectic of the slave. . . . A spectre haunts Europe: the dissident. Give voice to each individual form of the unconscious, to every desire and

need. Call into play the identity and/or the language of the individual and the group. Become the analyst of every kind of speech and institution considered socially impossible. Proclaim that we reveal the Impossible.[4]

Thus, although *Tel Quel*'s renunciation of the collective never led to an in-depth analysis of the effects of its political ideology on the specifics of *Tel Quel* theory or practice, the move in the direction of dissidence contained an implicit recognition, not necessarily of its political idealism, for the group had not yet abandoned completely its revolutionary rhetoric,[5] but of a certain theoretical inadequacy whose outlines are only barely visible in the comments of Guy Scarpetta:

> To hear the discourse of the dissidents, to risk hearing it, is obviously to call into question a certain number of our certainties and of our progressivist biases; . . . it is to ask how our own theories . . . can also share in the very logic of an ideology of the totalitarian State. . . . Let us therefore, first of all and with humility, know how to *listen* to the dissidents. . . . [T]heir language has come in time to remind us of the murderous character of the social bond and, simultaneously, of the necessity of daily, obstinate, rebellious resistance toward all dogmas. [The dissidents have confronted us with] this truth to which decades of Marxist conformity have blocked our access: that as soon as there is a *reduction* of language and literature to ideology, totalitarianism and murder by the State are already there in full force.[6]

The diverse languages of dissidence would thus come to replace *Tel Quel*'s conceptual authoritarianism, leading to a renewed interest in literature for its own sake, unsubordinated to a theoretical program and therefore "subversive in itself," and to an exploration of the subversive possibilities within a diverse range of signifying practices, including religion, psychoanalysis, and art. Indeed, it can be argued that the focus in the 1980's on the psychology of religion in the writings of both Sollers and Kristeva represents a significant turning point in their thinking. Although neither advocated a return to the tradition and a reaffirmation of religious faith, religion, particularly in Kristeva's analysis of the discourses of love in Western culture, acquired a more positive value and was discussed in terms dramatically different from her earlier rejection of the monotheistic tradition in which poetic language was "the enemy of religion" and "the only language that uses up transcendence and theology to sustain itself."[7] Religion, first regarded as working in complicity with the state and the family to impose social constraints, later became for both Sollers and Kristeva not so much "an enemy to be evaded" (*un ennemi à fuir*), as a discourse that needed to be analyzed: "Theology interests me most right now," Sollers said in 1981. "The initial hypothesis is very simple: two thousand years of Christianity remain unreflected. Nobody has really taken a good look at the way Christianity functions."[8] The notion that Judaism and Christianity were signifying practices whose analysis might shed light on the contradictions and repressions involved in the formation of the Western subject acquired perhaps greater urgency after *Tel Quel*'s flirtation with Marxism, when the group discovered that the Marxists had not dissolved the religious phenomenon but had actually reproduced it: "Marxism is a religion," Sollers asserted, "and worse than a religion, in a way, because it is even more impoverished than what religion stratifies on the symbolic level" (p. 43). Analyses of the "religious factor" thus gained greater prominence in the writings of Sollers and Kristeva, whose two studies in the 1980's of the psychic underpinnings of the various discourses of love in Western culture allowed her to examine the psychology of religious love as well.

Love, Psychoanalysis, and Religion

In *Tales of Love*, for example, which examines Western images of love as elaborated in the writings of Plato and certain Christian theologians, as well as in a wide range of literary texts, and in her subsequent work, *In the Beginning Was Love: Psychoanalysis and Faith*, which focuses on the psychology of religious love and Christian faith, religion is considered in a very different light. Its role in the preservation of the social order and in the repression of unconscious heterogeneity is no longer Kristeva's primary concern.[9] On the contrary, she now sees religion as a practice that, far from repressing instinctuality, reveals the continuity of the instinctual, heterogeneous economy. Using Freud's analysis of narcissism as a point of departure, Kristeva indeed claims that the different expressions of love throughout Western civilization, and this includes Christian *agapē*, are in a sense all reconstructions of the unconscious, pre-Oedipal stage of psychic development, when the subject's narcissism determines the choice of a love object and sets into motion the identifications essential to the subsequent development of the ego.

Addressing her readers now as a practicing psychoanalyst but revealing an interest, which has grounded all of her writings, in the status of the speaking subject and in Western notions of identity, Kristeva shifts her attention away, in this later work, from the question of poetic language and its disruption of traditional representational or mimetic logic in order to focus on the interpersonal structuring relations constituting the human psyche. This change in emphasis does not mean, however, that Kristeva has abandoned the question of traditional notions of the mimetic and its identifying mechanisms. Although she never speaks directly of the question of mimetic representation in her analysis of the idealizing identifications necessary for psychic development, she reveals a continuing interest in the same problematic, one that manifests itself not simply in a linguistic sense but in a sociopsychological sense as well. Tracing the outlines of what will be developed more fully in the writings of Lacoue-Labarthe and Nancy, who deal expressly with the question of mimesis as it functions in an explicitly cultural context, Kristeva analyzes narcissistic identification and shows that the traditional mimetic precepts governing linguistic representation (understood either as a simple imitation of a preexistent psychological, social, or conceptual reality, or as what constitutes reality in accordance with a predetermined concept or idea) are also evident in sociopsychological relations. Whether one is speaking of the individual psyche, when the child's narcissistic identifications with an idealized "other" allow for its own identity to be constituted, or of the structuring of communal identity through its identification with a political model or ideal, the underlying mechanism is the same. Each takes as its point of departure the structure of mimesis itself, which, when understood in its traditional sense as an infinite repetition of the same, involves the appropriation or reproduction of a predetermined model or concept (thus indicating that self-identity is dependent on the existence of an other) while denying the contradictory and destabilizing elements that the relation to otherness implies.

It is interesting to note that in Kristeva's critique of the Western philosophical, theological, and literary tradition for its common tendency to cover over the problematic of the self that is implied in this narcissistic relationship to the other, she reveals that her own thinking about the subject has taken on a significantly different coloration. Her analysis in *Tales of Love* of the narcissistic (that is, mimetic) relations necessary to the constitution of the human psyche seems to have led her away from her previous emphasis on the uniformly cohesive character of the symbolic order of identity and its structuring representations toward a deepened awareness of those destabilizing elements that have always undermined symbolic and representational unity. By bringing into focus the centrality of the narcissistic experience to the very existence of the subject as a conscious speaking being, Kristeva discusses human subjectivity less in terms of enclosures that need to be torn down and more in terms of the subject's internally fragmented existence as "one open system connected to another." Insofar as the narcissistic "opening up to the other" plays a decisive role in the constitution of the self, the movement of idealizing identification necessary to the ego's formation as a conscious speaking identity exposes an emptiness at the root of the human psyche. The self that emerges is never whole but divided, traversed by an otherness that constitutes at the same time that it problematizes self-contained identity.

Although Kristeva's analysis of the unconscious foundations of the amatory experience and of the crisis in identity that its relation to "otherness" reveals does reflect her gradual shift from semiotics toward a more psychoanalytical focus, it can also be traced to her work of the 1970's, *La Révolution du langage poétique,* in which she examines the psycholinguistic processes structuring both the sign and the speaking subject. In this work, she draws extensively upon Freud's theory of the unconscious, as well as on Lacan's interpretation of that theory, to wage an assault on the Western humanist tradition with its view of the subject as a fully coherent, self-sufficient identity. In Kristeva's later work, however, she continues to explore the mechanisms of the unconscious, pre-Oedipal stage, but her affirmation of its revolutionary potential is replaced by different concerns. No longer sure of the radically revolutionary possibilities of her own and the *Tel Quel* enterprise, Kristeva returns to an area she claims she and the members of the *Tel Quel* group had never really left, to that of psychoanalysis and its investigations of the "internal experience," of the inner workings of the individual psyche.[10] This reevaluation of her position and the fact that she became a practicing psychoanalyst in 1979 affect her later work in a very interesting way. In Kristeva's concern as an analyst for the "outbreak" of psychic disorders that Western society is witnessing today, her study seems to reveal a nostalgia for the traditional myths that support individual fantasies of wholeness. It shows, in contrast to her earlier work, a curious desire to shore up the subject rather than break it down, an effort to restore those feelings of self-sufficiency even as she shows them to be illusory. Thus, while exposing the "narcissistic wound" at the center of psychic experience, Kristeva finds in psychoanalysis the possibility for a "cure." Recognizing that love is essential to the structuration of the self, Kristeva argues that the aim of psychoanalysis today must be to reconstitute the narcissistic relationship through the "transference love" that inevitably arises between analyst and patient. The comforting presence of our religious illusions, which offered protection against the void of primary narcissism, is thus to be replaced by the psychiatrist's couch, by the work of the analyst whose role is to affirm, albeit provisionally, our imaginary constructions. The goal, however, is not to restore the plenitude that has supposedly been lost, but to allow the subject to construct some measure of subjectivity and thus to function, however tentatively, within the social system. The modern subject thus becomes what Kristeva calls a "work-in-progress," constantly constructing itself as a necessarily false identity while recognizing and indeed accepting the inauthenticity of its imaginary constructions.

To say, then, that Kristeva seeks to restore the humanist myth of psychic unity or that she hopes to strengthen the ego in the manner of the American ego-psychologists would be a serious distortion of her work, and in this sense Kristeva's two studies of love remain consistent with her earlier objectives. There is, however, a difference that has important consequences for her formulation of the distinction between the semiotic and the symbolic. In *Tales of*

Love, the movement of idealizing identification, which Kristeva previously associated with the Oedipal father and the order of the symbolic, is now part of the preliminary disposition of the semiotic, where the pre-Oedipal stage of primary narcissism incorporates the notion, developed by Freud, of a loving, archaic paternity. This introduction of the Freudian "father of individual pre-history" into a space previously reserved for the maternal "semiotic" complicates her earlier distinction, as does her recognition that Christianity plays out the dynamics of primary narcissism and thus shows the eruption of the "repressed" semiotic within monotheism itself. Indeed, often criticized for her tendency to define the semiotic and the symbolic in essentialist, "phallocentric" terms,[11] in her latest work, though certainly not free of the phallocentrism implicit in her acceptance of the Freudian Oedipal framework (the notion of identity is still paternally grounded and depends upon the rejection of the mother as "abject"), Kristeva comes to look differently at the relationship between the semiotic and the symbolic, stressing less the separateness and more the interrelatedness of the two functions and ultimately problematizing, perhaps even more than Kristeva herself recognizes, the very terms of the opposition.[12]

Indeed, if Kristeva's distinction contained certain inconsistencies on the level of language, its psychoanalytical implications proved for many critics to be even more troublesome. What resulted in the course of Kristeva's elaboration of the processes constituting the individual "unitary subject" was a reinforcement, once again, of the logic of identity that she hoped to call into question, not simply because it led to an essentializing celebration of the semiotic, as some have claimed.[13] In arguing for a return of this repressed instinctuality, which presumably remains outside the symbolic, Kristeva also seemed to conclude that the structures within the symbolic are themselves unified and whole, that the ego, for example, in opposition to what she herself claimed we have learned from the more revolutionary aspects of Freud's writing, successfully represses the disruptive instinctual impulses of the pre-Oedipal stage and emerges from the Oedipal drama as a fully constituted, more or less stable identity. The idea of an unproblematic integrated ego is not, of course, what Kristeva set out to affirm in the course of her analysis, and we find as a result, even as she moves into the 1980's, a certain oscillation on her part between a concept of the subject as a permanently fragmented identity and one that reveals, through its exclusion of the drive-dominated instability of the pre-Oedipal stage, its unitary structure. In this case, the instability of the ego is not a "permanent condition of the speaking being," as she claims in *Powers of Horror* and in *Tales of Love*, but a stage to be passed through, a form of "abjection" that, again in *Powers of Horror*, must be "permanently thrust aside in order (for the subject) to live." Thus, the "abject," which for Kristeva is not an object but part of the pre-objectal relationship to the mother, must be "radically excluded" so that a presumably stable identity might ultimately emerge:

> The abject is not an ob-ject facing me, which I name or imagine. Nor is it an ob-jest, an otherness ceaselessly fleeing in a systematic quest of desire. What is abject is not my correlative, which, providing me with someone or something else as a support, would allow me to be more or less detached and autonomous. The abject has only one quality of the object—that of being opposed to *I*. If the object, however, through its opposition, settles me within the fragile texture of a desire for meaning, which as a matter of fact, makes me ceaselessly and infinitely homologous to it, what is *abject* . . . the jettisoned object, is radically excluded and draws me toward the place where meaning collapses. A certain "ego" that merged with its master, a superego, has flatly driven it away. It lies outside, beyond the set, and does not seem to agree to the latter's rules of the game.[14]

This tendency to see the constitution of subjectivity in terms of precise developmental stages taken from a rather conservative reading of Freud thus leads her, in some respects, to posit a view of the subject that supports rather than dismantles Western illusions of unity. The threats to the subject's identity come not so much from its idealizing identifications with an "other" (that is, with the Oedipal father), which would indicate that the fragmentation of identity is inherent in the symbolic itself; it comes, rather, from the restoration of what has supposedly been left behind, from the return of the boundaryless, instinctual heterogeneity in which the necessary distinction between the subject and the outside world have not yet occurred.

In her work of the 1980's, however, and particularly in *Tales of Love*, we begin to see a certain shift in emphasis. Rather than positing, as she does in her earlier work, a subjectivity constituted by a radical break with the instinctual heterogeneity of the maternal phase, Kristeva in her analysis of the narcissistic underpinnings of love in Western culture aims to show that drive-dominated narcissistic impulses continue to structure adult relationships to the other. In this case, every experience of love (and this includes Christian love, where the Holy Father replaces the archaic father as the site of the subject's identifications) ultimately plays out the dynamics of primary narcissism and, in so doing, incorporates not only the idealizing identifications through which the subject gains its identity but also the instinctual impulses that generate such an amorous interaction with another. Kristeva claims, following Freud, that all forms of love, whether of self, of another person, of God, or of an abstract idea, are expressions of the individual's libidinal impulses when he or she first focuses autoerotically on the self before the drives are diverted to other objects. This drive dynamic is thus what "feeds" the amatory identifications so essential to subjectivity, according to Kristeva, and it means that, far from repressing instinctuality, the subject in its very essence as a being for another reveals the continuation of the narcissistic experience.

Given, then, that primary narcissism is a permanent structure of the speaking being, that its instinctual as well as idealizing formations continue to manifest themselves after the subject's entry into the symbolic, it seems, in opposition to what Kristeva maintained in her earlier work, that there would be no need for a poetic discourse that would "restore" the semiotic instinctuality that the representations of the symbolic supposedly excluded. As her own analysis of the amatory experience indicates, the pulsional semiotic is already inscribed within the symbolic itself. Indeed, love's inscription of the instinctual forces that impel the subject toward the other and the focus in *Tales of Love* on the problematical nature of otherness itself (which I discuss in greater detail later) reveal that the instability of the narcissistic non-ego is not a stage that has been left behind. Instability resides instead at the very center of psychic experience and has therefore never stopped undermining the integrity of the post-Oedipal ego.

Thus, in her analysis of the amorous dynamic, Kristeva comes to conclusions that alter significantly her earlier distinction between the semiotic and the symbolic. In exposing the problematic of the self that is implied in this relationship to the other, and that the Western philosophical, theological, and literary tradition has tended to conceal, she stresses not so much its revolutionary potential but seeks to support through psychoanalysis the fantasies of wholeness and self-sufficiency that the tradition has always provided. Psychoanalysis thus becomes, in Kristeva's words, "the lay version, the only one, of the speaking being's quest for the truth that religion symbolizes,"[15] causing "truths to emerge but also [trying] to alleviate pains":

> The analyst . . . is duty bound to help [his patients] in building their own proper space. Help them not to suffer. . . . Help them, then, to speak and write themselves in unstable, open, undecidable spaces. . . . While waiting for social institutions to integrate such extraterrestrials, those survivors of primary narcissism, it is still in the imagination and symbolic realizations that their faltering identity will best find a way to construct itself as necessarily false—imaginary. . . . Let them speak, the ET's shall live.[16]

In contrast, then, to her earlier works, from *Séméiotiké* up to and including *Powers of Horror*, Kristeva focuses less on the dynamics of exclusion and more on the inclusive character of the various signifying practices, which are now seen as incorporating heterogeneity into their very structure. Although Kristeva's analysis of the subject in its relationship to otherness is rich in possibilities for the elaboration of a more global notion of the political, which she will indeed some years later examine more fully, her discussion for the moment is confined to reflections on interpersonal relationships among individuals and on a more personalized ethics of love as it presumably resists the homogenizing logic of identity.[17] Expressing in "Psychoanalysis and the Polis" (1981) her own resistance to the homogenizing forces of the political and her fear of the "totalitarian results: Fascism and Stalinism," which the "political interpretations of our century have produced," Kristeva sees psychoanalysis as "an antidote to political discourse," as that which "cuts through political illusions" by countering the belief that one "uncriticizable ultimate Meaning" can be used to influence human behavior.[18] Although it may be true that, as one critic points out, Kristeva seems to be "replacing the master narrative of Marxism . . . with that of psychoanalysis,"[19] it signals a change in her thinking that will ultimately have important political consequences. At this point, however, her renunciation of the political was unequivocal. Speaking in "Mémoire" (1983) of her disillusionment with the Chinese experiment, she writes: "Politically, I saw nothing that might possibly prevent the Cultural Revolution from becoming a national and socialist variation, whose basic reference point remains the province of the Soviets. It marked my farewell to politics, including feminism."[20] Significantly, her essay appears in the first issue of L'Infini immediately following the dissolution of Tel Quel. The journal's change of nomenclature, a result of its move from Les Editions du Seuil to Les Editions Denoël, signaled the reemergence of Tel Quel's original eclecticism and the utter renunciation of its former compulsion to make declarations and political pronouncements. Indeed, the newly formed L'Infini offered in its inaugural issue its first and last editorial, a dialogue between anonymous speakers whose laconic style speaks largely for itself:

—"Tel Quel is finished. L'Infini has begun." What are you trying to say?
—We were not the ones who brought an end to Tel Quel.
—The former editor?
—Yes. He insisted absolutely on keeping the title. It's dead.
—Do you want to make a declaration about that?
—No. No one wants to. That's old.[21]

CHAPTER 4

'Tel Quel' and Deconstruction

Tel Quel's reevaluation of its position, its loss of interest in the political following its renunciation of Maoism in 1976, did not constitute a resolution of the numerous problems that plagued the group's revolutionary project. It raised questions that continue to preoccupy us today, questions relating to the possibility of responding to any call for collective political action without succumbing to the demand for communal uniformity upon which politically constituted collectives often depend. These questions have been central not only to Kristeva's more recent writings, in which she reverses her earlier renunciation of the political and attempts to translate her more personalized ethics of resistance once again to the sociopolitical realm, but also to one of the earlier *Tel Quel* contributors, Jacques Derrida, whose reluctance to align himself with any political movement or group continues to generate considerable debate. Indeed, in light of the rather divergent paths taken both by Derrida, who never openly embraced *Tel Quel*'s revolutionary politics, and the other members of the group, an examination of the relationship between the two might prove useful for an analysis of the difficulties inherent in *Tel Quel*'s failed experiment, and for a consideration of a less rigid notion of the collective whose openness to the strangeness of the Other presents possibilities for a discourse that is more ethically and politically responsible than the more overtly political discourse of the early days of *Tel Quel*.

Although the question of the political in Derrida's writings gained greater urgency after the discovery in 1987 of Paul de Man's wartime journalism, it was often a topic of contention even in the earliest days of Derrida's association with *Tel Quel*. The debates and discussions generated then by Derrida's writings provide a foretaste of the polemics that took shape in strikingly similar ways some twenty years later. There were those, like Jean-Pierre Faye, who saw in Derrida's work an extreme right-wing political agenda and others, like the members of the *Tel Quel* group itself who came to believe that his work was not political enough, who thought that his notion of *différance*, which played an important role in the questioning of metaphysics and the disruption of its logic, failed to account for the position of the subject and thus had no grounds for theorizing the possibility for social change.

It should be noted, however, that during the early days of Derrida's collaboration with *Tel Quel*, his seminal essay, "La Différance," first published in *Tel Quel*'s *Théorie d'ensemble*, was valued for its politically subversive capabilities and was thus incorporated into *Tel Quel*'s revolutionary program.[1] As a notion that refers to the spatiotemporal movement within language that both generates and defers meaning, Derrida's *différance* was important to *Tel Quel* for its capacity to function as a kind of unconscious infrastructure of language, working in conjunction with Marxist and Freudian theory to disrupt capitalist/patriarchal institutions whose authority depends upon traditional notions of the sign and its assumptions of absolute presence. What formed, however, the basis of an alliance between *Tel Quel* and Derrida also contributed to the eventual break between the two. Not only did the journal criticize Derrida's refusal to embrace revolutionary Marxism,[2] at which time Derridean theory came to be referred to as "affected Derridean gobbledygook," but Kristeva, in a far less polemical way, began critiquing what she saw as the dissolution of the thetic in Derrida's grammatological project:

> [G]rammatology denounces the economy of the symbolic function and opens up a space that the latter cannot subsume. But in its desire to bar the thetic and put (logically or chronologically) previous energy transfers in its place, the grammatological del-

uge of meaning gives up on the subject and must remain ignorant not only of his functioning as social practice, but also of his chances for experiencing jouissance or being put to death. Neutral in the face of all positions, theses, and structures, grammatology is, as a consequence, equally restrained when they break, burst, or rupture: demonstrating disinterestedness toward (symbolic and/or social) structure, grammatology remains silent when faced with its destruction or renewal.[3]

The possibility for political action and social change is undermined by Derrida's theory because his term *différance*, according to Kristeva, turns the Hegelian notion of negativity into a positive or affirmative concept. Negativity, in this case, becomes drained of its "potential for producing breaks" and thus fails to account for the splitting that produces the speaking subject: "[S]ince *différance* neutralizes productive negativity, it is conceived of as a *delay* [*retard*] that comes *before* . . . the sign, *logos*, the subject, *Being*. . . . If in this way the trace dissolves every thesis . . . , it can do so because it grasps the formation of the symbolic function preceding the mirror stage and believes it can remain there, even while aiming toward that stage."[4] Recognizing, however, that Derridean grammatology would "undoubtedly not acknowledge the pertinence of this psychoanalytic staging [*stadialité*], which depends on the categories and entities of beings" (p. 143), Kristeva reveals once again that her revolutionary project is dependent on such distinctions and categories. Not only do transgressive strategies require a notion of the subject for their conceptualization and implementation, but they would indeed be worthless if there were no way to theorize the linguistic and social constraints that are meant to be transgressed. This is implied in Kristeva's critique of deconstructive analyses of Husserlian phenomenology:

> [S]uch "deconstructions" refuse (through discrediting the signified and with it the transcendental ego) what constitutes one function of language though not the only one: to express meaning in a communicable sentence between speakers. This function harbors coherence (which is indeed transcendental) or, in other words, social identity. Let us first acknowledge, with Husserl, this thetic character of the signifying act, which establishes the transcendent object and the transcendental ego of communi-

cation (and consequently of sociability), before going beyond the Husserlian problematic to search for that which produces, shapes, and exceeds the operating consciousness (this will be our purpose when confronting poetic language). Without that acknowledgement . . . any reflection on significance, by refusing its thetic character, will continually ignore its constraining, legislative, and socializing elements.[5]

In seeking to preserve the position of the subject by acknowledging its constraining, legislative power, Kristeva also aims to safeguard a place for those heterogeneous elements that are meant to break down the boundaries that the subject imposes, for it is her view that deconstruction's denial of the thetic constitutes a denial of heterogeneity as well. Indeed, if *différance* is a movement that always "precedes" the sign and subject, if, that is, there is no subject that has been saved from "foundering in inarticulable instinctuality,"[6] then there can be no thought of the semiotic heterogeneity in which the differential movement of the trace supposedly takes place. Consequently, and more importantly, without the possibility of "experiencing" semiotic heterogeneity and its drive-related effects, there can be no affirmation of its transgressive capabilities:

> Although it begins by positing the heterogeneity in which *différance* operates, doesn't grammatology forget this heterogeneous element the moment it neglects the thetic? Doesn't it indefinitely delay this heterogeneous element, thus following its own systematic and philosophical movement of metalanguage or theory. Indeed grammatology seems to brush aside the drive "residues" that are not included in the *différance* toward the sign, and which return, heterogeneous, to interrupt its contemplative retention and make language a practice of the subject in process/on trial.[7]

Although *différance* in this case seems paradoxically to have acquired the constraining capabilities that Kristeva previously claimed it lacked and thus reinstates a notion of the thetic in a theory that presumably dissolves such possibilities, Kristeva's point is to show that grammatology, in failing to account for the subject *and* for its "object," heterogeneity, thus undermines any possibility of a political role for Derrida's notion of *différance*. In making this argument, however, she not only moves *différance* out of the realm of heterogeneity by linking it more closely to that of the symbolic, but she shows once again that her own and *Tel Quel*'s revolutionary strategy is dependent on the preservation of these two categories and on the logic of contradiction that allows one to "subvert" the other. If, therefore, as Toril Moi has stated, Kristeva's "insistence on the *reality* of the drives" is what "forces her to oppose Derrida's grammatological project,"[8] if, that is, Kristeva speaks of the existence of "nonsymbolized," "nonsymbolizable," "nondeferred energy charges," which *différance* as a process of deferral or "symbolic becoming" has presumably "effaced," the principal reason is that in order for instinctual heterogeneity to maintain its status as a radically disruptive force, it must be preserved as an unmediated space of pure drive uncontaminated by symbolic structurations (including those of *différance* itself). It depends as well on a logic of negation whose potential for instituting the break between the semiotic and the symbolic is not only what constitutes the subject but also what allows it to be put "in process/on trial."[9] This is why Kristeva believes that the revolutionary potential of the Derridean project is still unrealized. Although she affirms that project at the outset of her argument, claiming that it is "the most radical of all the various procedures that have tried, after Hegel, to push dialectical negativity further and elsewhere," she finds that its range is too limited, that it must be pushed even further to a point where the unleashing of heterogeneous "energy discharge" within the movement of *différance* itself brings about a full realization of its disruptive capabilities:

> This instinctual heterogeneity—neither deferred nor delayed, not yet understood as a becoming-sign—is precisely that which *enters into contradiction with différance* and brings about leaps, intervals, abrupt changes, and breaks in its spacing [*espacement*]. Contradiction can only be the irruption of the heterogeneous which cuts short any *différance*. . . . The return of the heterogeneous element in the movement of *différance* (symbolic retention, delayed becoming-sign-subject-Being), through perception and the unconscious (to use Freudian categories), brings about the *revolution of différance* [my emphasis]: expenditure, semantico-syntactic anomaly, erotic excess, social protest, jouissance.[10]

Différance has thus been radicalized or even "heterogenized" by Kristeva's reworking of Derrida's notion. As a form of "erotic excess" or *jouissance*, it becomes an instrument of "social protest" and is thus made to work in closer conformity with *Tel Quel*'s revolutionary program. This effort to push Derrida's grammatological project in a more explicitly political direction was made in an even more direct way several years earlier in an interview, published in *Positions*, between Derrida and two members of the *Tel Quel* group, Jean-Louis Houdebine and Guy Scarpetta.[11] Here, some of the theoretical questions Kristeva raised were placed in the context of Derrida's commitment to Marxism, and it showed that points of divergence, even when Derrida was still expressing his "solidarity" with the *Tel Quel* group (p. 78), were increasingly apparent as the interviewers grew more insistent in their effort to pin Derrida down on the question of dialectical materialism. Anticipating the questions Kristeva posed later in *Revolution in Poetic Language*, they confronted Derrida directly on the issue of heterogeneity as it relates to both Marxist theory and Derrida's own texts. They objected that, despite the many points of convergence between Derrida's notion of "writing" and the "materialist text," there was a curious lack of explicit reference to Marxist theory in Derrida's work and a reduction of the "motif of heterogeneity" to a "theme of spacing" whereby the "differences" articulated in Derrida's analysis lost their radicality by becoming merely another variant of the Lacanian symbolic.

Claiming that his work challenges the very logic of Lacanian categories (certain aspects of which Kristeva also embraced) Derrida insisted that the movement of *différance*, as *dissemination*, as that which remains irreducible to a single unity of meaning, actually "resists . . . the order of the 'symbolic' " just as it undermines the possibility of any hypostatized notion of "heterogeneity" as the "symbolic's *simple* exterior" (pp. 84–86). Consequently, when Houdebine pressed Derrida further on the question of the text and its relation to dialectical materialism, whose logic, as Houdebine defined it, is to be "articulated on the basis of the conceptual series 'matter' (that is, an irreducible heterogeneity in relation to a subject-meaning)/contradiction/struggle of the contraries . . . in the process of their transformation" (p. 60), his comments elicited from Derrida the following response:

> It is not always in *the* materialist text (is there such a thing, *the* materialist text?) nor in *every* materialist text that the concept of matter has been defined as absolute exterior or radical hetero-geneity. I am not even sure that there can be a "concept" of an absolute exterior. If I have not often used the word "matter," it is not, as you know, because of some idealist or spiritualist kind of reservation. It is that in the logic of the phase of overturning this concept has been too often reinvested with "logocentric" values, values associated with those of thing, reality, presence in gen-eral. . . . In short, the signifier "matter" appears to me problemat-ical only at the moment when its reinscription cannot avoid making of it a new fundamental principle which, by means of theoretical regression, would be reconstituted into a "transcen-dental signified." . . . It then becomes an ultimate referent, . . . or it becomes an "objective reality" absolutely "anterior" to any work of the mark [pp. 64–65]. . . . I do not believe that there is any "fact" which permits us to say: in *the* Marxist text, contradiction *itself*, dialectics *itself* escapes from *the* dominance of metaphys-ics. (p. 74)

It seems clear, then, that Marxism or a certain reading of Marxist theory that posits the "triumph of materialism"[12] and the hier-archical oppositions matter/meaning, same/other, outside/inside, homogeneous/heterogeneous, upon which such a position rests, could itself be subject to a deconstruction of its precepts in Derrida's view—although Derrida himself had never engaged in a lengthy critique of Marxist theory (or of *Tel Quel*, for that matter) and claimed, at one point, that he would rather avoid contributing to the attacks so prevalent in the late 1960's directed at groups on the left. This does not mean, however, that the motif of "irreducible hetero-geneity" (which for Houdebine "constitutes the materialist motif *par excellence*") has been banished from the Derridean notion of *différance*. On the contrary, if the motif can be interpreted as a "radical alterity" that undermines and displaces such oppositions, Derrida's own work could, as Derrida himself indicated, be consid-ered "materialist" (p. 64). In this sense, however, Derrida's argu-ment goes further than that of *Tel Quel*, for he shows how the spacing that Houdebine and Kristeva find too closely associated with "linguistic differences" is not only compatible with the motif of heterogeneity; it also undermines the "purity" of such concepts as heterogeneity itself. One could even argue that Houdebine's version of heterogeneity, which he defines, citing Kristeva, as "without meaning, outside and despite it" (p. 74), ceases to be heterogeneous; it becomes instead self-identical, uncontaminated by those "linguistic" elements that presumably remain outside its borders. Consequently, when Derrida speaks of "radical alterity," he does not assume a pure exteriority whereby heterogeneity as a hypostatized "Other" would ultimately be subsumed under a notion of the Same; he points to an otherness that inhabits the self-identical, not as the result of some subversive or transgressive act but as an alterity that has always been internal to any closed structure, be it linguistic or otherwise.[13]

This inscription of otherness within the selfsame is indeed what is indicated by Derrida's notion of *différance*, with which the notion of spacing is associated.[14] As a movement within language that generates and is, at the same time, drawn into the play of differences that ultimately constitutes meaning, *différance*, although it precedes the production of meaning, cannot itself be looked upon as an absolute point of origin or causative agent, for it exists only as an operation that produces differences and is therefore continually caught up in the very process it has set in motion. The origin, or source of signification, in this case does not remain outside language but becomes a function within the differential movement of language itself. *Différance* as spacing is not therefore an entity; it in fact "designates *nothing*." By bringing the temporal deferral of presence and the spatial distinction that places it in relation to an other, *différance* marks the impossibility for an identity to close in on itself. In this sense, spacing becomes indissociable from the concept of alterity. As Derrida argues, "the irreducibility of spacing is the irreducibility of the other," but the other in this case functions not as an entity with a definable essence remaining outside the linguistic system but as a movement of alterity that is inserted *in it*, thereby displacing all forms of identity including that of the system itself. If, then, Derrida shows a certain reticence with regard to Houdebine's insistence on the "materialist position," it is because alterity (or heterogeneity), in his view, can never be "posed" as such. Indeed, to do so would be to reinstate the traditional subject/object relation and to remain inattentive to the differential relations that constitute as well as problematize the self-contained identity of the subject and of the object "positioned" before it:

> If the alterity of the other is *posed*, that is, *only* posed, does it not amount to *the same*, for example in the form of the "constituted object" or of the "informed product" invested with meaning, etc.? From this point of view, I would even say that the alterity of the other *inscribes* in this relationship that which in no case can be "posed." Inscription, as I would define it in this respect, is not a simple position: it is rather that by means of which every position is *of itself confounded* (*différance*): inscription, mark, text and not only *thesis or theme*-inscription of the *thesis*. (pp. 95–96)

What is required, then, according to Derrida, is both a rethinking of the "concept" of alterity and, perhaps more important, an interrogation of the idea of the "position" itself, and of the subject who "takes it," for these are also effects of *différance*, marked by the irreducibility of the other in the spacing relations that constitute them. To say, however, as Derrida does, that the subject cannot be conceived of in terms of a "pure self-presence" is not to indicate, as Kristeva has maintained, that *différance* "dissolves every thesis" or, in the words of Scarpetta, that for Derrida "the 'subject' of writing does not exist" (p. 87). What *différance* marks is not the disappearance of the subject; it challenges instead a certain notion of the sovereign subject as master of its discourse and fully present to itself. Derrida makes this point emphatically in his 1971 essay "Signature Event Context" and in his response to a critique of that essay by John R. Searle, who also objected to the disappearance of the subject, this time in relation to the question of intentionality and the "iterability" of the written sign. Derrida's claim that the written sign, as an infinitely repeatable structure, is ultimately "cut off from . . . *consciousness* as the ultimate authority"[15] leads Searle to take a stand that he assumes to be in opposition to Derrida's by arguing that there is "no getting away from intentionality," that "to the extent that the author says what he means the text is the expression of his intentions."[16] In responding to Searle's

objections, Derrida points out that, as far as the question of inten-
tionality is concerned, this is what he had been saying all along:

> *Sec* ["Signature Event Context"] has not simply effaced or denied
> intentionality. . . . On the contrary, *Sec* insists on the fact that . . .
> *"the category of intention will not disappear, it will have its*
> *place,* but from that place it will no longer be able to govern the
> entire scene and system of utterance . . . given that structure of
> iteration, the intention animating the utterance *will never be*
> *through and through present to itself and to its content.* The
> iteration structuring it a priori introduces into it a *dehiscence*
> and a cleft [*brisure*] which are essential." (pp. 58–59)

What is limited, then, by the differing-deferring structure of
iterability, which functions in a way that is analogous to Derrida's
notion of *différance,* is not the intentionality of the speaking or
writing subject, but "the simplicity of its features, its *undivided-*
ness" (p. 105). Given that the subject does not precede *différance,*
spacing, and iterability, but is dependent on them for the man-
ifestation or ex-position of its "presence," the subject is caught up
in a temporizing movement of deferral, constituted only as it is
divided from itself. Consequently, there can be no opposition or
contradiction between the subject and its heterogeneous "other,"
for heterogeneity and contradiction are already internal to its struc-
ture. As Derrida states in his interview with Kristeva, "[t]here is no
subject who is agent, author, and master of *différance,* who even-
tually and empirically would be overtaken by *différance.*" The
subject, like its object, has not been eradicated; it is seen as "an
effect of *différance,* an effect inscribed in a system of *différance.*"[17]

This means, however, that Derrida's notion of *différance,* which
shows that the subject is always already a "subject in process/on
trial," calls into question the principal assumptions structuring *Tel*
Quel's revolutionary project. If Kristeva and Scarpetta object to the
dissolution of the subject in Derrida's work, and if Houdebine tries
to retain heterogeneity by insisting on the difference between spac-
ing and alterity (which can only be associated in his view when
they confront each other as part of the "basic dialectical materialist
contradiction"), it is because the two concepts serve *Tel Quel*'s
political objectives, satisfying its need to preserve not only the

identity of the subject to be transgressed but the subversive position of what is in Houdebine's words "a 'something' (a 'nothing') 'that is *not nothing*' " and which is also "the *position* of irreducible alterity."[18]

If the members of the *Tel Quel* group thus refused to grapple with the questions raised by Derrida's essay, preferring instead to inscribe *différance* within their increasingly reductive conception of the Marxist dialectic (through which the "contradictions" outlined early on by Althusser and Sollers were functioning as little more than a simple conflict between two opposing forces), it was perhaps because Derrida's analysis of *différance* underscored the problematical nature of the hierarchizing oppositions upon which *Tel Quel*'s and indeed all conventional conceptions of the political depend. By showing that each element is always related to something other than itself, Derrida foregrounds the redundant (not to mention metaphysical) character of any concept of transgression that presumes the integrated status of an inside (in this case, of the subject and its mimetic representations) that has not yet been contaminated by what presumably remains outside the subjective enclosure. In marking heterogeneity as an otherness that inhabits all forms of identity, the movement of *différance* indicates that the subversion of the self-present subject has always already taken place. *Différance* must be seen, then, not as a movement that completely dissolves subjectivity but as one that interrogates, in a way that went beyond *Tel Quel*'s own investigations of the subject, the very essence of subjectivity itself.[19] Had the politics at *Tel Quel* permitted them to remain open to the implications of Derrida's analysis, they would have seen that *différance* had no need of being "heterogenized" or radicalized.[20] Although it works in service of no political program, and indeed calls into question such notions, *différance* marks an inscription of heterogeneity that is more radical, one that in fact anticipates a view put forth much later by Kristeva in *Strangers to Ourselves* and that comes to have, according to Kristeva, decidedly political implications. Insofar as Kristeva in this work sees "foreignness" or "otherness" as a fundamental yet destabilizing component of the human psyche, she offers a view of the subject that is not so different from the one that emerges in the course of Derrida's critique. Indeed, one could argue that subjectivity in Kristeva's recent analysis is, as Derrida would say, an "effect" of *différance*, the "product" of a relation to an other that constitutes but also problematizes the subject's integrated identity.

The "Other" Within:
Kristeva's Passage Through Narcissism

In *Strangers to Ourselves*, Kristeva examines the dissolution of traditional communal bonds within contemporary society and finds in it certain political possibilities. The growing multicultural character not only of contemporary French society but of so many other Western countries has given us, in Kristeva's view, a new "moral" or "ethical" imperative, one requiring reflection on the status of the foreigner and on our ability to accept his or her otherness "without ostracism but also without leveling," that is, without subsuming diversity under a new homogeneity.[21] This relatively recent work, along with her open letter to Harlem Désir, published soon after, can be taken as a response to the racism, anti-Semitism, and general xenophobia that, she says, have become in France "the manifest pornography of social mores."[22] Although her short letter to Harlem Désir, the founder of the anti-xenophobic group SOS-Racisme, provides only the most general outlines of her argument, it is in the former work that she examines in greater depth this new modality of "otherness," tracing the "changing representations" of the foreigner at various moments in Western history. What she finds stands in stark contrast to some of her earlier conclusions concerning the role of the "other" within the symbolic system. Indeed, a brief review of her earlier writings reveals the extent to which the concept of "otherness" has evolved in Kristeva's thinking—an evolution that can be attributed, in part, to her encounter with the complex dynamics of primary narcissism when she ultimately becomes caught up in the contradictory dialectics of narcissism and identification, in which Freud himself became embroiled.

Before we proceed to Kristeva's investigations, however, it would be useful to consider briefly the numerous, and by now familiar, revisions and corrections in Freud's own analysis, for they not only underscore the difficulties inherent in any attempt to deal with the problematic notion of "selfhood" upon which narcissism depends, but they bring into focus the extent to which narcissism undercuts the traditionally mimetic logic that supports such concepts as the unified "self." Whether the unity of the ego is seen as the outcome of the identificatory processes unleashed by the narcissistic relation, which then perform a primarily unifying, ego-consolidating function, or as an original plenitude to which subsequent reproductions remain ideally subordinate, both perspectives require a denial of the paradoxes and complexities of the mimetic relation through which the identity of the self is formed on the basis of its imitating appropriations of an other.

The difficulties in dealing with that otherness are evident in Freud's early elaborations of primary narcissism when he posits, in conformity with the most traditional of mimetic precepts, the existence of an originary presence or self-identical model preexisting the infant's narcissistic, mimetic identifications. Here, the infant focuses autoerotically on the self before moving on to a world of external "objects," which are then absorbed through "narcissistic identification" into the child's own ego. But by defining narcissism, as he does in *Totem and Taboo*, as a primitive stage following the infant's initial autoerotism, when the infant "behaves as though he were in love with himself," Freud seems to be implying that the constituted ego is there from the very beginning and ends up, as a consequence, countering his own theory of psychic development as a gradual, evolutionary process.[23] Perhaps recognizing, however, the problems inherent in the earlier definition, Freud clarified his position the following year in *On Narcissism: An Introduction*. He claims that the ego "cannot exist in the individual from the start," that there must instead "be something added to auto-erotism—a new psychical action—in order to bring about narcissism."[24] Modifying his position even further in *The Ego and the Id*, Freud makes an additional correction of his statement that the ego is the "true and original reservoir of the libido," whose energy charges later flow out onto objects,[25] by claiming that the "great reservoir of the libido" is now to be found not in the ego but in the id:

> At the very beginning, all the libido is accumulated in the id, while the ego is still in process of formation or is still feeble. The id sends part of this libido out into erotic object-cathexes, whereupon the ego, now grown stronger, tries to get hold of this object-libido and to force itself on the id as a love-object. The narcissism of the ego is thus a secondary one, which has been withdrawn from objects.[26]

Although this modification corrects the notion of a preconstituted, originary ego, many critics have pointed out that Freud's introduction of the term "secondary narcissism" serves only to obscure further the nature of primary narcissism. It becomes difficult to see how primary narcissism can be defined as a stage when the infantile ego is the "target of self-love," when there is no constituted ego, no "self" to become the object of one's infantile affections.

It is indeed this question of narcissistic identity that Lacan addresses in his theory of the "mirror stage," which, as the name suggests, draws out of Freud's analysis its specifically mimetic implications. Interpreting almost literally the myth from which the term "narcissism" was derived (according to which the beautiful lad, Narcissus, falls in love with his own reflected image), Lacan equates the Freudian notion of narcissism with the simulating mechanisms of the mirror stage when the child's perception of its own mirror image gives it its first sense of self as a corporeal identity. By stressing, however, the complexity of that early mimetic relation, Lacan underscores its potential for disrupting the hierarchical opposition between original and copy upon which traditional concepts of the mimetic rely. He shows that the originary presence posited initially by Freud becomes itself an imitation, a transparency that does not let an original plenitude emerge but that reveals instead a fundamental emptiness at the "origin" of the mimetic process.

Seizing upon what Freud himself saw but failed to elaborate in his effort to maintain the distinction between primary and secondary narcissism, Lacan claims that the love of self that the term narcissism implies is never primary. It can only be secondary, taking as its object an ego that, far from being originary, is constituted through its mirroring relations to the other.[27] By focusing, then, on the structuring relations of primary narcissism, which in his view announce the child's entry into the ordering realm of language, Lacan indicates that the process of self-organization initiated by the first love relationship poses a serious threat to the illusions of psychic omnipotence structuring the infant's and all humanist images of the self. Given its dependence on the other for its very existence, the self emerges from the process of narcissistic identification as a fundamentally alienated subject, constituted only in the process of becoming eccentric to itself.

Although the Lacanian conception of "otherness" clearly plays an important role in Kristeva's distinction between the semiotic and the symbolic, there are also significant differences in their approach to the problem. They both link the concept of the Other to language, to the symbolizations set in motion by the alienating division of the mirror stage, but Kristeva's earlier writings tended to underemphasize the self-alienation produced by this confrontation with otherness in order to focus on what she felt had been neglected by Lacan's interpretation of Freud, to go beyond Lacan's emphasis on language and the symbolic structurations of the thetic phase by restoring to the Freudian notion of the unconscious its instinctual, "drive-affected dimension."[28] Her accentuation of the instinctual, prelinguistic operations dwelling within the human unconscious is in fact what distinguishes her theory of the "semiotic" from the Lacanian "imaginary," whose idyllic visions of unity and wholeness are never really free of symbolic (that is, linguistic) structurations. Her effort to maintain this distinction is complicated, however, when, in the course of her elaboration of the different stages of psychic development, she attempts to situate the complex structurations of primary narcissism, and we shall see that the changes in her own analysis testify to her difficulty in defining this early pre-Oedipal stage.

In *Revolution in Poetic Language*, for example, narcissism is defined in Lacanian terms that emphasize the intersubjective, relational aspect of Freud's theory as developed in *Mourning and Melancholia*. Although Kristeva gives it only cursory treatment at this point, primary narcissism is nonetheless associated with the early narcissistic identifications of Lacan's mirror stage, when the child's reflected image serves as the model for all future identifications. This narcissistic contemplation of self as other signals for Kristeva the beginning of the thetic stage, which prepares for the final rupture (through castration) with the undifferentiated mother-child dyad (the semiotic *chora*) and initiates the child's entry as a separate identity into a "world of objects" that are "likewise separate and signifiable."[29]

In the course, however, of her analysis of the thetic phase, which she defines as "the place of the Other, as the precondition of signification, i.e., the precondition for the positing of language" (p. 48), Kristeva seems to suggest that otherness functions not so much as a destabilizing force but as an essential component in the constitution of the subject's identity. She concludes, in opposition to Lacan, that it is not the symbolic order of language and the relation to the other that decenters the subject, but the irruption within language of what remains outside it, the insertion of undifferentiated, non-relational drive heterogeneity, that prevents it from performing its signifying, socializing function:

> [W]hat remodels the symbolic order is always the influx of the semiotic. This is particularly evident in poetic language since, for there to be a transgression of the symbolic, there must be an irruption of the drives in the universal signifying order, that of "natural" language which binds together the social unit. . . . The semiotic's breach of the symbolic in so-called poetic practice can probably be ascribed to the very unstable yet forceful positing of the thetic. In our view, the analysis of texts shows that thetic lability is ultimately a problem with imaginary captation (disorders in the mirror stage that become marked scopophilia, the need for a mirror or an identifying addressee, etc.) and a resistance to the discovery of castration (thereby maintaining the phallic mother who usurps the place of the Other). These problems and resistances obstruct the thetic phase of the signifying process. (pp. 62–63)

In her effort, then, to preserve the subversive capabilities of Freud's theory of the drives, whose motility would be subdued by the symbolizations implied in any relationship to an other, Kristeva gives us in subsequent works a very different conception of narcissism, one that stresses less the Lacanian notion, with its links to the structurations of the mirror stage, and conforms more closely to the view developed by Freud in *Totem and Taboo* of a non-objectal primary narcissism, of that period of indifferentiation preceding all relations to an outside world of objects.[30] Countering, however, the notion, implicit in Freud's analysis, of a fully formed, originary ego, Kristeva uses the lack of objectality to emphasize the uncertainty of the ego's identity. As she writes in *Powers of Horror*:

> Two consequences seem necessarily to follow from [the structure of primary narcissism in Freud]. On the one hand, the non-constitution of the (outside) object as such renders unstable the ego's identity, which could not be precisely established without having been differentiated from an other, from its object. The ego of primary narcissism is thus uncertain, fragile, threatened, subjected just as much as its non-object to spatial ambivalence (inside/outside uncertainty). . . . On the other hand, one has to admit that such a narcissistic topology has no other underpinning in psychosomatic reality than the mother-child dyad.[31]

Thus, in this later text, narcissism is associated with the semiotic *chora*. Defined by Kristeva as a "receptacle of narcissism," it is a place of "imprecise boundaries" where the "[i]nside and outside are not precisely differentiated . . . nor is language an active practice or the subject separated from the other" (p. 60). Once again, the repressive mechanisms set in motion by the triadic relationship of the Oedipus complex extricate the subject from the dyadic relationship by throwing a "veil over primary narcissism and the always ambivalent threats with which it menaces subjective identity" (p. 63).

In "Place Names" as well, primary narcissism is considered to precede the symbolic structurations of the mirror stage, origin of the sign and subject: "To repeat the question that the infant-analyst puts to maternal attentiveness before any mirror shows him any presentation whatsoever, before any language begins to encode his 'idealities': what about the paradoxical *semiosis* of the newborn's body, what about the 'semiotic *chora*'; what about this 'space' prior to the sign, this archaic disposition of primary narcissism that a poet brings to light in order to challenge the closure of meaning."[32]

This view of the subject, in contrast to the one Kristeva put forth in *Tales of Love* and *Strangers to Ourselves*, tends to downplay the problematic nature of otherness. What threatens identity here is not "otherness" but the lack thereof, the absence of object relations and of a differentiating third party who would ideally prevent the return of that instinctual heterogeneity in which all distinctions are blurred. The differentiating "other," in this case, which is never part of the semiotic but which Kristeva always links to the father and to the symbolic order of identity, serves not to destabilize but to support the subject, and only when that triangular relationship fails to suppress the pre-Oedipal narcissistic pulsions does the subject's unitary structure find itself undermined:

> [T]he so-called narcissistic drive dominates only if instability of the paternal metaphor prevents the subject from finding its place within a triadic structure giving an object to its drives. . . . [I]f one takes the word object in its strongest acceptation, [it can be seen] as the correlative of a subject in a symbolic chain. The paternal agency alone, to the extent that it introduces the symbolic dimension between "subject" (child) and "object" (mother), can generate such a strict object relation. Otherwise, what is called "narcissism" . . . becomes the unleashing of the drive as such, without object, threatening all identity, including that of the subject itself. We are then in the presence of psychosis.[33]

This tendency in *Powers of Horror* to pit the anobjectal mother-child symbiosis of archaic narcissism against the structuring, ternary relationship of the Oedipal and symbolic realm of identity undergoes a series of modifications in *Tales of Love*, due in part perhaps to Kristeva's abandonment of her revolutionary goals, which require that the one be seen as opposing and possibly dismantling the other, but attributable also, it seems, to a more thorough investigation in *Tales of Love* of the complexities of primary narcissism itself. In her previous effort to place narcissism outside the symbolic and its structuring representations, to see it as a nonrelational space of drives and energy charges preceding the child's recognition of the symbolic "other," she neglected to answer the very question raised implicitly by Freud in his effort to define this early stage of psychic development, that is: if primary narcissism occupies a space where there is no sense of self because there is no other, then where does the love of self that the designation "primary narcissism" implies come from? Indeed, how can primary narcissism be defined as an archaic space before any relation to another when the very term "narcissism" already supposes that the infant, like the mythical Narcissus, sees itself as other and falls in love with its own specular image?[34]

The question of narcissistic "identity" that is dependent on the discovery of difference is thus what Kristeva is forced to confront in her study of the psychic underpinnings of love in *Tales of Love*.[35] After taking another look at the Freudian conception of narcissism, she alters the distinction between the semiotic and the symbolic, giving the semiotic a more "Oedipal" configuration (which for some critics may not constitute an improvement in her theory) and thus blurring the lines separating the two functions. Recognizing in *Tales of Love* that symbolic "otherness," a sense of identity and difference, already inhabits this early semiotic stage of development, Kristeva no longer defines primary narcissism in terms of an undifferentiated mother-child dyad; it becomes instead a ternary structure acquiring what she calls "an intra-symbolic status" through the intervention of an archaic paternal function, Freud's "father of individual pre-history" taken from *The Ego and the Id* (1923). Indeed, the triangulating instance of an archaic paternity, the child's identifications with an idealizable other who returns its own ideal image, gives rise to the love of self characterizing primary narcissism and prepares for the development of the ego. Thus, although *Tales of Love* still focuses on a stage that precedes both the Oedipus complex and the mirror stage and is therefore connected to the drives of the pre-Oedipal oral phase, Kristeva no longer regards primary narcissism and the archaic semiotic it occupies as radically distinct from the symbolic order that follows, for they contain many of the complex structurations that characterize the symbolic itself. The archaic inscription of the father interrupts the bodily exchange between mother and child and accomplishes, in Kristeva's words, "the very splitting that established the psyche and . . . bends the drive towards the symbolic of an other" (p. 31). Kristeva thus establishes even before the structuring relations of the Oedipal triangle and preceding the subjective, representational structurations of the mirror stage an even earlier instance of subjectivity, what she calls a "position of symbolicity" located within the semiotic itself and constituting "a fragile inscription of subjecthood" (p. 46) without excluding the drive heterogeneity that subtends it.

One can still object, of course, that Kristeva has not abandoned her tendency to see the formation of the ego in terms of psychoanalytic stages that depend on clear distinctions between maternal heterogeneity and the paternal order of identity. Indeed, she embraces as the core of her theory of the semiotic the Freudian notion of the mother as "abject," as a nonentity characterized by deficiency and lack. Although Kristeva claims that the archaic, imaginary father is a "mother/father conglomerate" with the attributes of both parents, the father's dual identity, which is none other than the maternal desire for the father's phallus, signifies once again that the mother is an "incomplete being" who wants, a "not-I" to be "ab-jected" through the transference of the child's identifications to the imaginary father himself who prepares the way for the Oedipal father and whose identity at this point no longer seems dual. Thus, the notion of identity in *Tales of Love* is, as it has been throughout her work, grounded in the paternal. The difference here, however, is that the father is for the first time not only the guarantor of the symbolic but also, along with the mother (although *he* is never encoded as abject), the target of the infant's primitive, drive-dominated impulses. In this sense, then, the "loving" father of archaic instinctuality represents a certain feminization of the paternal and is to be distinguished from the stern, prohibitive Oedipal father who requires the repression of the drives. Existing prior to the constitution of any relations to a person as object, the father of the semiotic disposition is a magnet for a more primitive, primary identification arising during the oral phase, when the object is not yet perceived as different from the self. As Kristeva writes: "This archaic identification, which is characteristic of the oral phase of the libido's organization where what I incorporate is what I become, where *having* amounts to *being*, is not, truly speaking, objectal" (p. 25). Instead, nonrelational, "non-objectal," "oral assimilation" of the archaic father (an identification, in reality, with the mother's desire for the father's phallus) is endowed with a "heterogeneous, drive-affected dimension," whose motility has not yet been completely subdued by language and its symbolizations.

In contrast, then, to Lacan, who excludes drive heterogeneity, according to Kristeva, by establishing the identifications structuring primary narcissism as intrinsically symbolic, as a function of separation and difference that is always mediated by language, Kristeva attempts to restore to narcissistic identification its "complex dynamics" by incorporating not only the early transference of the psyche to the "site of the Other" but also its "narcissistic, drive-animated pre-object orientation." By returning once again to the notion of an "anobjectal" archaic identification, which incorporates Freud's somewhat problematical characterization in *The Ego and the Id* of primary identification as "immediate and direct," Kristeva hopes to preserve the integrity of the drives and thus to counter the Lacanian notion, also implicit in Freud, that all relations to an object (or to a person as object) are necessarily mediated by language.

Ironically, however, Kristeva's effort to move beyond Lacan to a presumably more Freudian notion of the instinctual unconscious is undermined by Freud himself, whose recognition of the psychic reconstitution and, therefore, deferral of the drive raises questions about the possibility of gaining access to the drives outside the ordering law of language and about the ways the drives themselves are to be defined. For even Freud was forced to characterize his theory of the instincts as his "mythology" and came to see the drives as "mythical entities, magnificent in their indefiniteness."[36] The apparent inaccessibility of the drives is compounded when one considers that, for Kristeva, narcissism is also a ternary structure, that the semiotic, corporeal father is also one who separates and differentiates: "The archeology of such an identifying possibility with an *other* is provided by the huge place taken up within narcissistic structure by the vortex of *primary identification* with what Freud called a 'father of individual pre-history.' . . . [T]hat archaic vortex of idealization is immediately an *other* who gives rise to a powerful, already psychic transference of the previous semiotic body in the process of becoming a narcissistic Ego" (p. 33).

A curious juxtaposition of mediating otherness and non-objectal immediacy thus emerges in Kristeva's analysis of what she calls the "dynamics of metaphoricity" structuring archaic identification. Rejecting the Lacanian notion of "metonymical displacement," which installs the lack of being and therefore mediation and language in the archaic object-relation, Kristeva stresses the metaphorical operation of condensation that results from this paradoxically objectless identification with an other. With no object to lose, and therefore no need for mediation, the archaic relationship cannot be understood strictly in terms of language. It moves instead "from drives and sensations to signifier and conversely," causing the Other to be understood "not as a 'pure signifier' but as the very space of metaphorical shifting: a condensation of semantic features as well as non-representable drive heterogeneity that subtends them, goes beyond them and slips away" (pp. 37–38).

It may be difficult to accept the link that Kristeva establishes between primary identification, which is founded upon the recognition of difference, and the Freudian notion of an undifferentiated, anobjectal state, but one must admit that her effort to deal with the difficult question of the relationship between narcissistic drives and symbolic identifications has led her to make some significant changes in her thinking about primary narcissism and particularly about the semiotic *chora* with which it has been associated. In that the semiotic now contains the mediations of the symbolic, the two can no longer be viewed as radically opposed. By incorporating the symbolic idealizing identifications with an other, which give rise to the narcissistic sense of self, and the semiotic "non-representable drive heterogeneity," which is devoid of all notions of a separate identity, primary narcissism emerges as a complex, contradictory relationship, as an unstable and shifting dynamic where the semiotic and symbolic intersect.

By stressing, however, the interrelatedness of the two functions, Kristeva raises certain problems with regard to her previous characterizations of the psycholinguistic stages constituting the speaking subject. If the semiotic is no longer radically outside the symbolic, if the triadic structurations that guarantee entry into the symbolic order are already at work within the drive heterogeneity of the semiotic disposition, does this not ultimately call into question Kristeva's psychoanalytic stages as well as the distinction between the semiotic and the symbolic upon which the stages depend? In this instance, not only are the structurations of the symbolic injected by Kristeva into the semiotic, but we find that the semiotic, with its threats to the subject's identity, is also at work in the symbolic. Her analysis of the narcissistic underpinnings of love in Western culture shows that drive-dominated narcissistic impulses continue to structure adult relationships to the other, and it points to otherness itself, not simply as a "correlative of the subject" in its effort to establish a distinct identity, but also as a destabilizing force: "[I]n love, 'I' has been an *other*. That phrase, which leads us to poetry or raving hallucination, suggests a state of instability in which the individual is no longer indivisible and allows himself to become lost in the other, for the other" (p. 4). Insofar as the "I" is because the "I" loves, the speaking subject is inevitably and permanently caught up in a contradictory dynamic, one that incorporates both the idealizing mechanisms of the symbolic as well as the libidinal charges linked to the semiotic. The contradictory movement of the amorous dynamic, which Kristeva sees as a "permanent stabilization-destabilization" of the speaking being, thus blurs the boundaries separating the symbolic and the semiotic, and it calls into question, perhaps even more than Kristeva herself realizes, the very terms of the opposition. In this case, the semiotic can no longer be defined as a primitive stage of drives and energy charges if symbolic structurations and notions of identity have already restricted their libidinal flow. Nor can the symbolic be seen as a strict order of linguistic and subjective identity if semiotic threats to identity are already inscribed within the structure of the symbolic itself. We find, then, that like Freud, who revised his original opposition between sexual instincts and ego instincts as a result of his confrontation with narcissism,[37] so too has Kristeva, in her analysis of the narcissistic underpinnings of love in *Tales of Love*, come to look at her own distinction differently, leading to modifications that will have important political consequences by extending beyond the borders of the subject on the individual level to encompass the collective cultural subject as well.

A Politics of Otherness/An "Other" Politics

Kristeva's examination in *Strangers to Ourselves* of the concept of "nationhood" and of its relationship to the foreigner as "other" shows, in a manner similar to that of *Tales of Love*, that otherness, now absorbed into the destabilizing operations of the Freudian unconscious, is not a form of "abjection" that has been cast aside, nor is it a form of psychosis that reveals the failure of the symbolic to perform its censoring function; it remains an integral part of the symbolic itself:

> With the Freudian notion of the unconscious the involution of the strange in the psyche loses its pathological aspect and integrates within the assumed unity of human beings an *otherness* that is both biological *and* symbolic and becomes an integral part of the *same*. Henceforth the foreigner is neither a race nor a nation. The foreigner is neither glorified as a secret *Volksgeist* nor banished as disruptive of rationalist urbanity. Uncanny, foreignness is within us: we are our own foreigners, we are divided. (p. 181)

Psychic instability, which in *Powers of Horror* stemmed from disorders of the identifying mechanism, is thus no longer seen as a sign of potentially psychotic or pathological behavior. Whether on the level of the individual or the collective, the foreigner as "uncanny strangeness" is a "permanent presence in '*normal*' psychical [and, one could add, cultural] dynamics" (p. 189; my emphasis). Kristeva writes: "[T]he foreigner is a 'symptom' . . . : psychologically he signifies the difficulty we have of living as an *other* and with others; politically, he underscores the limits of nation-states and of the national political conscience that characterizes them and that we have all deeply interiorized to the point of considering it normal that there are foreigners, that is, people who do not have the same rights as we do" (p. 103).

In opposition, then, to her previous focus on the exclusionary logic structuring Western society, Kristeva traces those moments in its history when the foreigner gains acceptance and is even granted a certain legitimacy by the social system and its laws. Beginning with the Danaïdes, the first foreigners at the earliest stages of civilization, and then moving to the barbarians and the metics during the age of the Greek city-states, Kristeva shows that the foreigner was not simply viewed as a threat to the identity of the community and therefore rejected; he was often given a place within it and even protected by its members, sometimes only for reasons of economic usefulness, but other times in ways that offered a foretaste of the acceptance of foreignness, of the "cosmopolitanism" that was to emerge conceptually with the Stoics and more concretely with the Christian and Enlightenment traditions. It would appear, then, that Kristeva's earlier conclusions with regard to the repressive and tightly controlled structures of the Western social system have been replaced by a more nuanced analysis. Although she maintains that cosmopolitanism contains within it a "repressed, corrosive aspect"—a possibility, in other words, that its universalist principles could degenerate into dogma and lead, for example, to the persecutory practices of the Inquisition in the case of Christian cosmopolitanism or to the Reign of Terror following the Enlightenment's call for human equality—its libertarian ethic opens the social system by challenging its prohibitions and by affirming human dignity, which also includes strangeness.

Cosmopolitanism thus constitutes, despite its "limitations and shortcomings," according to Kristeva, a genuine defense against xenophobia because it involves extending the notion of love to a wider cultural sphere. This is what Kristeva suggests in her analysis of the universalist ethics of the Stoics, who gave us, in Kristeva's view, our first political cosmopolitanism. Their concept of *oikeosis*, or conciliation, understood as a "permanent taking hold of oneself," has narcissistic colorations that tie in with the notion of *amor nostri* or *caritas*, which for the Stoics was the "basis of conscious life":

> [T]hat original conciliation binds us not only to ourselves but also to the concentric spheres that would represent the arrangement of our fellow men—starting with close relatives and ending up with the whole of mankind. . . . That human universality, which is asserted in such manner for the first time, was founded on the community of reason. Because they are reasonable, men apply *amor nostri* and *caritas* to all of mankind: *caritas generis humani*. (p. 57)

With the Christian era and the foundation of the Pauline church, love became a fundamental principle, requiring that the believer love his neighbor as he loves himself. The alienation of the foreigner was, as a result, dissolved into "the universality of the love for the other" (p. 84), and an ecclesiastical community was formed of "those who were different, of foreigners who transcended nationalities by means of a faith in the Body of the risen Christ" (p. 77).

Christian love thus welcomed the stranger in his "otherness," not only as a person of different ethnic origin but as a being divided within himself. With both idealizing identification and drive-dominated orality converging in the image and body of Christ, that love assumed the foreigner's fragmented identity whose differences and imperfections were not to be erased but were to receive God's forgiveness.

And yet, while claiming that Christian love found a place for heterogeneity in its assumption of the foreigner's "passion-inspired division," Kristeva at the same time stresses that Christianity's cosmopolitan spirit could also work to dissolve all differences. Its principle of hospitality, which extended to those who made pilgrimages to its holy sites, displayed a side that was potentially "constricting and abusive," for the right to hospitality was granted only to Christians; the non-Christian was excluded. Dogmatism thus emerged from the heart of the Christian community; its cosmopolitanism "bore in its womb the ostracism that excluded the other belief and ended up with the Inquisition" (p. 87). Rather than functioning, however, as an exclusively repressive mechanism, which had been Kristeva's view of most cultural practices, cosmopolitan universalism, of which Christianity serves as an example, contains within it not one but several conflicting possibilities, leading to the disruption of the social order and its founding prohibitions (or to its opposite extreme, a strict totalitarian order), or to a reasonable middle ground where one finds "the elitism of lucid, self-controlled beings, of wise men who manage to be reconciled with the insane" (p. 61). The Stoics chose the latter possibility, according to Kristeva, as did the Enlightenment philosophers.

In signaling, however, the possibility of this "reconciliation" between reason and madness, Kristeva reveals that important changes have occurred in her characterization of the various "signifying practices" structuring Western culture, particularly since the Western philosophical tradition emerges here in a completely different light. Not only does it acquire a greater degree of complexity in the course of her analysis, but it shows that the forces of subversion do not lie outside culture but are an integral part of what she previously viewed as one of the most traditional cultural practices, that of the Enlightenment philosophers. No longer founded on the "unity of creatures belonging to God" and no longer serving the needs of an oppressive social order, Enlightenment cosmopolitanism, especially as expressed in the writings of Montesquieu and Diderot, points to the recognition of the strange and heterogeneous and, through that recognition, to the possibility of a political ethics that respects the "rights of those who are different." Taking Montesquieu's notion of "l'esprit général," which she opposes to the narrow, nationalistic conception of *Volksgeist* (as used by the National Socialists, for example, to exalt the German state), Kristeva argues that the political philosophy of Montesquieu offers a model of cosmopolitanism that allows for a different and more "supple" conception of nationhood unrestrained by the particularized needs of national politics. According to Kristeva, Montesquieu's "esprit général" includes the rights of the citizen of a given nation-state and of all human beings who become part of a vast and diversified "union of singularities." And if Montesquieu's borderless and integrative spirit expanded the limits of cultural identity, it also found a place within the community for the "strange" and "idiosyncratic," extending its laws to the private practices of the individual through the protection of religious, sexual, and moral differences.

Moving from Montesquieu's texts to the polyphonic discourse of Diderot, Kristeva finds in *Le Neveu de Rameau* this acceptance of individual differences raised to a new level where strangeness is actually internalized during the confrontation between the philosopher and his nephew. The peculiarities of the nephew's pantomime, his multiple postures and voices, insinuate themselves into the very syntax of the philosopher's sentences, bringing about a "dislocation of identity" that reveals a process of estrangement at its core, a sense of internal division that will emerge more fully, first in the image of the Romantic hero and then in the writings of Freud. Although Kristeva suggests that it was only through Freudian psychoanalysis, more than 100 years later, that we gained a genuine appreciation of the major implications of Diderot's insights for human subjectivity, she shows that Freud's discovery of the "uncanny strangeness" within the individual psyche was anticipated much earlier.

Kristeva's analysis also shows, and this is significant for my argument here, that her encounter with the Freudian "uncanny," in addition to her investigations of the narcissistic relations to an "other," brought about important modifications in her thinking. She comes to conclusions that differ dramatically from those of her earlier writings, not simply with regard to the repressive structures of the Western social system, but also concerning the monological structure of the traditional text. In contrast to her previous tendency to characterize "all 'literature' before the epistemological break of the nineteenth/twentieth centuries" as "closed and terminated in its very beginnings,"[38] she now finds at the heart of the rationalist Enlightenment tradition manifestations of difference and heterogeneity that have not been repressed but that have been integrated into both the polyvalent discourses of literature as well as the "polyphonic community" of Montesquieu's philosophical texts. Indeed, references to that epistemological break have all but disappeared from Kristeva's recent writings, and although she still stresses the importance of the Freudian "breakthrough," she no longer discusses Freud's work in terms of a radical rupture. As her argument in *Strangers to Ourselves* suggests, Freud clearly remained indebted to those who preceded him even as he greatly expanded on many of their insights, showing in what way foreignness is a fundamental component of the human psyche: "With Freud indeed, foreignness, an uncanny one, creeps into the tranquility of reason itself, and, without being restricted to madness, beauty, or faith any more than to ethnicity or race, irrigates our very speaking-being, estranged by other logics, including the heterogeneity of biology. . . . Henceforth, we know that we are foreigners to ourselves, and it is with the help of that sole support that we can attempt to live with others" (p. 170).

Additionally significant is Kristeva's modification of her conception of the cultural sphere, which had been seen as a uniformly repressive social enclosure. The Freudian notion of the unconscious and of the drive-dominated narcissistic impulses that impel the subject toward an other now has implications that extend beyond the individual to encompass intersubjective relations as well. And it leads, as a result, to an even broader, more fundamental understanding of the political possibilities that Enlightenment cosmopolitanism presented by pointing to the likelihood that once we understand that strangeness lies within the borders of the self, we become more tolerant of the stranger in the world outside:

> It is through unraveling transference—the major dynamics of otherness, of love/hatred for the other, of the foreign component of our psyche—that, on the basis of the other, I become reconciled with my own otherness-foreignness, that I play on it and live by it. Psychoanalysis is then experienced as a journey into the strangeness of the other and of oneself, toward an ethics of respect for the irreconcilable. How could one tolerate a foreigner if one did not know one was a stranger to oneself? (p. 182)

Enlightenment cosmopolitanism thus finds itself altered and in a sense revitalized in the course of its confrontation with Freudian psychoanalysis. Kristeva's discovery of otherness in the writings of Freud is indeed what leads her to elaborate a new cosmopolitan ethic, one that moves beyond the naive idealism of the eighteenth century and its subjectivist notions of fraternal solidarity, without, however, calling into question its principle of universal dignity. According to Kristeva's reformulation of the concept, political cosmopolitanism is founded on a notion of human dignity that would no longer be assimilated to some national, ethnic, or religious identity; it would stem from a recognition of the difference and estrangement that reside at the core of every entity and whose existence would be affirmed by those who share in its fragility. If a solidarity thus emerges, it is not motivated by the self-interested concerns of presumably autonomous subjects; it is founded instead on the awareness of individual limits, on this shared state of finitude in which the fate of the self is indissolubly linked to that of the "other": "By recognizing [the foreigner] within ourselves, we are spared detesting him in himself. A symptom that precisely turns 'we' into a problem, perhaps makes it impossible. The foreigner comes in when the consciousness of my difference arises, and he disappears when we all acknowledge ourselves as foreigners, unamenable to bonds and communities" (p. 1).

Kristeva's association of Freudian psychoanalysis and Enlightenment cosmopolitanism in the course of her elaboration of a new ethics of tolerance for today's emerging multinational societies thus restores to psychoanalysis its political or ethical dimension.

For it was Freud, according to Kristeva, who gave us the "courage to call ourselves disintegrated in order not to integrate foreigners and even less so to hunt them down, but rather to welcome them to that uncanny strangeness, which is as much theirs as it is ours" (pp. 191–92).[39] For this reason, "[t]he ethics of psychoanalysis implies a politics: it would involve a cosmopolitanism of a new sort that, cutting across governments, economies, and markets, might work for a mankind whose solidarity is founded on the consciousness of its unconscious—desiring, destructive, fearful, empty, impossible" (p. 192).

Kristeva's journey through psychoanalysis, which eventually led her away from the political, thus brings her back to her point of departure, not however without significant changes along the way. Her confrontation with destabilizing otherness initiated by her analysis of the amatory dynamic in *Tales of Love* and continued in *Strangers to Ourselves* has caused her to rethink the political itself. If cosmopolitanism has become for Kristeva a new moral or ethical imperative, the reason is precisely and paradoxically that it calls into question the political discourses of power and dominance upon which traditional programmatic imperatives rely. Indeed, far from calling for coordinated action in response to the subjective will of an individual or a group, Kristevan cosmopolitanism, in confronting us not with the mastery but with the fragility of the speaking subject, requires a politics that remains attuned to that fragility, that maintains an open and receptive attitude toward the difference of the other and of the self.

The inclusive operations uncovered by Kristeva's reworking of Stoic and Enlightenment cosmopolitanism, which it will be remembered were anticipated much earlier in the work of Pleynet, thus form the basis for a non-authoritarian approach to ethics and politics and point to modes of political thought and action that are responsive and enabling rather than controlling and coercive. In promoting a receptivity to otherness that does not fall victim to the oppositional and often exclusionary logic structuring traditional forms of collective political action, Kristeva underscores in an indirect way the dangers of conceptual imperialism inherent in the formation of any theoretically informed program for political action. In so doing, she offers an implicit critique of the *Tel Quel*

collective itself, whose revolutionary idealism ultimately perpetu-
ated rather than resisted the discourse of authoritarianism and its
movement toward closure. While the danger of theoretical closure
is always a possibility and can emerge in the thematization of
otherness itself, the faces of that otherness in Kristeva's recent
work are also variegated and multiple. No longer located simply in
the paternal symbolic where it functions as a correlative of the sub-
ject, and no longer seen as the radical Other of the symbolic in the
form of the unconscious drives of the maternal semiotic, otherness
emerges as a shifting, unstable, and indeed non-gendered "iden-
tity."[40] As Kristeva writes: "Let us not seek to solidify, to turn the
otherness of the foreigner into a thing. Let us merely touch it, brush
by it, without giving it a permanent structure. Simply sketching
out its perpetual motion through some of its variegated aspects
spread out before our eyes today, through some of its former, chang-
ing representations scattered throughout history."[41]

In tracing the history of those "changing representations," Kris-
teva in effect calls into question the bifurcated logic structuring the
entirety of *Tel Quel*'s revolutionary project, for she no longer sees
destabilizing heterogeneity as a subversive weapon to be wielded in
the assault on the Western tradition and its repressive structures.
Indeed, Kristeva's analysis shows that throughout the history of
Western culture, both in its judicial practices as well as in its
literary and philosophical texts, the subversive forces of otherness
were always already at work. That is why Kristeva is able to claim
in her open letter to Harlem Désir that the cosmopolitanism of the
Enlightenment continues to speak to us today. Although Freud and
Lacan deepened our understanding of the problematic of otherness,
the integrative spirit of political cosmopolitanism, from the time of
the Stoics to the Enlightenment and beyond, allowed for a loosen-
ing of communal bonds through the inscription of foreignness and
favored a tolerance for strangeness and difference from which non-
authoritarian conceptions of national identity might ultimately
emerge.

Indeed, one of the more interesting aspects of Kristeva's search
for new ways of thinking communal identity in *Strangers to Our-
selves* and in her open letter to Harlem Désir is that it seems to
have drawn her closer to the deconstructive perspective, particu-

larly as elaborated in recent years by Jean-Luc Nancy and Philippe Lacoue-Labarthe, for whom, as we shall see in the following section, the questions of nationhood and community have become central, and by Derrida, whose *The Other Heading: Reflections on Today's Europe* discusses the European Community and its cultural identity in terms that are at times quite similar to those of Kristeva. For Derrida, too, affirms the legacy of the Enlightenment tradition, whose democratic values and respect for human rights continue, in his view, to be valid today, but he warns that its principles should guide us only insofar as we also acknowledge their limits. We should remain wary of the possibility that any concept, even one that works in the service of the most liberal of democratic ideals, might harden into a "regulative idea," into a notion that is "simply given" as part of what is assumed to be a uniquely European heritage.[42] Here once again, as in the recent work of Kristeva, the question of identification (that is, of mimesis) comes into play, an identification, this time on a cultural level, with a certain concept of European identity, which, in serving as a model for others to reproduce or imitate, assigns to Europe an exemplary role as the cultural leader or "head" of world civilization. Capitalizing on the multiple meanings of the term "heading" (*cap*) as it has been applied to Europe—first, in the geographical sense, as a cape or headland at the extreme end of the continent from which voyages of discovery and colonization have taken place; and second, in the figurative sense, as a "spiritual" heading or governing idea through which Europe's cultural identity and position of privilege have been established—Derrida proposes an "other" thought of the heading. That thought would counter such Eurocentric projections and mimetic logic by acknowledging what these projections or self-representations overlook, that is, the experience of the other that both constitutes a culture and opens its borders to the *promise* of "that which is not, never was, and never will be Europe" in any reified sense of the term (p. 77):

> [W]*hat is proper to a culture is to not be identical to itself*. Not to not have an identity, but not to be able to identify itself, to be able to say "me" or "we"; to be able to take the form of a subject only in the non-identity to itself or, if you prefer, only in the difference

with itself [*avec soi*]. There is no culture or cultural identity without this difference *with itself*. . . . This can be said, inversely or reciprocally, of all identity or all identification: there is no self-relation, no relation to oneself, no identification with oneself, without culture, but a culture of oneself *as* a culture *of* the other, a culture of the double genitive and of the *difference to oneself*. (pp. 9–10)

The promise of which Derrida speaks refers to the opening toward an "identity" that is yet to come ("à-venir"), one that does not locate all difference under the heading that names "Europe," but is implicit in the opening itself, that is, in what opens itself without being able to gather itself in its relation to an other. This does not mean that we should abandon our role as "the guardians of an idea of Europe, *but*," as Derrida insists, the idea for which we are to become guardians is one that "consists precisely in not closing itself off in its own identity and in advancing itself in an exemplary way toward what it is not, toward the other heading or the heading of the other, indeed—and this is perhaps something else altogether—toward the other *of* the heading, which would be the beyond of this modern tradition, another border structure, another shore" (p. 29). The promise of the "other heading," which gives us new ways of thinking cultural identity, does not, then, constitute a radical eradication of our European heritage. It is, Derrida claims, something for which we bear a certain responsibility and through which the Enlightenment value of responsibility itself can be affirmed, not as a *demand* for responsible action but as a call for an "opening and a non-exclusion" in which the responsibility of Europe itself would also be implicated. At this point in Derrida's argument, when he enumerates the duties and obligations that such a redefinition of European identity implies, we are reminded of Kristeva's recent writings. Derrida reveals concerns that are not unlike those put forth in *Strangers to Ourselves*, in which Kristeva articulates her conception of a new cosmopolitanism and its tolerance of the foreign. As Derrida writes:

[T]he *duty* to respond to the call of European memory, to recall what has been promised under the name Europe, to re-identify Europe . . . dictates welcoming foreigners in order not only to integrate them but to recognize and accept their alterity: two concepts of hospitality that today divide our European and national consciousness.

The *same duty* dictates *criticizing* ("in-both-theory-and-in-practice," and relentlessly) a totalitarian dogmatism that, under the pretense of putting an end to capital, destroyed democracy and the European heritage. But it also dictates criticizing a religion of capital that institutes its dogmatism under new guises. . . .

The *same duty* dictates respecting differences, idioms, minorities, singularities, but also the universality of formal law, the desire for translation, agreement and univocity, the law of the majority, opposition to racism, nationalism, and xenophobia. (pp. 76–78)

Reevaluating 'Tel Quel'

What permitted this theoretical rapprochement between Derrida and Kristeva is difficult to say, but a possible answer might lie not so much in Kristeva's reappraisal of Derridean theory—given that no mention of *différance* is made in either of her recent works—as in her immersion in psychoanalysis where she came up against a similar problematic, that of the idealizing identifications of narcissism that constitute but also destabilize traditional notions of identity through the confrontation with otherness. And as her understanding of the subject and of its linguistic representations deepened through her encounter with primary narcissism, so too, as we have seen, did her understanding of the political. This led her to what she had been aiming at all along, to the possibility of a non-dogmatic politics that comes, this time, from a more profound appreciation of human finitude and of the necessary attenuation of subjective authority. It could be argued that had that appreciation emerged in the early stages of *Tel Quel*'s history, had the group been ready to embrace the more radical implications of the motif of *différance* and its problematization of identity, they might have avoided some of the difficulties plaguing a project whose goal, from the moment Sollers first announced *Tel Quel*'s political program, was to question the logic of identity structuring the entirety of Western culture and thought. Guided by the assumption that such a logic is inherently political, that it serves an essentially capitalist social system whose ideology permeates every level of Western life, from its political and religious institutions to the objectivist precepts of its representational discourse, they understood that no critique of the political system and its ideology could take place without a thorough interrogation of the language in which that ideology is embedded as well as of the subject who perpetuates it through his subjective projections of meaning.

If it is agreed, however, that *Tel Quel* failed in the realization of its objectives, perhaps the reason is that its investigation did not go far enough. The group's questioning of the politics inhering in the Western principle of identity never led to an interrogation of its own political practice or, more important, to an examination of the extent to which politics is by its very nature dependent on that principle as well as on the instrumentalist view of language upon which any notion of the political is based. Indeed, if the *Tel Quel* experience demonstrates nothing else, it shows that the very concept of directed political action presupposes all the "bourgeois capitalist" notions they had hoped to contest. It assumes a conscious, rational subjectivity as a self-present determining center in control of its discourse and whose struggle for dominance establishes the character of the political as binary, as a site of confrontation, antagonism, and conflict. Thus, although the group attacked the privileging of identity as the expression of the capitalist system's will to dominate, the fact of *Tel Quel*'s adherence to a political program suggests a limited awareness of the degree to which revolutionary politics and political action in general are complicitous with the "politics of identity" the group called into question.[43] Consequently, despite *Tel Quel*'s attempt to overcome such limitations by avoiding the political dogmatism associated with orthodox Marxism, the group's adoption of a common political strategy led it to engage in a politics of the most orthodox kind, involving the exclusion of those who threatened the uniformity of its practice and unleashing an exaggerated binarism in the form of the polemical justifications of its political position.

Given the problems plaguing the *Tel Quel* project, it is no wonder that Derrida resisted demands by both *Tel Quel* and others for

an explicit politicization of his work. While he never directly dis-
credited *Tel Quel*'s revolutionary activism, his refusal to give in to
what he later described as a "certain Marxist intimidation"[44] stems
from a deep suspicion of the "all or nothing" logic that structures
the political itself. Moreover, if Derrida was himself a victim of
that logic, as the object of rather hostile remarks in some of *Tel
Quel*'s editorials, that merely lends further support to what Derrida
has been maintaining all along through his analysis of *différance*
and other analogous motifs such as iterability, the supplement, the
mark, the trace, and so on. What Derrida's analysis shows is that
although *différance* makes the conceptual oppositions "all or noth-
ing," "for or against," possible, it is also what renders impossible
their rigor and purity, because the concept that emerges as an effect
of relations is never entirely safe from contamination.

Indeed, the *Tel Quel* experience itself illustrates what Derrida
has called the "law of undecidable contamination" at work in the
movement of *différance*. To the extent that *Tel Quel*'s editorials
testify to a certain will to "purify," to subordinate difference to the
political identity of the group, their discourse had been tainted by
the very subjectivist and representationalist precepts it claimed to
denounce. Derrida's reluctance, however, to embrace the "mate-
rialist position" was not so much due to a complete lack of affinity
for *Tel Quel*'s political objectives, for, as we have seen, his de-
construction of phonocentrism and its metaphysics of presence
provided the theoretical impetus to the group's revolutionary proj-
ect. Rather, it stemmed from an awareness that no political "posi-
tion" can avoid this kind of contamination, that every position
taken against ideology is itself ideological, grounded in a philo-
sophical tradition that privileges the conceptual powers of a will-
ful, rational subject and his utilitarian view of language:

> I persist in believing that there is no theoretical or political
> benefit to be derived from precipitating contacts or articulations,
> as long as their conditions have not been rigorously elucidated.
> Eventually such precipitation will have the effect only of dogma-
> tism, confusion, or opportunism. To impose this prudence upon
> oneself is to take seriously the difficulty, and also the hetero-
> geneity, of the Marxist text, the decisive importance of its histor-
> ical stakes.[45]

What should accompany, then, according to Derrida, any recognition of the need for political action is a rigorous examination of the ideological or metaphysical precepts grounding the political itself. Not, of course, to free oneself from the constraints of such precepts, for that would be to posit once again the possibility of a conceptual purity that has not been inscribed in a web of differential relations, but to recognize the risk, which is in a sense unavoidable, of reproducing the homogenizing, totalizing logic one claims or intends to deconstruct.

The work of deconstruction thus calls for a strategic analysis of the precepts that *Tel Quel* also questioned but that would also be extended to encompass the political as well, remaining all the while as "vigilant as possible," keeping one's "eyes wide open" in an attempt to ward off (but never absolutely) such reappropriations. Derrida's resistance to *Tel Quel*'s politicization of his work does not therefore signify that deconstruction is *opposed* to the political as such or that it seeks refuge in some apolitical realm. Although it serves no existing political code or program, its radical questioning and ultimate destabilizing of the founding and organizing schemas that make such programs possible introduces a "principle of dislocation" whose effects are clearly political. Deconstruction cannot, then, be placed in opposition to the *Tel Quel* project as the expression of a purely textual and apolitical "gla-gla précieux derridien." The strategies of the one project conflict with but are also implicated in the strategies of the other, not only in terms of their destabilizing function, but also in light of the stabilizing effects that are contained within it. This is a point that Derrida makes in his 1990 essay on the states of theory in which he uses the term "jetty" instead of theory to stress the fact that no theory can close itself off from and remain unaffected by one that presumably opposes it. Derrida's description of the jetty's deconstructive operations underscores the degree to which deconstruction aimed at destabilizing effects that were quite similar to those of *Tel Quel*, including the questioning of the closure of theory itself:

> [T]he *destabilizing* and *devastating* jetty . . . resists theorization first because it functions in a place which the jetty questions, and destabilizes the conditions of the possibility of objectivity, the

relationship to the object, everything that constitutes and institutes the assurance of subjectivity, in the indubitable presence of the cogito, the certainty of self-consciousness, . . . the principle of reason and the system of representation associated with it, and hence everything that supports a modern concept of theory as objectivity. Deconstruction resists theory then because it demonstrates the impossibility of closure, of the closure of an ensemble or totality on an organized network of theorems, laws, rules and methods.[46]

The deconstructive jetty's interrogation of the power of the thetic in all its forms, whether it is manifested in theory, political dogma, scientific discourse, or the literary text, is thus what gave both projects their critical force, and in this sense, one could say that both *Tel Quel* and deconstruction functioned in a way that was essentially political. One could also argue that the moment *Tel Quel* abandoned the perpetually self-critical methodology of Kristeva's revisionary semiology, that is, when its destabilizing resistance hardened into an oppositional logic by taking a position *against* those who refused to embrace revolutionary Marxism, was the moment *Tel Quel* ceased to be political and assumed instead what Derrida has described as the jetty's stabilizing, consolidating function, a function whose possibility is contained within the structure of the jetty itself and with which it remains indissolubly linked:

> [In] the word "jetty" . . . I distinguish, on the one hand, the force of the movement which throws something or throws itself (*jette* or *se jette*) forward and backwards at the same time, prior to any subject, object, or project, prior to any rejection or abjection, from, on the other hand, its institutional and protective consolidation, which can be compared to the jetty, the pier in a harbor meant to break the waves and maintain low tide for boats at anchor or for swimmers. Of course, these two functions of the jetty are ideally distinct, but in fact they are difficult to dissociate, if not indissociable. (p. 84)

Thus, the very thing that resists and destabilizes the theoretical, the thetic, the philosophical, and the political can at the same time provoke, "as gestures of reappropriation and suture," a reconstitution of the thetic in the form of theorems, treatises, and political movements, leading to situations like those of *Tel Quel*, where the political "effects" of the deconstructive jetty hardened into polemical statements and political pronouncements. Derrida's retreat from *Tel Quel*'s revolutionary Marxism is not therefore a retreat from all forms of political practice but a resistance, through a constant interrogation of its premises, to the jetty's capacity to reconstitute the political as a stabilizing, reappropriating force. In this sense, then, and in contrast with the assertive politics of *Tel Quel*'s stabilizing jetty, the deconstructive jetty plays a more radically destabilizing role. This is not to suggest, however, that the "politics" of deconstruction is more "effective" than *Tel Quel*'s, for that would simply reproduce the stabilizing jetty's theorizing and reifying logic and thus demonstrate the persistence and ease with which that logic exerts its considerable force. What is at stake here is not a game of oneupmanship to determine who can be more political than the other, but the question of the political itself and its complicity with the stabilizing jetty's need to solidify and consolidate. Indeed, if the assertions and declarations necessary for coordinated political action can be said to institute the consolidating structure of the jetty and make it function in the name of a cause, doctrine, or some unifying "ism" (Marxism, socialism, fascism, republicanism, and even, as Sollers came to say, "Telquelism"), then deconstruction does not escape its fortifying constructions. As Derrida points out, the deconstructive jetty stabilizes and closes itself the moment one begins to make assertions about it and leads to what some people have called "deconstructionism" whose stabilizing effects are both necessary and unavoidable:

> The closest type, the stabilizing jetty which resembles the destabilizing jetty most, is what is called poststructuralism, alias deconstructionism. It's not bad, it isn't an evil, and even if it were one, it would be a necessary evil. It consists in formalizing certain strategic necessities of the deconstructive jetty and in putting forward . . . a system of technical rules, teachable methodological procedures, a discipline, school phenomena, a kind of knowledge, principles, theorems, which are for the most part principles of interpretation and reading (rather than of writing). (p. 88)

Given, however, the ease with which the stabilizing jetty "asserts" itself—for its closural effects are evident even in Derrida's own assertions that deconstruction cannot constitute closure, that it is not a theory, a philosophy, a school, or a method—one should proceed with caution, remaining aware of the necessity of such assertions and of their risks. Although assertions are clearly necessary, and indeed one cannot proceed without them, one should always be suspicious of their content, aware that their borders are never as well defined and stable as they appear. The quotation marks used so frequently in "deconstructive" texts are markers of this instability, for they carry with them the recognition that no concept is safe from contamination, that the stabilizing jetty's assertions, concepts, and theories are also what the destabilizing jetty firmly resists. Assertions thus call for the "strictest vigilance" in the form of a quotation that indicates a certain "reservation or distance" with regard to traditional words and concepts. If *Tel Quel* succumbed to the stabilizing jetty's consolidating effects and allowed a Telquelism ultimately to prevail, the reason was that it failed to sustain, through the vigilant use of quotation marks, its initial mistrust of all theoretical or political concepts.

To pit, however, deconstruction, as a discourse *with* quotation marks, against Telquelism, as a discourse *without*, is to sum up the relationship a bit too neatly and to forget what the quotation marks themselves indicate: that the deconstructive jetty destabilizes all concepts and all conceptual oppositions, even ones affecting the destabilizing purity of deconstruction itself. Thus, as Derrida points out, the quotation marks themselves must be placed in quotation marks, without, for all that, warding off completely the possibility of a reappropriation:

I would say that even on the side where one generally tries to situate "deconstruction" (quotation marks within quotation marks), even there, "deconstructionists" and "deconstructionism" represent an effort to reappropriate, tame, normalize this writing in order to reconstitute a new "theory"—"deconstructionism" with its methods and its rules. . . . This distinction between, on the one hand, deconstruction or deconstructions, the effects or processes of deconstruction, and, on the other hand, the theorems or theoretical reappropriations of "deconstructionism," . . . doesn't have the reality of a border which some would cross and others wouldn't. It is always being crossed, erased and retraced, retraced by being erased. (pp. 75–76)

Because of the "instability of the borderline" distinguishing the two discourses, Tel Quel and deconstruction do not stand in direct opposition to each other as pure representatives of the jetty's stabilizing or destabilizing function. Not only was the Tel Quel phenomenon itself not monolithic (and we have seen the various destabilizing elements structuring both its theory and its practice—as in Kristeva's theory of intertextuality, for example, or in the multiple "positions" of Pleynet's Stanze), but the stabilizing force of what Sollers referred to as Telquelism is a potentiality within deconstruction itself, for it points to what deconstruction could have, could always, and, in the eyes of some, has already become. Derrida's call for the generalized use of quotation marks is thus a way of resisting that potentiality, of conveying a distrust toward any concept that is used uncritically and that, as a consequence, imposes its restrictive effects.

In the context of the Tel Quel experience, whose failed politics provides an example of what can occur when one presupposes notions such as the political without analyzing them critically, a case for Derrida's insistence on quotation marks as the "only 'theoretical' attitude possible" could easily be made. If words such as "the political" rarely appear in his writing unadorned by these marks of resistance, it is not, however, to keep "an impure concept at a distance" so as to avoid, as one critic suggests, "dirtying any hands."[47] On the contrary, one could argue that the deconstructive project, by problematizing the conceptual purity of those oppositions upon which political struggle and confrontation depend, is directly engaged in the political, that indeed no attitude is more political, more responsible before the political than "that which puts into practice a vigilant but, in its very principle, a general use of quotation marks. Responsible before history and before the political-socioinstitutional 'realities' which constitute the solid jetty of these concepts."[48]

The very impossibility of a rigorous conceptual purity as suggested by the "law of undecidable contamination" opens the field of ethical-political responsibility, in Derrida's view. Undecidability is the necessary condition of responsible action insofar as a decision to behave responsibly, to exercise one's moral or political responsibility can only be made when it "exceeds the calculable program." If everything is decided in advance, determined by a preestablished set of rules, responsibility becomes irresponsibility, transformed into a "programmable effect of determinate causes." As Derrida writes, "[T]here can be no moral or political responsibility without this trial and this passage by way of the undecidable."[49] Echoing his remarks some years later in one of his more explicitly political essays on the question of European identity, Derrida adds:

> I will even venture to say that ethics, politics, and responsibility, *if there are any*, will only ever have begun with the experience and experiment of the aporia. When the path is clear and given, when a certain knowledge opens up the way in advance, the decision is already made, it might as well be said that there is none to make: irresponsibly, and in good conscience, one simply applies or implements a program. Perhaps, and this would be the objection, one never escapes the program. In that case, one must acknowledge this and stop talking with authority about moral or political responsibility. The condition of possibility of this thing called responsibility is a certain *experience and experiment of the possibility of the impossible: the testing of the aporia* from which one may invent the only *possible invention, the impossible invention.*[50]

Considering Derrida's remarks in the context of the *Tel Quel* experience, one could argue that the possibility for the political emerged at *Tel Quel* only *after* the group's dissolution, when a more thoroughgoing analysis of the mechanisms of identification and its opening toward the other underscored not only the intellectually repressive measures the group had to take in order to affirm its common political identity but also its blindness to the "law of undecidable contamination" at work in its own distinction between the semiotic as transgressor and the symbolic as that which needed to be transgressed. Through Kristeva's increased interest in the dynamics of narcissism and her perhaps unintentional discovery that the "purity" of the drives finds itself contaminated by symbolic identifications with an other, she comes face to face with the "experience of the aporia" and arrives at a point in her thinking that approaches more closely that of Derrida. If Derrida's concerns can be more directly related to language, the underlying question for both approaches is essentially the same. Whether one is examining the identificatory mechanisms essential to the constitution of the human psyche or the role of language in reproducing some psychological, sociopolitical, or conceptual reality, the question to be addressed is that of *mimesis* itself, which, when subjected to what can only be described as *Tel Quel*'s rather superficial critique, can, as we have seen, have disturbing political consequences. Without a painstaking analysis of its most basic precepts, traditional mimesis with its logic of identity not only supports in the name of some individual or communal identity the quest for uniformity that ultimately unraveled the *Tel Quel* collective, but it also has the potential, in its most extreme manifestations, to unleash, in Derrida's words, "the worst violences, those that we recognize all too well without yet having thought them through, the crimes of xenophobia, racism, anti-Semitism, religious or nationalist fanaticism."[51]

The way that the deconstructive approach responds to the possibility of such violence will thus be the focus of the third section of this book, which argues, in opposition to those who denounce deconstruction for its so-called textualization of reality at the expense of the social, the historical, or the political, that it is precisely this focus on language, on the logic of mimesis and its inscription of alterity that problematizes such distinctions between the textual and the nontextual, and makes the question of our moral and political responsibility in effect unavoidable. As Derrida points out, we are "invested in an undeniable responsibility at the moment we begin to signify something," for that is when we are faced with what amounts to an ethico-political summons, one that comes, as we shall see, from the inevitable exposure to an other.

PART III

Deconstructive Poetics

CHAPTER 5

Deconstruction on Trial

If the issue of responsibility has come to occupy an increasingly prominent place in Derrida's writings in recent years, it is because the accusations either of deconstruction's political disengagement or of its sympathies for the wrong kind of politics did not, as anyone with the slightest interest in Derrida's work well knows, cease with the demise of *Tel Quel*. With attention shifting from Derrida's relationship to Marxism, which by the 1980's had become a dead issue for many French intellectuals disillusioned by the terroristic practices of Soviet communism, to Derrida's so-called Heideggerianism, the debate concerning deconstruction's political allegiances (or lack thereof) took on a new intensity. Ignoring the complex nature of Derrida's relationship to Heidegger (and of a work just as diligent in its critique of many of Heidegger's assumptions as in its recognition of the importance of Heidegger's thought), certain of Derrida's detractors have used that relationship and Farias's rehashing of the question of Heidegger's prewar Nazi involvement to indict the whole of deconstruction, which was seen as compromised by Heidegger's unsavory politics.

The de Man and Heidegger Controversies

The details of that debate are more familiar to American audiences than those of the earlier disputes involving *Tel Quel*, due no doubt to the involvement of deconstruction's leading proponent in the United States, Paul de Man, whose collaborationist contributions to a Belgian newspaper during the German occupation attracted a considerable amount of journalistic attention. With the appearance shortly after the publication of Victor Farias's *Heidegger et le nazism*[1] of a *New York Times* article exposing de Man's early collaborationist essays, the debate moved beyond Parisian intellectual circles to gain widespread and often sensationalized coverage in the American press, where columns fed upon the comments of those academic critics who reveled in the idea that deconstruction might, as one *Newsweek* reporter put it, "self-deconstruct" in the wake of Heidegger's and de Man's disgrace. After claiming, for example, that the de Man affair had become "one of the most serious intellectual scandals of the decade," that same *Newsweek* reporter gives the following account of his interview with one of de Man's critics:

> "There's no doubt that de Man was a gung-ho collaborator," says Jeffrey Mehlman, a professor of French at Boston University. In Mehlman's view, there are even "grounds for viewing the whole of deconstruction as a vast amnesty project for the politics of collaboration during World War II." . . . Opponents of deconstruction think the movement is finished. As one Ivy League professor gleefully exclaims, "deconstruction turned out to be the thousand-year Reich that lasted 12 years."[2]

Other critics, who were somewhat less hasty in their judgments and more willing to grapple seriously with the issues raised by the de Man and Heidegger affairs, were concerned not so much with Derrida's or deconstruction's link to Nazism as with what they perceived as Derrida's reluctance to make a strong political statement against it. Their attention was directed primarily at Derrida's essay "Like the Sound of the Sea Deep within a Shell: Paul de Man's War," in which he attempts to account for the complexities and ambiguities in de Man's wartime journalism. By developing a strategy of reading that alternates between opposing points of view, between one that shows de Man's commentary conforming to "the official rhetoric" of the occupation forces in Belgium and one that uncovers the "counterpropositions" that address de Man's pro-German, anti-Semitic remarks, Derrida became the center of a controversy whose repercussions can still be felt today, through the proliferation of books and articles that continue to raise the question of the political in Derrida's texts. Shortly after its publication, however, first in *Critical Inquiry* and later in the revised edition of *Memoires for Paul de Man*,[3] critics began to object to a tendency they found in Derrida's analysis to "de-emphasize" or "diminish" the most incriminating aspects of de Man's articles. The "recurrent alternation" of "on the one hand . . . on the other hand," which was meant to underscore textual heterogeneity and the ways in which de Man's writings also distance themselves from all forms of "totalizing violence," tended, in the view of critics such as David Carroll, for example, to give greater weight to the second "counterpropositional" part of the "on the one hand . . . on the other hand" equation, and, in so doing, to "seriously distort" or "cover over" their "dangerous nationalist, fascist . . . anti-Semitic arguments." As Carroll writes in his open letter to Derrida:

> [T]he "one hand" dominates and renders practically insignificant whatever it is the "other hand" is doing. . . . [Y]ou give so much weight to "the other hand" and in this way de-emphasize (not deny the existence of) the "one hand" and its effects. This ends up reversing the imbalance of the hands actually at work in de Man's texts themselves, in which potential countering effects are always tightly controlled and dominated by the hegemony of the nationalist, profascist, pro-German hand. . . . [T]his strategy is highly questionable. . . . It can't help but "attenuate the fault" and begin to pardon the unpardonable—whether you "intended" it to do so or not.[4]

Similar objections were raised in the issue of *Critical Inquiry* devoted entirely to the controversy generated both by the revelations concerning de Man and by Derrida's response. One article extended the previous critique by suggesting that Derrida's emphasis on the undecidable logic of the *double bind* at work in de Man's newspaper articles not only "lessens de Man's responsibility" because he stresses unduly the ambiguity of de Man's political commitments but also casts doubt upon deconstruction itself, and the claims Derrida makes for it, in terms of its ability to stand as a "bulwark against totalitarianism." Despite Derrida's insistence that it is by way of the undecidable that one avoids the totalizing gesture, of which Nazism is only the most extreme example, the article suggests that his "construction of ambiguity" in de Man's writings constitutes a "methodological error" that renders deconstruction powerless in the struggle against fascist ideology:

> Derrida has responded [in his essay on de Man] with two very large claims. He claims, first, that deconstruction provides the instruments of interpretation and habits of analysis without which the practices of a fascist intellectual like the young de Man cannot be understood. And, further, that the mode of philosophical and literary analysis embodied in his own and the later de Man's work is a bulwark against totalitarianism, including fascism itself. With these claims Derrida puts the prestige of deconstruction on the line: its political significance, its power to explain political and cultural conjunctures, and its capacity for self-understanding. If these remain staked on the procedures and outcomes of his account of "Paul de Man's War," the wager will be lost.[5]

The question of whether the deconstructive approach, particularly with its emphasis on "undecidability" and on the possible complicities in one's own discourse with the political position that one seeks to oppose, can provide an adequate response to ethical and political issues becomes even more urgent in the context of Heidegger's Nazism. If the flurry of commentary and protestation generated by Derrida's response to the accusations directed at de Man seems to have died down in recent years, the controversy surrounding Farias's book and the response of the so-called French Heideggerians has not. Richard Wolin, for example, who continues certain aspects of Luc Ferry and Alan Renaut's earlier critique of French Heideggerianism—a designation that lumps together indiscriminately the writings of Derrida, Heidegger, and Jean-François Lyotard[6]—argues in his preface to the 1993 edition of *The Heidegger Controversy* that deconstruction's unwavering commitment to the Heideggerian critique of philosophical humanism has led to an "apologetic and relativizing treatment of Heidegger's ties to Nazism."[7] Referring specifically to the writings of Lacoue-Labarthe and Derrida, who are described, in his contribution to the above collection of essays, as the "two leading representatives of Heideg-gerianism working in France today," Wolin acknowledges their willingness to confront the disturbing evidence of Heidegger's po-litical affiliations, but argues that they do so in order to "allow the vultures to feed on Heidegger the contingent, empirical individ-ual . . . while saving the philosophical oeuvre itself—especially Heidegger's work following *die Kehre* (the 'Turn'); where—so the argument runs—Heidegger freed himself from the vestigial anthro-pocentrism" dominating his early work.[8]

Although Wolin counters to a certain extent the chronology he has constructed when he views Derrida's analysis of the various permutations of the word *Geist* (spirit) in Heidegger's work as an attempt to get the *"early* Heidegger partially off the hook" (p. 289), he is particularly disturbed by the "defense" of Heidegger that he finds both in Derrida's *Of Spirit* and in a 1987 interview with *Le Nouvel Observateur*. Referring to his controversial English transla-tion of that interview, which appeared in the first edition of *The Heidegger Controversy* but was withdrawn by Derrida from the second, Wolin sees in the following comments by Derrida a "quasi-exoneration" of Heidegger's philosophical commitment to Na-tional Socialism:

> As Derrida himself explains the rationale behind his "spirited" defense of Heidegger: one must preserve the "possibilities of rupture" in a "variegated Heideggerian thought that will remain for a long time provocative, enigmatic, worth reading." In his Rectoral Address, "Heidegger takes up again the word 'spirit,' which he had previously avoided, he dispenses with the inverted commas with which he had surrounded it. He thus limits the movement of deconstruction that he had previously engaged in. He gives a voluntaristic and metaphysical speech [whose terms] he would later treat with suspicion. To the extent that [Heideg-ger's discourse] celebrates the freedom of spirit, its exaltation [of spirit] resembles other European discourses (spiritualist, reli-gious, humanist) that in general are opposed to Nazism. [This is] a complex and unstable skein that I try to unravel [in *De l'esprit*] by recognizing the threads in common between Nazism and anti-Nazism, the law of resemblance, the fatality of perversion. The mirror images are at times vertiginous." (p. 289)[9]

Finding that these remarks leave us with the "far-fetched and illogical conclusion" that an excess of metaphysical humanism led to Heidegger's endorsement of National Socialism, Wolin claims that Derrida's line of argument and Lacoue-Labarthe's as well, constitute a "strategy of denial" that not only blurs many of the essential differences between humanism and antihumanism, and thus robs us of the possibility of taking a stand against Nazism, but also exonerates Heidegger of any personal responsibility for his extreme right-wing politics. "[It] was ultimately Western metaphysics that was at fault," Wolin writes, "since this was the intellectual framework that stood behind [Heidegger's infatuation with] Nietzsche's thought. Heidegger had been misled and duped (first by Nietzsche, then by the Nazis), but he was not 'responsible for,' let alone 'guilty of' any misdeeds" (p. 289):

> Through a brilliant piece of hermeneutical chicanery, they [Derrida and Lacoue-Labarthe] intentionally seek . . . to link up the philosophy of the early Heidegger with his pro-Nazi phase in order the better to save him: the early Heidegger, whose thought is in any case overly saturated with superfluous metaphysico-humanist residues, can be safely jettisoned in order that the post-humanist Heidegger . . . can be redeemed unscathed. And thus by an ingenious interpretive *coup de maître*, the troubling "question" of Heidegger and politics can be neatly brushed aside, since the post-1935 Heidegger abandoned the philosophical paradigm that led to his partisanship for Hitlerism in the first place. (pp. 285–86)

In an effort, then, to sever the link that Derrida and Lacoue-Labarthe establish between Heidegger's metaphysical discourse and his commitment to National Socialism, Wolin sees himself countering their argument by claiming that those very "metaphysico-humanist residues" prevented Heidegger from "identifying wholesale with Nazi ideology" by allowing him to contest, through an appeal to spirituality, the racist, biologist thinking upon which that ideology is based. Wolin, for the sake of his argument, never points out, however, that Derrida makes a similar case, that, indeed, this might even be Derrida's point when he refers to the "terrifying contaminations" that can taint even the most vigilant discourse. In tracing the duplicitous twistings and turnings in Heidegger's notion of "spirit" (in which we see the "on the one hand . . . on the other hand" alternation at work once again), Derrida indicates a myriad of conflicting possibilities, involving Heidegger's attempt to confer "spiritual legitimacy" on National Socialism and to "spiritualize" Nazism itself, thus saving it from its more racist manifestations:

> [B]y taking the risk of spiritualizing nazism, [Heidegger] might have been trying to absolve or save it by marking it with this affirmation (spirituality, science questioning, etc.). By the same token, this sets apart [*démarque*] Heidegger's commitment and breaks an affiliation. This address *seems* no longer to belong simply to the "ideological" camp in which one appeals to obscure forces—forces which would not be spiritual, but natural, biological, racial, according to an anything but spiritual interpretation of "earth and blood."[10]

Derrida thus concurs with Wolin that it was indeed Heidegger's humanism that allowed him to denounce the more terrifying aspects of National Socialist doctrine. He is quick to point out, however, that such denunciations have a price, insofar as the very thinking that permits a resistance to Nazism also runs the risk of perpetuating its logic by "reinscribing spirit into an oppositional determination":

> The constraint of this program remains very strong, it reigns over the majority of discourses which, today and for a long time to come, state their opposition to racism, to totalitarianism, to nazism, to fascism, etc., and do this in the name of spirit, and even of the freedom of (the) spirit, in the name of an axiomatic— for example, that of democracy or "human rights"— which, directly or not, comes back to the metaphysics of *subjectity*. All the pitfalls of the strategy of establishing demarcations belong to this program, whatever place one occupies in it. The only choice is the choice between the terrifying contaminations it assigns. Even if all forms of complicity are not equivalent, they are *irreducible*. (pp. 39–40)

Thus, rather than simply equating one phase of Heidegger's writing with metaphysics and another with the deconstruction of its precepts "in order the better to save" it, as Wolin has claimed,

Derrida underscores the complex interweaving of both throughout Heidegger's work by marking the "spectral duplicity," the shadowy figure of spirit's "metaphysical ghost," that haunts Heidegger's discourse even during those moments "pre-1935" or "post-1935" when Heidegger engaged in his most serious attempts to deconstruct the metaphysical tradition. Contrary to Wolin, then, who argues that there are "some binary oppositions that need to be strengthened, rather than 'deconstructed' and, hence, relativized" (p. xviii), Derrida insists that whether one is speaking *for* Nazism or *against* it, one must be wary of the inversions and complicities that inevitably contaminate oppositional logic. The irreducibility of such complicities "calls more than ever . . . for absolutely unprecedented responsibilities of 'thought' and 'action.' This is what we should have to try to designate, if not to name, and begin to analyze."[11] Consequently, far from constituting an apologia for Heidegger, as Wolin and others have argued,[12] Derrida's *Of Spirit* sets out to show that a simple, unexamined opposition to Heidegger's Nazism can never suffice, that we must analyze the conditions and thinking that make the sanctioning of National Socialist doctrine possible, conditions that, in Derrida's view, have not yet been sufficiently thought through.

Jean-François Lyotard's 'Heidegger and "the jews"'

The need to "think Nazism through" is a position taken up by Jean-François Lyotard, who is one of the more interesting critics of deconstruction primarily because he embraces many deconstructive "strategies" himself, but who can also be included among those who have denounced deconstruction for its failure to come to terms with the sociopolitical. Unlike Wolin, however, Lyotard is concerned not so much with Derrida's critique of the metaphysical tradition and its leveling of the distinction between Nazism and anti-Nazism, as with the possibility that the deconstructive critique is too limited in scope, that metaphysical residues within Derrida's own thinking prevent him, like Heidegger, from adequately responding to the imperative to speak out against the Nazi atrocities. Lyotard claims in his relatively recent *Heidegger and "the jews"* that Heidegger's failure to address the question of Auschwitz even after his break with National Socialism was due not simply to a "deconstructionist lapsus," as he calls it, but rather to a flaw within deconstruction itself. In focusing too persistently on the question of Being, deconstruction remains tied, in Lyotard's view, to a tradition that refuses to think the possibility of nothingness, of something "unpresentable" or ungraspable within Being itself.[13]

As Lyotard points out, this is all the more curious given that Heidegger's own critique of the metaphysical tradition, of its focus on being's "thingness" and its forgetting the fundamentally enigmatic essence of Being as such, taught us to think the unthinkable, to preserve the memory of what is necessarily missing, forgotten, and utterly unrepresentable in both language and thought. In failing, however, to push his deconstructive project far enough, preferring instead to embrace notions of authenticity and the ultimate "destiny" of Being, Heidegger remains complicitous, according to Lyotard, not only with the Western philosophical tradition but also with its politics, a politics whose rejection of heterogeneity and otherness, or indeed of anything that disrupts conceptual, representational, or social homogeneity, can have Nazism as one of its possible consequences. Although that politics is obviously not always identical with that of National Socialism, although it does not necessarily authorize such monstrosities as Nazism's "final solution," it nevertheless finds its place within a conceptual framework that can always permit such a possibility. For, if the Jews were to be eliminated without leaving a trace or memory, it is because of a "politics of absolute forgetting" that was in effect made possible by the Western philosophical tradition, by its effort to eliminate from thought the unrepresentable itself.

In Lyotard's text, it is indeed "the jews" who come to signify this problematic of the unrepresentable. In placing his term in lower case, however, as well as in the plural and in quotation marks, he does not aim to designate the Jewish people alone or some form of "political . . . religious . . . or philosophical . . . subject," but to signify that unnameable otherness, the forgotten unrepresentable that the West has tried to eradicate from thought. And although Lyotard claims that the term should not be confused with real Jews, there are obvious parallels between the two in that both have become objects of a radical exclusion. Given that the condition of being Jewish is one of continual "emigration" and "dispersion," the Jews are seen to " 'thwart' every program of mastery" (p. 81). They are never at home even within their own tradition, because it includes, in Lyotard's words, "exodus as its beginning, excision [and] impropriety" (p. 22).[14] The specter of anti-Semitism has, as a consequence, haunted the West, not simply because of Western xenophobia, according to Lyotard. It is, rather, the means by which the stabilizing structures of Western culture try to protect themselves by actively forgetting the "impropriety" that "the J/jews" (in both upper and lower case) have come to represent.

Although there are moments in Heidegger's writings that suggest this thought of unthinkable "impropriety," there are others, in Lyotard's view, that miss entirely this problematic of the unpresentable, certainly during his association with the Nazi Party but even after the break when his discourse on art and technology ignored, for the most part, what Lyotard calls the "thought of 'the jews,' " taking it to the point of suppressing to the end the Extermination itself (p. 4). And while both Lacoue-Labarthe and Derrida have tried to respond to this question of Heidegger's silence and have, over a period of many years, attempted to distance themselves from the more "mythical" aspects of Heidegger's thinking, their effort has done little to satisfy Lyotard. He claims that the fault lies with the deconstructive approach itself, which is still too philosophical, too "respectfully nihilist" (in other words, too forgetful of the oblivion of Being) to ever address what constitutes the very epitome of unrepresentability, the event for which no discourse can ever be adequate: that is, the Holocaust itself. Indeed, if the Holocaust is to be addressed, and with it the thought of "the jews," it cannot be done, according to Lyotard, through a philosophical critique, from which deconstruction has not succeeded in liberating itself, nor can it be done through the more traditional forms of representational discourse. Transforming the event into images and words makes us forget that there is a forgotten, something that has eluded the structures of language and thought. This something can as Lyotard indicates, never be inscribed within a representation or concept because it is in reality nothing that can be stored in memory. One can only remember it "as forgotten 'before' memory and forgetting" (p. 5), as an absence that is there nonetheless, residing within the "deep unconscious where," according to Lyotard, "there are no representations."

In this sense, then, Lyotard's notion of "the jews" takes on a significance that extends far beyond the physical reality of the Jews as a people. Related by Lyotard to the Kantian sublime and more specifically to Freud's notion of the "unconscious affect," the term refers to something that exceeds the powers of the human psyche, to a kind of "excess" that in the Freudian context takes the form of an "initial" shock to the system that the psychical apparatus is unprepared to deal with and of which it is in fact unaware. For Freud, that shock or trauma might originate in the "scene of seduction," whose traumatic effects can only be registered after the fact when the child, having reached puberty, is capable of understanding its sexual implications. This deferred reconstitution or revision of what Freud came to regard as a fantasied past "event" occurs because the "original" event was never truly assimilated; it becomes an event for which there are no representations and whose delayed reconstitution serves only to "neutralize," according to Lyotard, "the 'initial' violence," staging a recollection that can only be a "reappropriation of the improper" (p. 16) of what, in Lyotard's words, "has never been there in any other way than forgotten" (p. 29). Although Lyotard does not locate the source of this "initial" trauma in any particular event, nor does he situate it within a specific stage of psychic development, this notion of a past as forgotten but whose repercussions are still felt as a symptom or phobia in the present is what is suggested by Lyotard's notion of "the jews." In its relation to the interminably deferred, the term designates an origin without origin or an "originary terror" that the Western philosophical and literary tradition, in its obsession with foundational thinking, has worked so actively to forget.

What Lyotard calls for, then, is a thinking of a different sort, one that acknowledges the inescapable necessity of representing the "forgotten" while remembering that what it "represents" can never be represented in writing (p. 26). Writing, in this sense, which opens to a more " 'archaic,' " "prehistoric," "immemorial dispossession" becomes what Lyotard calls a "writing of the ruins," an "after-Auschwitz aesthetics" or "anaesthetics" that in guarding the memory of the forgotten advances toward the "insensible secret," the "cloud of terror" that lies hidden within language. Indeed, Lyotard claims that this writing of the immemorial has always been the objective of literature, and that it is the French in particular, writers such as Rimbaud, Mallarmé, Flaubert, and Beckett, who are the most inclined toward this "naming" of the unnameable. Lyotard's remarks are not, however, confined to the French alone, for his list includes such "great non-German Germans, non-Jewish Jews" as Freud, Benjamin, Adorno, Arendt, and Celan, who, in contrast with Heidegger's deconstructive approach, give voice to the forgotten by not only questioning but also "betray[ing] the tradition, the *mimè-sis*, the immanence of the unfolding, and its root" (pp. 92–93).

If in seeking, as an alternative to deconstruction, a discourse that "bears witness to the unnameable," Lyotard's effort bears a certain resemblance to that of Kristeva, who not only sought to give voice to the unrepresentable but assigned a position of privilege to certain kinds of literary texts. And if, as David Carroll writes in his introduction to *Heidegger and "the jews,"* Lyotard's "defense" of the forgotten suggests a certain forgetting of the irretrievability of the forgotten itself, one must keep in mind, as Carroll suggests, that the content of the forgotten in Lyotard's work is unidentifiable as such. Although Lyotard does refer to a "content" such as the unconscious in his work, as does Kristeva, he makes no attempt to restore it as unmediated heterogeneity. Lyotard sees Freud's "unconscious affect" as inscribed in a movement of deferral, one that, as a consequence, places the outside of representation within representation itself. For "writing," as Lyotard states in reference to the French writers of the past, represents "in words, what every representation misses, what is forgotten there: this 'presence,' whatever name it is given by one author or another . . . persists not so much at the limit but rather at *the heart of representation*" (p. 5; my emphasis).

In this sense, one could argue that Lyotard's thinking is more closely attuned to the various critical approaches of deconstruction than it is to the early semiological analyses of Kristeva, and yet his insistence on distinguishing his own "remembrance" of the forgotten from deconstructive amnesia has led to another significant lapse in memory. Although Lyotard's list of those writers who do give voice to the unnameable is hardly exhaustive and elsewhere in the text includes Kafka, Céline, Bataille, and Char, there is one important non-French French, non-Jewish Jew who is conspicuously absent from Lyotard's text. That writer is Edmond Jabès. As a nonpracticing Egyptian Jew who first confronted the condition of being Jewish in his early forties when he and the other members of the Jewish community were forced by the Nasser regime to leave Egypt, Jabès, from the moment of his exile in France, never ceased addressing the very questions that preoccupy Lyotard. Although Lyotard's "forgetting" Jabès may not have been deliberate, it was clearly convenient: Jabès, who died in January 1991, was, as one critic put it, a "deconstructionist by his own admission,"[15] one who addressed the question of the Holocaust and who also lent a forceful voice to what Lyotard refers to as "the thought of 'the jews.'" Indeed, as I shall argue in the pages that follow, in opposition to those like Lyotard, Wolin, and others who stress the political inadequacies of deconstructive thought, the voice of "the jews" can be heard not just in the texts of Jabès but in the theoretical writings of Lacoue-Labarthe, Derrida, and Nancy as well. They each show, in their very different ways, that the political questions raised by the experience of Auschwitz (and of the exclusionary modes of thought that ultimately produced that atrocity) were at the very center of their preoccupations, leading not to a strategy of avoidance or withdrawal but to an unmistakable engagement in political issues.

"Sharing the Unshareable": Deconstruction, Edmond Jabès, and the "Thought of 'the jews' "

While it is possible to argue that a certain remembrance of the unrepresentable can be found in the deconstructive texts of Edmond Jabès, his work, like that of other writers associated with deconstruction, has become the object of criticism for its presumed silence on the Extermination. Berel Lang in his "Writing-the-Holocaust: Jabès and the Measure of History" claims that the "question of whether writing centered in the Holocaust, in the Nazi genocide against the Jews is even possible: literally and morally *possible*" is never uttered in Jabès' *The Book of Questions*. It is, according to Lang "unhappily repressed," dissolved into a more generalized problematic of language which makes it disappear as a unique historical event.[1] Lang is, of course, correct when he points out that the question of writing and of language in general is a major preoccupation for Jabès. It propels the work through the production of volume after volume—all of which testify to the inadequacy of representational discourse.

Beginning with the seven texts that comprise *Le Livre des questions* and continuing through the three-volume *Le Livre des ressemblances* and the four-volume *Le Livre des limites*, Jabès' work accentuates on the most basic structural level the problematical nature of language itself.[2] The work seems an endless proliferation of words, with a total of fourteen volumes circling one another, each repeating and transforming the other in continuous search of its elusive center. Incapable, however, of establishing a totality, the writing of the book becomes an activity that can never be finished; the rupture necessary to the dissemination of the word prevents the constitution of a unified entity. For this reason, the work itself remains for the most part unclassifiable, offering no possibility of determining its status as either poetry or prose. Although each individual text bears a superficial resemblance to the novel in terms of length at least, there is only the barest existence of a plot. The first cycle ("The Book of Questions," "The Book of Yukel," and "The Return to the Book") is concerned in part with the Nazi Holocaust and with the separation of two lovers, Sarah and Yukel, which occurs when Sarah is placed in a concentration camp. The madness and eventual death of Sarah and the suicide of her lover Yukel are suggested, but they are never developed in a logical, orderly sequence, for the events and the characters themselves are often confused. Three different versions of Sarah's arrest are given, with no clear indication which version is correct; the circumstances of Yukel's suicide become interwoven with the death of the narrator himself. The identity of Yukel, as a result, can never be established with certainty: "Yukel, you have never felt at ease in your skin. You have never been *here*, but always *elsewhere*" (*BQ*, 1: 32). We are told that we will be given a portrait of Sarah and Yukel, and yet there is no portrait. Memory fails, "Was it yesterday? Today? Where was it?" (*BQ*, 1: 49), and stories are never told, "You have not told us the story of man. . . . You hardly talked about Sarah and Yukel" (*BQ*, 1: 121–22).

In the context, then, of this constant questioning of the powers of representational discourse, Lang's critique seems quite legitimate. Yet to accuse Jabès in particular and deconstruction in general of erasing or "repressing" the memory of the Holocaust and thereby leaving us vulnerable, unable to protect ourselves against its possible recurrence, is to cover over once again the problematics of representation that the Holocaust itself brings into particularly sharp focus. Indeed, Lang has himself described this problem most convincingly:

> We understand here the dilemma that Jabès—and any writer who
> takes the Holocaust as subject—confronts. On the one hand, it is

difficult, perhaps impossible, for a writer to meet the Holocaust face to face, to re-present it. The events themselves are too large for the selective mirror of fiction, too transparent for the un-avoidable conceits of literary figuration; linguistic representa-tion is in any case redundant, thus an impediment, when the events that converge on a subject speak directly and clearly for themselves. On the other hand, to write about the Holocaust obliquely, by assumption, leaves the task that had been declined by the author to the reader, who can hardly—if the *writer* will not—hope to find a passage from personal emotion and imagery to artifice. Where then is the work of literary representation to be done? (p. 194)

Clearly, the "work of literary representation" can only be done in the context of a Jabesian questioning that in acknowledging the impossibility of writing about the Holocaust becomes at the same time the only means by which its memory can be preserved. While it is true that the names or dates representing the event may ul-timately annihilate what they save, they also, as Jabès' texts show, save what they annihilate, permitting, as Derrida writes, "alli-ances, returns, commemorations, even if there should be no trace scarcely an ash of what we thus date" or thus name.[3] The failure of the Holocaust "to write itself," as Lang puts it, in Jabès' work cannot therefore be attributed to the failure on Jabès' part to as-sume his "moral responsibility." Indeed, the inscription of the Holocaust as that which resists conceptualization and the limiting representations of traditional discourse requires an investigation of the concept of responsibility itself. Almost no one, least of all those who embrace deconstructive theory, denies that the Holocaust is an issue that must be addressed, but one cannot avoid asking how it is possible to fulfill one's responsibility without reaffirming the concepts of representation that the Holocaust itself calls into ques-tion. And, more important, how does one *impose* such an impera-tive without reinforcing the oppressive and dictatorial logic that the imperative itself was meant to counter?

The contradictory possibilities that these questions raise are inscribed in what Derrida calls the "terrifying ambiguity" of the Hebrew word *Shibboleth*. Used by the army of Jephthah as a pass-word or watchword to exclude its enemy, the Ephraimites, who were known for their inability to pronounce the "shi" sound, the term *Shibboleth* served as both a sign of membership and a "discriminatory limit," for failure to pronounce it correctly meant exclusion from the group or, in some cases, death. The *Shibboleth* is therefore a sword with a "double edge," "the mark of an alliance" but also an "index of exclusion," of "discrimination," indeed, as Derrida writes, of "extermination." Thus, although the condemnation of all silence on the Holocaust seems to have become the "password" in the struggle against "fascism, racism, oppression, and exclusion," it must be remembered that the password contains the possibility of being "tragically inverted," used to reimpose the exclusionary, discriminatory logic it so valiantly resists. Derrida's own response in an interview with Jean-Luc Nancy to the question of Heidegger's silence points to this possibility:

> The excess of responsibility of which I was just speaking never authorizes silence. . . . I suppose, I hope that you are not expecting me only to say that "I condemn Auschwitz" or that "I condemn all silence on Auschwitz." Concerning the latter phrase or its equivalents, I find the mechanism of the trials organized against all those who one believes can be accused of not having named or analyzed "Auschwitz" a bit indecent, even obscene. . . . If we admit . . . that the thing remains unthinkable, that we do not yet have discourse that can measure up to it . . . then let people stop diagnosing the so-called silences and making the "resistances" and "nonthoughts" of just about everyone be confessed. Of course silence on Auschwitz will never be justified, but neither will the fact that people speak of it in such an instrumental way and to say nothing, to say nothing that is not self-evident, trivial, and that does not serve primarily to give themselves a good conscience, in order not to be the last to accuse, to give lessons, to take positions or to show off.[4]

How, then, does one *demand* that condemnations of this monstrous event be "pronounced" without producing such a tragic inversion, particularly when additional requirements are often imposed as to the form that pronouncement should take? Consider, for example, the current debate among traditional historians and Jewish scholars who argue over questions of the Holocaust's uniqueness or comparability as if there were only one appropriate category, one truly adequate representation that could actually contain such an event. Although the establishment of correct categories and comparisons is not Lang's intention in his analysis of the Holocaust as it functions in Jabès' work, for he is well aware of the problems of representation that traditional historians tend to ignore, he finds that one way of writing about the Holocaust is preferable, indeed more valid than another. Despite his acknowledgment that allusions to the genocide of the Jews permeate *The Book of Questions* and that "events verge continually on this background," he condemns nonetheless the lack of direct reference in Jabès' texts to the Holocaust itself, claiming, "[b]ut never is the Holocaust or any pieces of history that make it up given by name or identified in those terms" (p. 193). Should, however, the silence be broken, how is one to represent the Holocaust as a concrete historical event without affirming the naive notions of history and representation that Lang himself calls into question? If one were to affirm such notions, would pronouncing its name really tell us more about the event? As though in answer to this question, Jabès uses the word "Auschwitz" in his more recent *The Book of Shares*, but the reference is, as in his other texts, just as elliptical: "At Auschwitz, the eyes of all the lined-up prisoners hung on the guard's right thumb. To the left, death; to the right, life, for the time being. But newcomers to the camp would only see the incomprehensible, regular back and forth of an official's finger."[5] The technique here of leaving it to the reader to fill in the blanks is one that Lang finds objectionable, but what more, in this case, can effectively be said? Is further elaboration necessary for us to understand the significance of that horrific gesture? Not according to Jabès: "For the Jews, unfortunately, after all the camps and all the horrors, it is an all too banal story. It isn't necessary to go into details. When you say: they were deported—that is enough for a Jew to understand the *whole* story.... [I]f these are things that cannot be expressed, they are also things that cannot be emptied of meaning."[6]

The oblique references to the Holocaust in Jabès' texts, which Lang finds far too elliptical, are not therefore signs of Jabès' failure to assume his moral responsibility. Jabès' response to Adorno's injunction against the writing of poetry after Auschwitz states just the opposite, for he claims that "we must write" while acknowledging that "we cannot write like before."[7] One could indeed argue that Jabès does not repress the question of writing on the Holocaust; rather, that question is at the very "center" of his work. It takes the form of an almost obsessively recurring but necessarily indirect reference whose very obliqueness raises Lang's question: "Is writing centered in the Holocaust even possible?"

If, then, we are to address the issue of Auschwitz, and we must, as Jabès and Derrida's remarks clearly indicate, it perhaps can never be done "directly." It requires, in Derrida's words, "another rhythm and another form," a kind of writing that takes into account the complex problematics of the *Shibboleth* and leads not just to the formulation of condemnations and imperatives, although that too is one of its possibilities, but to a questioning of the modes of thought that make atrocities such as the Holocaust possible. For the Nazis, according to Jabès, were not an aberration or, as he puts it, "some brutes descended from another planet." Their activities must be considered in the context of a culture that allowed fascism to flourish:

> How does one forget that [the Nazis] were supported by a large majority of the German people, including, with a few exceptions, its intellectual elite? It is therefore the culture in which we live that must be interrogated. We must try to understand *how* it could have given birth to the worst and not only *in what ways* it revealed itself as incapable of preventing it; because is it possible to separate man from his culture? The most important texts written since Auschwitz are engaged in this interrogation.[8]

Lacoue-Labarthe, Heidegger, and National Socialism's Misapprehension of 'Technē'

The need, underscored by Jabès, to interrogate fascist ideology through an investigation of its wider philosophical and cultural context, while always implicit in the deconstructive enterprise, has been addressed more directly in recent years particularly by Philippe Lacoue-Labarthe, who attempts to understand how one member of the German intellectual elite, Martin Heidegger, was able to accept Nazi doctrine. In his recent *Heidegger, Art and Politics*, he claims, like Jabès, that Nazism was not a "pathological phenomenon" but was rooted in a body of thought that spans the entire history of Western metaphysics.[9] Indeed, it is his view that despite Heidegger's complicity with Nazism and his later inability or unwillingness to deal with its disastrous effects, his tracing the changes throughout Western history of our understanding of the term *technē*, a notion that in his later work constituted the essential ground of modern technology, can provide insight not only into the profound nature of Nazism but also into Heidegger's own political involvement. Through such a meditation on the essence of technology, which, according to Lacoue-Labarthe, ultimately betrays Heidegger's acceptance of a very traditional concept of the mimetic, we come to see the identificatory (that is, mimetic) mechanisms that prepared for the rise of Nazism, mechanisms that Heidegger himself, despite his persistent interrogation of the metaphysical tradition, never subjected to any kind of thoroughgoing critique.

In his critique of the fundamentally nihilistic essence of modern technology, Heidegger claims that nihilism, the definition of which he derived from his interrogation of the Nietzschean version, results from the persistent failure of the metaphysical tradition to think Being *as such* unhindered by the tendency toward human mastery that is evident even in its earliest formulations by Plato and Aristotle. The history of Western thought, which for Heidegger includes Nietzschean thought as well, can thus be defined as the history of the oblivion of Being, which culminates in the modern technological age when "man brings into play his unlimited power for the calculating, planning, and molding of all things"; that is to say, when Being is subsumed under the ordering objectifications of a self-conscious, representing subject.[10] Modern science and technology thus belong to an age that constitutes for Heidegger the "accomplishment of nihilism," bringing the history of metaphysics to its fulfillment as the ultimate expression of the human "will to power." In an apparent endorsement of certain aspects of the Heideggerian critique, Lacoue-Labarthe claims that while Heidegger's reduction of the Extermination, in his one meager reference to the event,[11] to a mere technological phenomenon was "scandalously inadequate," he insists that it was at the same time "absolutely correct," for it was at Auschwitz, according to Lacoue-Labarthe, that the West in its nihilistic essence "revealed itself":

> [T]his *operation*, in which what was calculated coldly and with the maximum efficiency and economy (and never for a moment hysterically or deliriously) was a pure and simple *elimination*. Without trace or residue. And if it is true that the age is that of the accomplishment of nihilism, then it is at Auschwitz that that accomplishment took place in the purest formless form. God in fact died at Auschwitz. . . . That is why this event—the Extermination—is for the West the terrible revelation of its essence. (p. 37)

Although the statement "God died at Auschwitz" is, as Lacoue-Labarthe points out, one that Heidegger himself never made, his analysis of the formation of modern metaphysics and its grounding in the will to power, interpreted by Heidegger as absolute subjectivity, indicates to Lacoue-Labarthe that Heidegger *could have* made such a statement if he had had the *courage* to do so. His later writings in which the theme of technology becomes particularly explicit suggest a certain understanding of the mental processes that prepared for the emergence of Nazism, despite Heidegger's curious inability to deal with Nazism's devastating consequences or, for that matter, to understand the more radical implications of his own analysis. Indeed, Heidegger's characterization of the Holocaust as a technical phenomenon, however shocking it may be, contains insights that signify for Lacoue-Labarthe far more than a trivialization of the event. Technology, in the Heideggerian sense, is not to be equated with modes of production and machine-powered equipment but is to be understood more fundamentally as incorporating the history of modern metaphysics and the collapse of transcendental values. With the death of God—and this includes not simply the God of the Judeo-Christian world, but all aspects of the suprasensory world, including the realm of Platonic *ideas*—man has, according to Heidegger, been placed in a position of absolute dominance as "the measure and center of all things":

> Man has become *subjectum*. Therefore he can determine and realize the essence of subjectivity, always in keeping with the

way in which he himself conceives and wills himself. Man as a rational being of the age of the Enlightenment is no less subject than is man who grasps himself as a nation, wills himself as a people, fosters himself as a race and, finally, empowers himself as lord of the earth.[12]

If the age of modern technology in which "the subjectivism of man attains its acme" through the "unconditional rule of calculating reason" thus represents the completion of the modern metaphysics of "subjectness," begun with Descartes, then the relationship Heidegger establishes between mass extermination and technology must be taken far more seriously than Heidegger himself appeared willing to do. Despite his refusal to acknowledge the wholesale massacres that resulted from this "deployment of technology," in its most literal as well as metaphysical sense, much in his later writings suggests that he could have claimed that Auschwitz, in marking both the moment of God's withdrawal and the ascendancy of modern technological man, was that moment in Western history when the metaphysics of subjectivity found its fulfillment, culminating in what Lacoue-Labarthe describes as the Nazi myth of the "Aryan type, as absolute subject, pure will (of the self) willing itself" (p. 95).

Lacoue-Labarthe argues that Heidegger's meditations on the essence of modern technology, whose origins can be detected in the early Greek notion of *technē*, a word that encompassed both art and knowledge, can give us an understanding not only of National Socialism but of the modern political sphere in general. Through such meditations, which become prominent in his writings after his break with the Nazi Party, we come to see the program of National Socialism as a process of political fictioning or of what Lacoue-Labarthe calls a "national aestheticism," where the formative or fashioning power of the German myth is what constitutes national identity, producing the "subject of absolute self-creation" in the form of the German people and the Aryan race. Lacoue-Labarthe, as a first step in support of his thesis that the "aestheticization of politics" determines the very essence of the National Socialist program, provides evidence demonstrating the extent to which the regime's major ideologues looked to art in their efforts to shape the German state, offering, as an example, the words of Goebbels, who regarded politics as one of "the highest and most all embracing" forms of art: "Art and artists are not only there to unite; their far more important task is to create a form, to expel the ill trends and make room for the healthy to develop" (p. 61).

This constitution of the political "in and as a work of art" is not, however, as Lacoue-Labarthe points out, an accident of history or an invention confined to National Socialism. It is an outgrowth of a fundamental "will-to-identity" that has shaped the history of Western thought, culminating in the absolute "presence-to-itself" of modern metaphysics in the form of the individual or of the total state:

> The infinitization or absolutization of the subject, which is at the heart of the metaphysics of the Moderns, finds [in National Socialism] its strictly operational outcome: the community creating, the community at work creates and works itself, so to speak, thereby accomplishing the subjective process *par excellence*, the process of self-formation and self-production. This is why that process finds its truth in "a fusion of the community" . . . or in the ecstatic identification with a Leader who in no way represents any form of transcendence, but incarnates, in immanent fashion, the immanentism of a community. And this is also why a will to immediate effectuation or self-effectuation underlies national aestheticism. (p. 70)

Thus, although Nazism does not "sum up the West," in the sense that the metaphysical tradition is to be equated with fascism, it represents that point in Western history when the metaphysics of subjectivity finds its ultimate and most extreme expression and reveals in exaggerated form the structuring power of myth upon which traditional notions of the subject, in the form of the individual or the collective, are grounded. Developing this idea in *The Inoperative Community*, Jean-Luc Nancy, a writer with whom Lacoue-Labarthe has often collaborated in his investigations of the political in general and of the mechanisms of fascism in particular, claims that there can be no humanity that is not "properly speaking *mything* humanity, humanity acceding to itself . . . being born to itself in producing myth—a truly *mything* humanity becoming truly human in this *mythation*."[13] Myth is a "fiction that founds," but what it founds "is not a fictive world"; it is instead "fictioning as the fashioning of a world . . . for the subject, the becoming-world of subjectivity" (p. 56).

This belief in the power of myth, or what Nancy calls "the myth of myth" (that is, the myth of the formative power of myth), is essential to the traditional concept of community, but when it is taken to the extreme, it undergirds the totalizing, mythizing logic of which fascism is a possible outcome. Nancy calls this the logic of "immanentism," a term he prefers to the less precise "totalitarianism" because it suggests the internal workings of a community whose work (*oeuvre*) is the creation of its own essence. This "will to absolute community," to total self-fulfillment through fusion with a collective identity, structures the National Socialist program, culminating in its visions of fusional communion in the formation of a pure Aryan essence. As Lacoue-Labarthe and Nancy write in their essay "The Nazi Myth": "Nazism is above all . . . a construction and confirmation of the world according to a vision, an image of the creator of forms, the image or the type of the Aryan."[14]

In *Heidegger, Art and Politics*, Lacoue-Labarthe takes this argument even further (and here Heidegger's insights come more directly into play), by showing that the identification of the political with the aesthetic is made possible by the structure of *technē* itself, that indeed Nazism's vision of "community" as a political work of art is rooted in a tradition that in fact goes back 2,000 years. In its earliest Greek determination as both art and knowledge, *technē* was a mode of revealing, of truth as *alētheia*, which allows Being, conceived as *physis* or "emerging power," to be brought out of concealment into unconcealment. Heidegger points out that *physis*, in the course of its "appearing," contains a "reservoir of the not-yet-uncovered" and therefore can never be perceived as immediately present-at-hand, but its essence as concealed unconcealment "comes to shine" only in the work of a *technē*, which refers in its broadest sense to "every sort of human capacity to bring forth": "Unconcealment occurs only when it is achieved by work: the work of the word in poetry, the work of stone in temple and statue, the work of the word in thought, the work of the *polis* as the historical place in which all this is grounded and preserved."[15]

Heidegger's analysis shows, according to Lacoue-Labarthe, that the political or the formation of the political community belongs "to the sphere of *technē* in the highest sense of the term, that is to say in the sense in which *technē* is conceived as the accomplishment and revelation of *physis* itself": "If *technē* can be defined as the sur-plus of *physis*, through which *physis* 'deciphers' and presents itself—and if, therefore, *technē* can be said to be *apophantic* in the Aristotelo-Heideggerian sense of the term—political *organicity* is the *surplus* necessary for a nation to present and recognize itself. And such is the political function of art."[16] In accordance with the traditional notion of art as a form of mimesis that provides an unproblematized presentation of reality, *technē* was, in this case, never seen as a work of pure fiction. It was the means by which the "natural" or the "physical" was given form and brought to light. This is why the Greeks did not look upon the polis as an "artificial or conventional formation." It was "also 'natural'"; it was, as Lacoue-Labarthe tells us, the "beautiful formation" that sprang from the " 'genius of a people' (the Greek genius) according to the modern—but in fact very ancient—interpretation of Aristotelian mimetology" (p. 66). And while the thinking of *technē* incorporates a logic of mimesis, or what Lacoue-Labarthe calls a "mimetologic," that may have received its first rigorously theoretical formulation in the writings of Aristotle, it can be revealed in Plato's politico-pedogogic writings as well. Even though Plato constructed the political by excluding the art of poetry and its "deceitfully" mimetic practices, the notion of the political as a form of "plastic art," that is, as a mimesis in the strictest sense, is apparent in the concepts of configuration or fashioning that shape Plato's political project:

> Oversimplifying to excess, it can be said that, at least since Plato, education or training, political *Bildung*, has been thought taking the mimetic process *as starting point*. . . . *Bildung* is always thought on the basis of archaic mythic *paideia*, which is to say that it is thought on the basis of what the Romans were to understand as *exemplarity*. It is not by chance that the "myth" of the

Cave—a myth that has no "mythic" source, a myth that is self-formed and self-grounded—lays the foundations of Plato's political project. Identification or appropriation—the self-becoming of the Self—will always have been thought as the appropriation of a model, i.e. as the appropriation of a means of appropriation, if the model (the example) is the ever paradoxical imperative of pro-priation: imitate me in order to be what you are. (pp. 80–81)

The political fiction of the German myth, which involves the projection of a model, image, or type (that is, the Aryan type) with which one identifies and through which the identity of a people or race is fashioned and ultimately realized, thus has its origins in Plato, according to Lacoue-Labarthe, not simply in his construction of the political model but in the very philosophy that grounds it, in the determination of Being as *eidos*. For here too, Lacoue-Labarthe points out, citing Heidegger, one finds the fashioning or fictioning of the self-identical in Plato's reinterpretation of Being as *idea*, whose permanence and selfsameness remain unaffected despite the many changes in its outward appearance. As that which can be approached only as it becomes visible in the sensuous realm of things and objects, Being as nonsensuous or supersensuous *idea* must first be posited as a unity, as a oneness that remains constant in order for it to be seen in the multiplicity of the individual things that are modeled after it. And yet, in order to "see" the immutable essence of the thing itself (the essence of the tree, for example, in the multiplicity of birches and oaks), that essence must be deter-mined beforehand, one must posit in advance an identity of the tree that lies beyond the variability of what is given to the senses. Such a positing of something identical, Heidegger shows, must therefore be a "creation" or an "invention": "In order to determine and think the tree in its actually given appearance, its sameness must have been created beforehand. This irrepressible presupposing of a self-same . . . is the essence of reason and thinking. . . . What properly appears to us and shows itself in its outward appearance, this same thing in its thinghood thus constituted—in Greek, this 'Idea'—is of a created origin."[17]

Such is the fictioning or "poeticizing essence of reason" as Hei-degger formulated it in his writings on Nietzsche. Incorporated by Lacoue-Labarthe into his earlier *Typography: Mimesis, Philosophy,*

Politics, the term underscores the powerful role that figuration has played throughout the history of Western thought in the shaping of both individual and national identity.[18] For it is this "fashioning and fictioning of the same," as manifested in Plato's eidetic ontology, what Lacoue-Labarthe calls "onto-ideo-logy," that lays the foundation for the age of modern metaphysics when the thought of Being, following the "Cartesian reversal," will be grounded in the objectifying representations of a Subject: "Indeed, up to and including the reversal of Platonism and the mutation of onto-ideo-logy into onto-typo-logy, thought as *stabilization* corresponds to Being as *stele*. Something like an *onto-steleo-logy* sustains, *stays* or *shores up* [*étançonne*], throughout its unfolding, the history of metaphysics—and delimits this metaphysics as the space . . . of 'theoretical fiction' in general" (p. 71). In the more specifically political context of his *Heidegger, Art and Politics*, Lacoue-Labarthe adds: "[S]uch an eidetics underpins mimetology in the form of what I have felt might be called an onto-typology, that an entire tradition (the one that culminates in Nazism) will have thought that the political is the sphere of the *fictioning* of beings and communities" (p. 82).

At stake, here, in Plato's dream of a "(philosophical) self-grounding of the political" is thus the structure of mimesis itself with all the duplicities that such a structure or logic entails.[19] Not only does the self-formation of the political community involve the appropriation of a model, thus showing that self-identity is dependent upon the existence of an other, but the *idea* itself is caught up in a duplicitous "mimetologic." As Heidegger has demonstrated and as anyone familiar with the writings of Plato knows, the *idea* becomes for Plato a "*paradeigma*" that unleashes a process of identification by functioning as a model or prototype to which every disclosure of being must be assimilated. What is disclosed, then, is no longer *physis*, the emerging power, but an image or copy that must correspond to, but is always inferior to, the "pure appearance" of the *idea*: "Being as *idea*," Heidegger asserts, "is exalted, it becomes true being, while being itself . . . is degraded. . . . [I]t always deforms the *idea*, the pure appearance, by incorporating it in matter."[20]

It is this transformation of being from *physis* to *idea* that set the stage, according to Heidegger, for the modern age of representation when the "truth of *physis*, *alētheia* as the unconcealment that is the essence of the emerging power, now becomes *homoiōsis* and *mimēsis*, assimilation and accommodation. . . . [I]t becomes a correctness of vision, of apprehension as representation."[21] For Lacoue-Labarthe, it is the means by which the identificatory mechanism founding national identity, which is, according to both Nancy and Lacoue-Labarthe, the mimetic mechanism par excellence, is put into place. Insofar as that mechanism is governed by a logic of the identical, according to which one moves "endlessly from the same to the other—under the authority of the same,"[22] it requires a gesture of exclusion or denial for which Plato, as one who condemned art as the mimetic form the most distant from and therefore the least faithful to the *idea*, serves once again as the model. Indeed, the history of Western metaphysics will be structured on this gesture of exclusion, on the refusal to recognize that "impropriety," the "lack of being-proper," is supposed by the mimetic act itself. If, as Heidegger has shown, the *idea* to be copied is itself "originally fictioned," if there is no self-identical model or prototype preexisting the mimetic process, then the copy must inevitably come before the model itself and function in a way that is not originary and but is in fact secondary.

Plato's banishing of the arts, his condemnation of mimesis as an inevitable distortion of the "pure appearance" of the *idea*, is thus motivated by a desire to cover over what could be viewed as an originary contamination of that purity, the insertion of "the abyssal ground of mimesis" into the *idea* itself. What must be expelled, then, is nothing other than "mimetic representation 'itself,' that is, mimesis as the *unassignable* danger that representation [*le représentatif*] might be primal, or, what amounts to the same thing, the danger of an originary absence of subjective 'property' or 'propriety.' "[23] Indeed, if the poet-mimetician is expelled by Plato from the city, it is because the cohesiveness of the social organization, the very foundation of the state could only be realized on the basis of that exclusion. For this reason, Lacoue-Labarthe claims that the problem of mimesis is not simply a philosophical problem but a political problem as well. The philosophical condemnation of the mimetic, which will prevail throughout the history of the Western philosophical tradition up to and including Heidegger himself, is essential to any process of national identification. Given that the contradictions implied in the mimetic relation serve only to de-stabilize the identificatory mechanisms essential to the self-for-mation of a political community, people or race, the "law of the proper" must prevail; there can be no admission of duplicity within the mimetic process itself. As Lacoue-Labarthe argues in *Heidegger, Art and Politics*, "[M]imetological law demands that *imitatio* rid itself of *imitatio* itself, or that, in what it establishes (or has imposed upon it) as a model, it should address something that does not derive from *imitatio*" (p. 79).

Thus, although significant changes have occurred as one passes from Platonic "onto-ideo-logy" to the "onto-typo-logy" of modern metaphysics, Plato's anti-mimetic discourse and his philosophical grounding of the political have repercussions that will reverberate some 2,000 years later. If Lacoue-Labarthe is right in saying that fascism is "the mobilization of the identificatory emotions of the masses" (p. 95), it can be looked upon as one of the possible consequences of this attempt to overcome or erase mimetic paradoxality. This is why Lacoue-Labarthe differs somewhat from Nancy in claiming that the logic of "immanentism" and the exclusion of the other did not by themselves lead to Nazi Germany and its "final solution"; he sees it originating in an operation that both allows and dislocates such an immanent community. It originates, in other words, in a certain concept of the mimetic, in what Lacoue-Labarthe calls "mimetology":

> This topological monstrosity has its origins in a quite other logic than that of immanence; it originates in fact in a mimetology, which means that the frenzied or delirious immanentism of the *organic* community is itself governed by a double bind which divides or "schizes" the intimacy of the community as soon as its project is formulated. . . . I would happily speak of a violent *abortion* of Germany in its frenzied attempt to appropriate itself as such (to identify itself) and to step into the light of history. (pp. 75–76)

If the Jews were eliminated for posing a threat to national identity, the reason was not that they were the enemy in the traditional sense, for they could hardly be said to have constituted an organized political or military force challenging the authority of the

German state. Instead, they were perceived to be entirely without identity. They were "unlocatable," functioning neither as an integral part of the community nor as an adversary standing outside it. Citing the anti-Semitic writings of one of the leading Nazi theoreticians, Alfred Rosenberg, Lacoue-Labarthe points out that the Jew was not seen by Rosenberg as standing in opposition to the Nazi dream of self-realization in the superior Aryan *type*; the Jew figured as its "contradiction," "the very absence of type," a "formless, unaesthetic 'people,' which by definition [could] not enter into the process of self-fictioning and [could] not constitute a subject, or, in other words, a being-proper [*être-propre*]." The Jews thus represented for the Nazis the process of "destabilization" itself. Their capacity to insert themselves into every culture and state defined them as "infinitely mimetic beings, as the site of an *endless mimesis*, which is both interminable and inorganic" (p. 96).

By offering this case as an example of what he refers to as a "Nazi onto-typo-logy," Lacoue-Labarthe thus shows to what extent the metaphysical notion of imitation, which tries to eliminate the "improper" by presupposing a unifying and stabilizing return to the Same, can have monstrously political implications. And while it did not lead to a similarly racist discourse in the writings of Heidegger, who attempted to counter the biologist thinking of the Nazi theorists, that notion was nevertheless decisive in the formation of Heidegger's politics as well. Indeed, in taking up the question of Heidegger's political engagement of 1933 not only in *Heidegger, Art and Politics* but in an essay published six years earlier in *Rejouer le politique*, Lacoue-Labarthe bases his critique of Heidegger's approval of National Socialism on what he sees as a fundamental flaw in Heidegger's thinking, one that endured even in his later meditations on the essence of technology, long after he had abandoned National Socialism.[24] Although Heidegger later denounced the entire onto-typological thematics perpetrated by Nazism's inversion of Platonism, with its conscious construction of the political through fiction, he remained himself an "unwitting prisoner" of a traditionally Platonic mimetology. Indeed, what subsists in Heidegger's writings, according to Lacoue-Labarthe, is a constant refusal to deal seriously with the questions raised by Plato's treatment of the mimetic; as a consequence, one encounters throughout Heidegger's work a "pure and simple acceptance of its Platonic depreciation."[25]

Heidegger's own rejection of the mimetic originates paradoxically in his critique of Platonic mimetology, for he sees in Plato's interpretation of Being as *eidos* a covering over or a forgetting of the truth of *physis* as *alētheia*, as "emerging-into-unconcealment." Insofar as truth has become *homoiōsis*, mimesis, or correctness of vision, Plato has led us away from the original Greek understanding of *alētheia* (through which man remained attuned to the openness and to the concealedness of emerging being) and inaugurated the eventual decline into representation when "man becomes the measure of all things." Lacoue-Labarthe points out, however, that in Heidegger's critique an attitude toward the mimetic emerges that is in many respects not dramatically different from Plato's own. Mimesis comes to be seen, as it is in Plato, as a process of obfuscation or falsification. This time it is not the *idea* but the essence of *alētheia* itself, the "original" Greek experience of reality that has presumably been lost. Mimesis for Heidegger thus constitutes the "decline of *alētheia*"; it "disinstalls" or diverges from the "truth," and is inscribed, as a result, into the traditional problematic of "(in)adequation," the object of a Platonic and now of a Heideggerian gesture of expulsion. What Heidegger refuses to acknowledge in his elaboration of the notion of truth in "The Origin of the Work of Art," for example, where it becomes a site of conflict or rift (*Riss*) between "world and earth," between "lighting and concealing," is that *alētheia* is *from the very beginning* traversed by mimetic "impropriety," that the process of disinstallation is already at work in the "self-secluding factor" that *alētheia* also brings forth.

Thus, underlying Heidegger's privileging of the ancient Greeks' responsiveness to the presencing of Being is a belief that *alētheia* has not itself been contaminated by the mimetic economy. This position Heidegger maintains with great consistency despite the fact that, as Lacoue-Labarthe argues, "nothing . . . more *resembles* mimesis than *aletheia*" primarily because *aletheia*, as Heidegger's texts never fail to indicate, "does not resemble *itself*." In the very process of its unveiling, it "endlessly withdraws, masks itself, desists."[26] Consequently, in spite of a lengthy critique of Plato's "fall" into the mimetic, one finds, according to Lacoue-Labarthe, that a "fundamental *mimetology*" is at work in Heidegger's thought as well. Nowhere is this more evident than in Heidegger's "The Origin of the Work of Art":

> What [Lacoue-Labarthe asks] is the *world* if not the product of what we should indeed agree to call an "original mimesis"? What is the world, if not an *original mimeme*? There would be no "real" . . . no "nature" in the accepted sense. . . . [P]*husis* itself could not break out in (and from) its unfathomable retreat, there would be no "earth" . . . if there were not, projected from the unpresentable "milieu of what is" . . . an "image," itself moreover imperceptible (unpresentable), of a possible presentation of what is. If there were not, in other words, a "schematization" or, which is the same thing, a *techne*.[27]

Herein, then, lies one of the fundamental differences between Lacoue-Labarthe's thinking and Heideggerian deconstruction—a difference whose importance should not be underestimated. Although Lacoue-Labarthe has been criticized for what Wolin has described as a "strikingly *orthodox* Heideggerian reading of the 'destiny of the West,'" where the "decline" into technology brings the oblivion of Being,[28] it should be recognized that Lacoue-Labarthe actually deconstructs Heidegger's "destinal historialism" by exposing a thought of mimesis that disorganizes Heidegger's historical schema.[29] Indeed, Lacoue-Labarthe points out that Heidegger's refusal to examine more critically traditional notions of the mimetic, which would have allowed him to see in the relation between *physis* and *technē* the very structure of mimesis itself, has important *political* ramifications insofar as it provides the philosophical basis for his commitment to National Socialism. Heidegger saw in the Nazi Party a means of reversing this decline into the mimetic, of breaking the "headlong rush" of *technē* toward the mathematical-technical thinking of the modern age and thus of awakening the German *Volk* to its "spiritual-historial destiny." Given Heidegger's exalted view of the "Greek beginning" as a time anterior to representation when thought or knowledge (*technē*), not yet compromised by the mimetic, maintained a more authentic relation to Being, he believed that the refoundation of Germany and the fulfillment of its spiritual mission was to be accomplished through the reenactment of that pre-Platonic heritage. Indeed, Heidegger found in the National Socialist revolution and its appropriation of Greece as the historical model a possibility for the German *Volk* to rise up against the spiritual decline of western Europe, where "men cling to familiar essents,"[30] to "stand firm in the face of German fate . . . in its extreme distress [*Not*]"[31] and accede to its own truly spiritual essence, one that would no longer be bound by the encapsulating representations of rational analysis but that would maintain instead a "fundamental knowing resolve" toward Being in its essence.

In calling upon Germany to recommence the Greek beginning, Heidegger underscores once again the extent to which his thinking remains tied to a tradition dominated both by a conventional notion of the mimetic and by what traditionally accompanies it, the inevitable covering over of mimetic duplicity. If in the course of European history, from the Renaissance to the neoclassicism of the Napoleonic era and beyond, the construction of national or cultural identity has been governed by the appropriation of the classical model of Greek or Roman antiquity, then Heidegger's solution to the German political problem presents us with the same, and by now, familiar problematic. By placing the National Socialist movement and the fate of Germany within the historical context of this "mimetic rivalry" with the ancients, Heidegger shows that national identification is essentially a problem of imitation.[32] The process of political structuration, the founding of a new and uniquely German identity on the basis of an identification with Greece, takes mimesis as its point of departure ("imitate me in order to be what you are") and assumes that the "mimetological double bind" that such a paradoxical imperative expresses can be overcome. Heidegger's political position thus leads to the erasure of mimetic duplicity on at least two fronts. It occurs not only in relation to the political identity of the German *Volk*, which is viewed as uncompromised by the identificatory mechanisms that constitute it, but also, as we have seen, in relation to the philosophical concepts upon which Heidegger's political thought is grounded. In claiming that access to the primordial knowledge (*technē*) of the Greeks is what will shape the spiritual destiny of Germany, Heidegger denies the mimetic inhering in the structure of *technē* itself.

What this shows, then, as Lacoue-Labarthe has consistently argued, is that the political is indissolubly joined to the philosophical in Heidegger's writings, and it means that insights can be gained into his politics even after his withdrawal from National Socialism, particularly from his discourse on *techne* in which the political and the philosophical are clearly intertwined. Whether *techne* is linked to science, as in his Rectoral Address, where the effort to bring knowledge back to its Greek origins is meant to expose the German *Volk* to a more authentic understanding of Being, or to art and poetic thinking, which assume that role in his later work, it is always a means of realizing the West's "spiritual-historial destiny," of saving Germany and/or the Western world from technological nihilism and its blindness toward Being. Although the focus moved, after the war, from the destiny of Germany to that of western Europe as a whole, *techne*, in this context at least, is consistently conceived in the same, nonmimetic terms. Defined as a mode of revealing, of bringing forth into presencing (that is, of *aletheia*), *techne* takes us back to a time before representation when it did not stand apart from *physis* in a secondary, reproductive sense, but was the means by which *physis* was brought into the open for the first time:

> It is of utmost importance that we think bringing-forth in its full scope and at the same time in the sense in which the Greeks thought it. Not only handcraft manufacture, not only artistic and poetical bringing into appearance and concrete imagery, is a bringing-forth, *poiesis* [a term Heidegger later equates with *techne*]. *Physis* also, the arising of something from out of itself, is a bringing-forth, *poiesis*. *Physis* is indeed *poiesis* in the highest sense. For what presences by means of *physis* has the bursting open belonging to bringing-forth, e.g., the bursting of a blossom into bloom, in itself (*en heautoi*). In contrast, what is brought forth by the artisan or the artist, e.g., the silver chalice, has the bursting open belonging to bringing-forth not in itself but in another (*en alloi*), in the craftsman or artist. . . . Thus, what is decisive in *techne* does not lie at all in making and manipulating nor in the using of means, but rather in the aforementioned revealing. It is as revealing, and not as manufacturing, that *techne* is a bringing-forth.[33]

This statement was cited at length because it contains at least two completely different and conflicting possibilities. On the one hand, it suggests that *technē* becomes manufacturing, reproduction, or fabrication (that is, mimesis) only as it is carried forward into the age of modern technology. This is when the original interconnectedness of *physis* and *technē*, both of which belonged equally to the disclosure of being, gives way to an increasing concealment of *physis*, to a process of "Enframing" (*Ge-stell*) that blocks the experience of *poiēsis* and unleashes a "frenziedness of ordering" that ultimately entraps Being in oblivion.[34] Defined by Heidegger as a "challenging revealing" that calls upon man to order the real as "standing-reserve" whereby everything is to be regulated and made available for human use, Enframing, as the essence of modern technology, is a mode of revealing that not only estranges man from Being by allowing his own ordering representations to subsume it but also conceals the process of revealing itself. The revealing that rules modern technology is a "setting-in-order," a structuring that hides technology's own essence as the site out of which the truth of Being emerges by allowing the appearance of Being to be grounded not in Being itself but in the perceptions of a subject. Modern technology and its mode of revealing, which is Enframing, thus become a debased form of *technē*, a decline into subjectness and representationality that, in transforming everything into "assured availability," into an object that is immediately "present-at-hand," forgets the essential hiddenness of Being, the movement not just of clearing but also of concealing that is intrinsic to Being's unfolding. For Heidegger, then, technology in its original sense as a primordial belonging together of man and Being, or of *technē* and *physis*, has not yet been contaminated by the mimetic. As Heidegger claims, the essence of technology is in itself "nothing technological"; the Greek mode of apprehending Being has not yet given way to "Enframing" and man's structuring representations.

On the other hand, when Heidegger claims that the decline into representational thinking is not an accident that befalls Being but is that to which Being is ultimately destined, his purely "derivative schema" becomes a bit more complicated. Insofar as the withdrawal of Being in the age of modern technology is seen as a "necessary consequence," an inevitability stemming from the very essence of Being itself, which "inclines intrinsically to self-concealment," and insofar as Being is "sent out" from its origin in concealment, which means that concealment, as Heidegger writes, "belongs to it essentially," then the concealment of Being brought on by modern technology was a possibility that structured the relationship to Being from the very beginning.[35] This is a point that Derrida makes in *The Postcard*:

> [T]he very idea of the retreat (proper to destination), the idea of the halt, and the idea of the epoch in which Being holds itself back, suspends, withdraws, etc., all these ideas are immediately homogenous with postal [that is, technological] discourse. . . . This is serious because it upsets perhaps Heidegger's still "derivative" schema (perhaps), upsets by giving one to think that technology, the position, let us say even metaphysics do not overtake, do not come *to determine* and to dissimulate an *"envoi"* of Being [that is, the original "sending forth" of Being] (which would not yet be postal), but would belong to the "first" *envoi*—which is obviously never "first" in any order whatsoever. . . . If the post (technology, position, "metaphysics") is announced at the "first" *envoi*, then there is no longer A metaphysics, etc. . . . nor even AN *envoi* but *envois* without destination.[36]

The "first envoi" has, thus, already been traversed by the mimetic, and it points, not to the unconcealed essence of Being, but to a fundamental deficiency, to an originary lack or insufficiency that must be *supplemented* by a *technē* in order for *physis* to be brought to light. This is why Lacoue-Labarthe claims that the structure of the relation between *physis* and *technē* in Heidegger's thought is the very structure of an "original supplementarity," a logic of the supplement rooted in Aristotelian mimetology. Aristotle maintained that art not only imitates nature but also accomplishes what nature itself is unable to carry out, that "*techne* carries to its end [accomplishes, perfects, *epitelei*] what *phusis* is incapable of effecting [*apergasasthai*]."[37] Thus, when Heidegger states that "art is the bloom, the fulfillment of nature," that "each is bound to the other" and makes up "the lack of the other . . . in order entirely to be what it specifically can be,"[38] he shows that the schematizing operations of a *technē* are essential to Being's unfolding and that mimetic impropriety consequently ceases to function as a pure derivation but becomes itself originary, an "originary secondarity," which ultimately displaces, divides, or defers the origin by disclosing that the technological oblivion of Being was marked at the outset.

At this point, Heidegger's thinking of *technē* opens onto a radically different possibility, one that works in contradistinction to the Platonic mimetology that structures his political thought (and continues to do so, according to Lacoue-Labarthe, even after his break with Nazism). It offers a thought of the origin "in *différance*" and of *technē* not as a "gathering apprehension" that marks the original togetherness of *technē* and *physis* but as an " 'inaugural' " or more originary "tracing," a differential "trait" that opens the relation to language while withdrawing itself in the very process of its tracing (p. 85). The work of *technē* in this sense as "trait" or as "silent tracing" is thus neither wholly originary nor simply derivative. Rather, it "cuts" a path, "incises" an opening that places what has not yet become Being in relation to its other, allows it to be marked by that other and thus to emerge, never as a full presence, but as that which bears the trace of that marking. Lacoue-Labarthe argues that when Heidegger speaks of the work of art or *technē* in terms of the "rift" (*Riss*) or "rift-design"—which belongs in the German language to the family of *reissen* ("to tear, rip, split, sketch, draw, trace, etc.")—he comes closest to a thinking of the "differential trait" or "archi-trace" in the Derridean sense (p. 85), and thus opens the field for a very different relation to the "political"—and, as we shall see in the section that follows, for a Lyotardian "thought of 'the jews.' "

With regard to the question of mimesis in Lacoue-Labarthe's work, Lyotard himself has never admitted such a possibility, even though he clearly acknowledges his own indebtedness to certain aspects of Lacoue-Labarthe's analysis. Addressing in *Heidegger and "the jews"* what he considers to be one of the major weaknesses of Lacoue-Labarthe's focus on the mimetic as a fundamental component of the political, he argues that Lacoue-Labarthe neglects what can never be inscribed in a representational determination, that in remaining too preoccupied by what is an essentially philosophical/representational problematic (by Heidegger's question of Being and its relation to the mimetic), Lacoue-Labarthe forgot the question of "the jews" and the possibility that the West, whose history Lacoue-Labarthe traces in essentially philosophical terms, might be "inhabited, unknowingly, by a guest . . . that is neither 'Western' " (pp. 83–84) nor reducible to what can be represented conceptually. Lyotard believes that the "West is thinkable under the order of *mimèsis* only if one forgets that a 'people' survives within that is not a nation (a nature)" (p. 94). In making a claim such as this, however, Lyotard seems unwilling to account for the possibility that this very interrogation of mimesis, and Lacoue-Labarthe's radicalization (through Derrida) of the Heideggerian problematic of the trait (that is, of the *Riss*), allows, as I shall argue in the following section, a thought of this "people without nature," of the "forgotten," "unthinkable," "immemorial dispossession" that is inscribed within the very heart of representation itself.

Of Ashes and Holocaustal Fire: 'Technē,' the "Trait," and "the jews"

Discussed initially by Heidegger in "The Origin of the Work of Art" in terms of a primal conflict between "earth" and "world," between veiling and unveiling that becomes the condition of Being's disclosure, and referred to later in "The Way to Language" as that which cuts "a furrow into the soil to open it to seed and growth,"[39] Heidegger's notion of the rift not only questions but also (and here Lyotard's own words can be appropriated) "betray[s] the tradition, the *mimèsis*, the immanence of the unfolding, and its root" (p. 93). It does so by pointing to the mimetic as inaugural depropriation, to the possibility that no "presence" is to be found at the origin—whether it take the form of nature or language or, as the more conservative Heidegger would have it, of a primordial unity of the two. For, if Heidegger's politics and his condemnation of mimesis are structured by a belief in a more authentic and originary "Saying" whose power of "gathering" makes manifest the "original togetherness of Being," his notion of the trait (*Riss*) suggests a very different dynamic. Such a dynamic indeed undermines the very principle of the political by disrupting its models of fashioning, by showing that the original "model" around which a political unity is constituted is the very thing that also divides and disseminates. In tracing a relation to language that allows Being to come to the fore, the differential trait, as Derrida describes it in "The *Retrait* of Metaphor," "incises" as much as it allies; it is the means by which two yet to be formed entities (the relation between what will be "art" and "nature," for example, or "word" and "being") "cut each other . . . re-cut, split and sign in some way the one in the body of the other, the one in the place of the other, the contract without contract of their neighborliness."[40] This "neighboring proximity" and the "trait of the incision" that makes the relation to the other possible thus mark the impossibility of original unity. Not only is that which is drawn into proximity without a preexistent identity, and is indeed cut, incised, divided, and dispersed, but the trait, as a movement within the unfolding of Being, is, as the following remarks by Derrida indicate, itself "improper," emerging only in the course of its being effaced:[41]

> The trait of the incision . . . does not precede the two properties which it causes to come to their propriety, for it is nothing without them. In this sense it is not an autonomous, originary instance, itself proper in relation to the two which it incises and allies. Being nothing, it does not appear itself, it has no proper and independent phenomenality, and in not disclosing itself it withdraws, it is structurally in withdrawal, as divergence (*écart*: splitting aside), opening, differentiality, trace, border, traction, effraction, etc. From the moment that it withdraws in drawing itself out, the trait is *a priori* withdrawal, unappearance, and effacement of its mark in its incision.[42]

Considered from the perspective of the trace, then, *technē* is not only more "originary" than the "unifying unity" of art and nature, but it is also more "violent," for "Being" comes into existence not as the result of a primal gathering but through conflict and struggle. "*Technē*," Heidegger writes in *An Introduction to Metaphysics*, is the "violence of knowledge" (p. 165). With no already present being preceding its movement, it forces being out of itself, wrests it, in the words of Heidegger, "from concealment into the manifestness as the essent" and, in so doing, thrusts it "into homelessness." The "event" of Being's emergence, which is here an "event of homeless-ness," a "happening of strangeness," thus demands the violence of a *technē*, a "naming [that] does not come afterward, providing an already manifest essent with a designation and a hallmark known as a word"; it is, in reality, "the other way around: originally an act of violence that discloses being." This violence, Heidegger adds, "is the strangest, the uncanniest thing of all" (p. 172), for in spite of his claim that the event (*Ereignis*)—which he defines as the "disclosing coming-to-pass" of Being—is what brings Being "into its own," it yields nothing present, reveals no gathering of Being in a self-enclosed presence, but produces a Being differed, one that is thrust into strangeness, taken out of itself in order to be:

> We shall fully appreciate this phenomenon of strangeness only if we experience the power of appearance and the struggle with it as an essential part of being-there. . . . Everywhere man makes himself a path; he ventures into all realms of the essent, of the overpowering power, and in so doing he is flung out of all paths. Herein is disclosed the entire strangeness of this strangest of all creatures: not only that he tries the essent in the whole of its strangeness, not only that in so doing he *is* a violent one striving beyond his familiar sphere. No, beyond all this he becomes the strangest of all beings because, without issue on all paths, he is cast out of every relation to the familiar and befallen by *atē*, ruin, catastrophe. (pp. 151–52)

Although Heidegger never fully understood the radical implica-tions of this thought of catastrophe and of *technē* as "(in)human and *unheimlich*"[43]—for that thought, as Derrida has consistently maintained, was overshadowed by his notion of the originary *logos* as "gathering"—it should be pointed out that for Heidegger the gathering *logos* (a notion with which *technē* stands in essential relation) was "never a mere driving-together"; it was also a conflict of opposites, a "gathering of the supreme antagonism" that, on the basis of his readings of the Heraclitean *Fragments*, Heidegger first equated with *polemos* and later with fire. Whether Heidegger is speaking of universal "conflagration" or of Heraclitean *polemos* whose warlike violence can never be understood in terms of human conflict (since it is older than both gods and humans), he confronts us in both cases with the "cata-strophic" non-origin of Being. The "origin" in this instance, particularly when it is thought in terms of fire, is shown to be an unstable movement of glimmering change-ability, at the same time life-giving radiant light and destructive, all-consuming heat: "In 'fire,' lighting, glowing, blazing, soft shining hold sway, and that which opens an expanse in brightness. In 'fire,' however, consuming, welding, cauterizing, extinguishing also reign. When Heraclitus speaks of fire, he is primarily thinking of the lighting governance, the direction [*das Weisen*] which gives measure and takes it away."[44]

The fiery *logos*, in this sense at least, cannot be thought in terms of a simple gathering, for it both gives and takes away, allowing Being to be brought forth to appearance in its radiant glow but also extinguishing it with its "revealing-concealing" light. Within lighting, then, darkness also resides, a darkness that not only conceals what is also brought into the open but that renders invisible the fire itself. Just as it is the nature of fire to maintain a core of impenetrability and ultimately to burn itself up in its flaming, devouring sweep, the movement of opening toward Being, which in Heidegger's words can have "a multiplicity of different names, [including] φύσις [*physis*], πῦρ [fire], λόγος [*logos*]," also recoils into itself, remaining hidden, in withdrawal, indeed, forgotten, as it radiates its invisible light:

> Mortals are irrevocably bound to the revealing-concealing gathering which lights everything present in its presencing. But they turn from the lighting, and turn only toward what is present, which is what immediately concerns them in their everyday commerce with each other . . . Λόγος, in whose lighting [mortals] come and go, remains concealed from them, and forgotten. . . . But the golden gleam of the lighting's invisible shining cannot be grasped, because it is not itself something grasping. Rather, it is the purely appropriating event [*das reine Ereignen*]. The invisible shining of the lighting streams from wholesome self-keeping in the self-restraining preservation of destiny. Therefore the shining of the lighting is in itself at the same time a self-veiling—and is in that sense what is most obscure.[45]

If mortals do not see the mystery of this "lightning-flash of Being," if the fiery *logos* as "revealing-concealing lighting" remains essentially "forgotten," it is not simply because of a refusal on their part to acknowledge it, but because the "event" of lighting itself is essentially ungraspable; in folding back on itself in the course of its emergence, it is drawn once again into hiddenness, consumed and consuming in the devouring movement of a sweeping conflagration. As Heidegger later wrote in his essay on Trakl: "[The] flame . . . inflames, startles, horrifies and shatters us. Flame is glowing lumination. What flame is the *ek-stasis* [passes ecstatically outside itself] which lightens and calls forth radiance, but which may also go on consuming and reduce all to white ashes."[46]

Fire's capacity for destruction, to which Heidegger refers only once in his 1943 lecture on Heraclitus, thus becomes much more explicit some ten years later when it is linked not to *logos* but, as Derrida has shown, to Trakl's understanding of the word "spirit" or *Geist*, when in answer to the question "What is spirit?" Heidegger offers, according to Derrida, a "[f]inal reply": "Der Geist ist Flamme." "How to translate?" Derrida asks. "Spirit is what inflames? Rather, what inflames *itself*, setting *itself* on fire, setting fire to *itself*? Spirit is flame. A flame which inflames, or which inflames *itself*: both at once, the one and the other, the one the other. Con*flagration* of the two in the very con*flagration*."[47]

Although Derrida's analysis of the motif of fire in Heidegger's 1953 essay does not make an explicit connection between the *logos* and *Geist*, it is clear that in its function as "animator," as that which "sets man on the way," spirit, as Heidegger interprets it, is analogous to *logos* itself, and allows the latter term to be understood in a more radical sense as a movement of opening in which not only the "gathering power of gentleness" but also "destructiveness" reside, a destructiveness that in the poetry of Trakl is linked, as the following statements by Heidegger indicate, to pain and evil:

> Trakl sees spirit in terms of that being which is indicated in the original meaning of the word "ghost"—a being terrified, beside himself, *ek-static*. Spirit or ghost understood in this way has its being in the possibility of *both* gentleness *and* destructiveness. Gentleness in no way dampens the ecstasy of the inflammatory, but holds it gathered in the peace of friendship. Destructiveness comes from the unbridled license, which consumes itself in its own revolt and thus is active evil. Evil is always the evil of a ghostly spirit. Evil and its malice is not of a sensuous, material

nature. Nor is it purely "of the spirit." Evil is ghostly in that it is
the revolt of a terror blazing away in blind delusion, which casts
all things into unholy fragmentation and threatens to turn the
calm, collected blossoming of gentleness to ashes.[48]

[Spirit's] flaming vision is pain . . . pain is the animator. . . . This is
why everything that is alive . . . is imbued with pain, the funda-
mental trait of the soul's nature. Everything that is alive, is
painful. . . . The primal early brightness of all dawning being
trembles out of the stillness of concealed pain.[49]

Through this vision of the "origin" as that which is consumed in
pain, fire, and ashes, Heidegger thus brings about a major disrup-
tion of traditional notions of the mimetic and its models of fashion-
ing. This is a possibility that even Lyotard acknowledges in his dis-
cussion of the "Turn" (*Kehre*) in Heidegger's thought when he
claims that Heidegger, having become aware of the extent to which
his philosophy of spirit was compromised by metaphysics, "took
up the task of thinking what . . . belonged . . . to the occultation . . .
of the unforgettable."[50] One could even argue that this is the "mo-
ment" in Heidegger's thinking when, as Lyotard would say, it
"touches the thought of 'the jews'" insofar as the "forgotten," in
this case, is "remembered" in fire's recoiling, invisible light. In-
deed, however inadequate that "Turn" might have seemed to Lyo-
tard, this image of the self-consuming, self-concealing flame of an
"originary" conflagration points to the unpredictable terror of an
"origin without origin," to an opening that not only gathers but also
divides while dividing itself in the process. In this sense, then,
although Lyotard never makes such a connection, fire in Heideg-
ger's essay on Trakl functions in a manner similar to that of Lyo-
tard's "unconscious affect." Like Lyotard's "initial" trauma, which
is never experienced directly and which signals itself only after the
fact in the form of a symptom or phobia, so too does fire, in its
retreat from man's representational formations, leave "traces" that
can only be felt symptomatically in the ghostly residues of pain and
ashes.

Indeed, given the catastrophic implications of Heidegger's
thinking of *logos* and more particularly of "spirit" in terms of fire
and ashes, one wonders how Heidegger could have failed to notice,

certainly by 1953, that the traces of that most terrifying of histor-
ical events could also be detected there. If, however, as Lyotard
indicates, Heidegger remained steadfast even to the very end in his
adherence to the notion of original authenticity, and if, as Derrida
argues, the motif of gathering governed Heidegger's writing even in
his essay on Trakl, then Heidegger's silence on the Extermination
may not be so entirely incomprehensible. One can see in it the
repetition of a very old and perverse logic, one that requires the
extermination of all forms of inauthenticity, be they linguistic,
conceptual, racial, or otherwise, while denying the very act of
extermination itself, erasing from memory all traces that could
testify to the slaughter of what Lyotard has called "the jews."

This is Lyotard's thesis, at least, one that provides valuable
insights into the interconnectedness between Heidegger's philoso-
phy and his politics but raises questions when it is used as an
indictment of deconstruction as a whole. When he suggests that
deconstruction's refusal to confront directly the issue of the Holo-
caust is rooted in the philosophical tradition's forgetting of Being as
nothingness, that it lies, in other words, in the denial of originary
inauthenticity, he not only collapses the many different practices
of deconstruction into a single, monolithic "Heideggerianism," but
he seems to forget the persistent critique in which both Derrida and
Lacoue-Labarthe have been engaged for some time now of the very
notions of authenticity that structured Heidegger's thought. More-
over, if it is true that Heidegger chose to remain silent on the
terrifying historical significance of his thinking of fire and ashes, it
is also true that Derrida did not. In *Of Spirit*, Derrida makes that
historical and political connection explicit by listening attentively
to the rumblings of the Holocaust that resonate faintly in Heideg-
ger's discourse on spirit.[51] "I shall speak of ghost [*revenant*], of
flame, and of ashes," Derrida writes on the opening page. "[T]he
whole of this discourse," he adds in a footnote, "will be surrounded
by fire" (p. 115 n. 4). When Derrida follows the trajectory that leads
Heidegger from the celebration of spirit during the highly charged
political period of the Rectoral Address to his later identification of
spirit with fire and ashes, there is no question of an evasion on
Derrida's part of that trajectory's historical and political signifi-
cance. He calls up the ghostly images of the Holocaust that pass

unnoticed by Heidegger, but whose traces are undeniably lurking in the shadows of Heidegger's discourse:

> [In the *Rectorship Address*] *Geist* affirms itself through the self-affirmation of the German university. Spirit's affirmation, in-flamed. Yes, *inflamed*: I say this not only to evoke the pathos of the *Rectorship Address* when it celebrates spirit, not only be-cause of what a reference to flame can illuminate of the terrifying moment which is deploying its specters around this theater, but because twenty years later, exactly twenty years, Heidegger will say of *Geist*, without which it is impossible to think Evil, that . . . *Geist* is flame. (pp. 31–32)

If Derrida's analysis of spirit in Heidegger is thus permeated with references to fire and ashes, it is because he sees in "the ambiguous clarity of the flame" a means of examining its more terrifying political implications and of gaining insight into what grounds the political itself, both as it is understood in its general sense and in the more specific context of Heidegger's Nazism. For Nazism, Der-rida argues, "was not born in the desert":

> We all know this, but it has to be constantly recalled. And even if, far from any desert, it had grown like a mushroom in the silence of a European forest, it would have done so in the shadow of big trees, in the shelter of their silence or their indifference but in the same soil. I will not list these trees which in Europe people an immense black forest, I will not count the species. For essential reasons, the presentation of them defies tabular layout. In their bushy taxonomy, they would bear the names of religions, philos-ophies, political regimes, economic structures, religious or aca-demic institutions. In short, what is just as confusedly called culture, or the world of spirit. (pp. 109–10)

Heidegger's discourse on Trakl indeed shows, as Derrida suggests, that the political, in its capacity for good as well as for evil, is grounded in the burning flame of spirit itself. As a "non-ground" that animates, spirit as flame, as that which "inflames or which inflames *itself*" (p. 84), is the movement that opens history and gives rise to an evil such as the Holocaust while also undoing the very logic that produced it. Spirit, in Heidegger's essay on Trakl, is thus marked by an "internal duplicity"; the destitution from which

Heidegger tried to save it when he embraced National Socialism is no longer viewed by Heidegger in terms of an eventual decline or fall into the realm of inauthenticity. As we have seen, and this is a point that Derrida stresses, the destitution of spirit, the possibility of evil, proceeds from within spirit itself:

> In the affirmative determination of spirit—*spirit in-flames*—the internal possibility of the worst is already lodged. Evil has its provenance in spirit itself. It is born of spirit but, precisely, of a spirit which is not the metaphysico-Platonic *Geistigkeit*. Evil is not on the side of matter or of the sensible matter generally opposed to spirit. Evil is spiritual, it is also *Geist*, whence this other internal duplicity which makes one spirit into the evil ghost of the other. (p. 97)

While sounding out the horrifying political resonances of Heidegger's discourse on spirit, Derrida also shows that the evil of which Heidegger speaks is directly linked to the depropriating "violence" of the mimetic. This linkage is particularly evident in *An Introduction to Metaphysics*, where, as Derrida points out, Heidegger associates evil with everything that constitutes the degradation or falsification of spirit's original essence, with the modern subject's assimilation of spirit to "utilitarian intelligence" that manifests, in Heidegger's words, only a "semblance of spirit, masking its absence" (p. 47). This means, however, that when Heidegger later exposes the spirituality of evil, when destructiveness is shown to be lodged in spirit as its "evil ghost," then we find that the "demon" of simulation, the "destructive," destabilizing force of mimetic "depropriation" has become an integral part of the very structure of spirit itself.

This, of course, as Derrida maintains, is only one of the directions in which Heidegger's thinking takes us, for the other returns to a thinking of spirit as gathering, but it is clearly the point where his thought rejoins not only that of Derrida but also that of Lacoue-Labarthe. In signaling that "other" origin, what is for Derrida "origin-heterogeneous [*hétérogène à l'origine*]," Heidegger shows that the duplicitous movement of spirit's burning flame contains a thought of the trait:

[In our reading of Heidegger, Derrida writes, let] us finally situate a last *trait*, the *trait itself*, *Riss*. This word also traces difference. It returns often to bespeak the retreat by which spirit relates to itself and divides in that sort of internal adversity which gives rise to evil, by inscribing it, as it were, right in the flame. Like fire-writing. This is not an accident. It does not befall, after the event and as an extra, the flame of light. Flame writes, writes itself, right in the flame. Trait of conflagration, spirit in-flames— traces the route, breaks the path . . . transposes, deposes, and deports into the foreign. . . . It is in the mark (*Riss*) of the flame that sadness [or pain] carries away, tears apart, or snatches at the soul. (pp. 104–5)

Technē, spirit, *logos*, and the trait are thus brought together in this thought of the flame, the radical nature of which Heidegger never fully understood. Not only did that thought fail to lead him to more than a superficial acknowledgment of the Holocaust, but it never prompted him to see that mimetic impropriety had, from the very beginning, contaminated the purity of many of his key concepts. Indeed, in denying both this originary "lack of being proper" *and* the Extermination, Heidegger shows in what way the two are, in a sense, subjected to the same logic, to what Lacoue-Labarthe has called a "mimetologic," which attempts first to eliminate the impure and improper and, then, in a second step, to erase the traces of that elimination. That this mimetologic is at the very root of the "politics of forgetting" is a point that Lyotard would certainly not contest, given his search for the disruption of that logic in his thought of the unrepresentable. And yet, when he cites Lacoue-Labarthe's insistence on the role of the mimetic in the construction of the political, Lyotard criticizes him for adopting a position that is still too philosophical, still too tempted by a representation that places Auschwitz, for example, through his notion of the "caesura," in the realm of art. In seeking, however, a thought that has, in Lyotard's words, "never been able to inscribe itself in the register of philosophy" (p. 84) or that indeed can never give rise to a theatrical "*mise-en-scène*," Lyotard runs the risk of forgetting that it is not by stepping outside representation that one approaches the unrepresentable; it is, rather, by marking the limits within the structure of representation itself. One could, in fact, argue that by questioning the very processes that make such a "politics of forgetting" possible, processes that cannot be dissociated from the mimetic, Derrida, with the help of Lacoue-Labarthe, addresses the issue of the holocaust in the two senses of the term, as Lyotard's "originary terror" and as that singular, never completely representable, but most terrifying of historical events. One could argue, in other words, that through that very questioning, Derrida arrives at a "thought of 'the jews.' "

Lyotard seems himself to suggest such a possibility, with reference to Derrida's *Of Spirit*: "When this meticulous and admirable archaeologist comes across the ashes of the Holocaust, how could he be surprised? Has he not always known that the 'spirit' of metaphysics builds its edifices on the denial of Being, on its *Verneinung* [negation], and that they are promised to the *Vernichtung* [extermination], the annihilation, to the ashes by the retreat of Being?" (pp. 81–82). When one considers, however, that Lyotard claims elsewhere in the text that the issue of the Extermination can never be addressed by Derrida "as long as he holds on to deconstruction" (p. 76), these questions are rather puzzling, especially since they seem to be soliciting an affirmative answer. Moreover, by implying that this was for Derrida an astonishing discovery, Lyotard overlooks the fact that Derrida's meditations on holocaustal fire and ashes did not emerge suddenly with his analysis of the word *Geist*. On the contrary, those meditations have been evident in his writings for quite some time. They appear certainly as early as *Glas* (1974), if not before, and bear many of the markings not only of Lyotard's "terror without origin" but also of Derrida's own notion of the trait:

> Pure and figureless, this light burns all. It burns itself in the all-burning [*le brûle-tout*]—("all [*holos*] is burned [*caustos*]")—it is, leaves, of itself or anything, no trace, no mark, no sign of passage. Pure consuming destruction. . . . A pure essenceless by-play, a play that plays limitlessly, even though it is already destined to work in the service of essence and sense. . . . The all-burning— that has taken place once and nonetheless repeats itself ad infinitum—diverges so well from all essential generality that it resembles the pure difference of an absolute accident. Play and pure

difference, those are the secret of an imperceptible all-burning, the torrent of fire that sets itself ablaze. . . . The pure play of difference is nothing, does not even *relate* to its own blaze [*incendie*]. The light envelops itself in darkness even before becoming subject. . . . [T]his example without essence, devoid of self (*Selbst*), is also a sort of signifier without signified. . . . [T]he total absence of property, propriety, truth, sense, a barely manifest unfolding of forms that straightaway destroy themselves; is a One at once infinitely multiple absolutely different, different from self, a One without self, the other without self that means (to say) nothing, whose language is absolutely empty, void, like an event that never comes about itself.[52]

Thus, by accentuating the more destructive aspects of Heidegger's thinking of fire, the differential "trait of the flame" marks in its retreat, in its "re-trait," an incendiary "destining" or "sending" of Being, one that in effect opens the history of Being but that at the same time sends nothing, nothing of itself nor of anything else that has not been scorched by the all-burning, turned into "fiery dust," cinders or ashes. Within these charred remains, which are nothing more than smoldering remembrances of what can never be remembered, one might find a Lyotardian image of the "immemorial," for they become, using Lyotard's terminology, "symptoms" of the holocaust as "originary terror," of a traumatic "event" that can never be inscribed in memory. As a self-incinerating, holocaustal non-origin, the originary "event" is instead "absolute nonmemory," a nonpresence that is at the same time never a pure absence; nor is it a single moment occurring strictly outside either Being or language. The heat of its incendiary "presence" makes itself felt "ad infinitum" as a burning nonpresence at the heart of Being.

If Derrida is thus, according to Lyotard, too preoccupied by the question of Being, it is surely not because he wants to mimic or duplicate the more conservative Heideggerian "position"; he proposes, rather, to examine the philosophical ground that makes the posing of such questions possible and also to delve more deeply into the very conditions of Being's emergence, into the meaning of that primordial "appropriating event" (*Ereignis*) that for Heidegger allows Being "to come into its own as presence" but that for Derrida is a moment of depropriation. In the latter case, the gift of the *es gibt* in the Heideggerian expression *es gibt Sein* can no longer be thought starting from Being but is instead replaced by Derrida's duplicitous reformulation, first in *Dissemination* and later in *Cinders*, of the expression *il y la cendre*, in which the inaudible difference between *la cendre* (the cinder) and *là cendre* (there cinder) places its meaning in withdrawal, giving us a phrase that has "decomposed from within":

> Cinders there are, the phrase thus says what it does, what it is. It immediately incinerates itself, in front of your eyes . . . the cinder is nothing that can be in the world, nothing that remains as an entity [*étant*]. It is the being [*l'être*], rather, that there is—this is a name of the being that there is there but which, giving itself (*es gibt ashes*), is nothing . . . remains unpronounceable in order to make saying possible although it is nothing.[53]

Cinders, according to Derrida, thus come "in place of the gift." The dispersion of their smoldering embers leaves only the faintest of traces, which erase but also testify to the memory of fire:

> Trace destined, like everything, to disappear from itself, as much in order to lose the way as to rekindle a memory [p. 57]. . . . The fire: what one cannot extinguish in this trace among others that is a cinder. Memory or oblivion, as you wish, but of the fire, trait that still relates to the burning. No doubt the fire has withdrawn, the conflagration has been subdued, but if cinder there is, it is because the fire remains in retreat. (p. 61)

As that which "remains without remaining from the holocaust," ashes, cinders, and fiery dust become, as Derrida himself has indicated, "the best paradigm for the trace" (p. 43). They are the dispersed traces of an "irruptive event" which requires that the meaning of the word "event" (*Ereignis*) itself be rethought with regard not only to what problematizes traditional notions of Origin, Being, and History but also to the trace's role in both constituting and providing access to the very events that those notions describe. Without the holocaust, Derrida maintains in *Glas*, "the dialectical movement and the history of Being could not open themselves, engage themselves in the annulus of their anniversary, could not annul themselves in producing the solar course from Orient to Occident" (p. 242). Without the holocaust, in other words, there could be no Holocaust; nor, on the other hand, could there be any means of opposing those forces that produced it. Although the "all-burning" may reduce everything to ashes, it is still the only means by which the holocaust (in the two senses of the term) can ultimately be thought. As Derrida writes: "[T]here is perhaps only one [word, one "cinder word"] worth publishing, it would tell of the all-burning, otherwise called *holocaust and the crematory oven*, in German in all the Jewish languages of the world" (p. 57; my emphasis).

In *Cinders*, a work first published in 1982 as *Feu la cendre*, Derrida's radicalization of Heidegger's thinking of ashes and fire renders the historical and political significance of that thinking particularly explicit.[54] Through the motif of the trait, of this "trait of flame," Derrida not only breaks Heidegger's silence on the Holocaust by giving voice to its terror, but, in analyzing the very conditions of its possibility, he points to a means of undoing the exclusionary logic, the "politics of forgetting," that might have permitted, if not necessarily authorized, such a catastrophe. Indeed, one could argue that it is only through a rigorous interrogation of that logic, which for Lacoue-Labarthe is an essentially mimetic logic insofar as it attempts to eradicate the improper both in its linguistic and real-world incarnations, that one arrives at the "thought of 'the jews.'" In this sense, then, as David Carroll suggests in his introduction to Lyotard's *Heidegger and "the jews"*, Derrida and Lacoue-Labarthe "are more Lyotard's allies than his opponents in the difficult task of rethinking the political" (p. xix). If, as Lacoue-Labarthe maintains, fascism resulted from a "misapprehension . . . regarding the essence of *technē*,"[55] understood more radically in its relation to Derrida's "trait of flame," if, that is, traditional notions of the aesthetic and of representational discourse are at the very root of the program of National Socialism, where the formative or fashioning power of the German myth constitutes national identity, then something approximating a Lyotardian "anaesthetics" or a Derridean "pyrotechnical writing," which bears within it the traces of the nonpresent otherness that "the jews" have come to represent, provides us with a means not only of undoing the political program of fascism but of resisting the logic of identity upon which all forms of totalitarianism depend.

The question to be raised at this point, then, is: given that the aesthetic and the political are, in Lacoue-Labarthe's view, essentially indissoluble, what is to be gained from an examination of a deconstructive "literary" text whose operations undo conventional notions of the aesthetic? This question, however, should not be understood as a means of finding a more perfect or privileged "example" of such a discourse of resistance; it is, rather, an effort to examine one of the many possible forms that such a discourse might take. The issue here is not to argue that "literature" is more effective or subversive in its resistance to programmatic politics but to ask, through an analysis of the texts of Edmond Jabès, for example, what additional insights can be derived from an encounter of deconstructive theory with "literary" practice, particularly since the work of Jabès offers one of the most compelling manifestations of the unraveling of the myths that shape national identity. Although Jabès, like so many other proponents of deconstruction, never saw himself embracing a deliberately transgressive or revolutionary strategy, his work clearly indicates that his persistent interrogation of the traditional notions of the mimetic allows for a rethinking of *technē* that can be linked throughout his texts not only to holocaustal fire, in its two very different but interconnected senses (that is, to the Holocaust as historical event and to the holocaustal non-origin), but also to the fate of the Jew.

The Cata-strophic Poetics of Edmond Jabès

In spite of Jabès' constant questioning of language's capacity to represent history, the Holocaust is a haunting presence/nonpresence that reverberates throughout the Jabesian corpus. It is manifested in the piercing sound of a scream whose shrill echo resonates in all fourteen volumes, carrying with it not only the fragmented memories of the Holocaust but the resonances of 2,000 years of Jewish history. It is a scream of madness—that of the Jewish woman, Sarah, who loses her sanity upon returning from the concentration camps. It is the collective scream of a people deprived of a communal or national identity and who, perhaps for that very reason, were persecuted for an identity of vileness that had been imposed by others. It is the cry of the newborn which, as it is ejected from the womb, is already a cry of "pain" and "exile"; it is also the cry of God whose withdrawal was made known to the world at Auschwitz; and lastly, it is the scream of the book, which in perpetuating itself in the course of its own destruction, has a destiny that becomes intertwined with that of the Jew. Indeed, if a history of suffering and persecution is contained in this screaming excess of language, which, as the "effect of a shock" (Lyotard) or of an "immemorial wound" (Jabès), remembers without remembering what both the mind and language are too overwhelmed to synthesize, it is because the Jew in Jabès' texts harbors within his very being everything that the Western tradition has tried to purge from thought, destabilizing all the identificatory mechanisms that support our notions of nationhood, of the individual subject, and of his language.

This occurs first of all because the Jew in Jabès' texts has no self-contained identity. One can never be entirely Jewish because one is never wholly oneself: "[W]ith, or for, others I am never *me*—I am *the other of me*," someone says in *The Book of Resemblances*.[56] "Are you Jewish?" another asks. "Will I have been? Only as the void torments the void?"[57] Dispersed throughout the five continents, condemned to a life of homelessness, wandering, and exile, the Jew can never serve as a stable model, a fixed image or type with which one identifies and through which the identity of a people is fashioned or realized, for his very existence problematizes such a traditional mimetologic. Indeed, the Jew in Jabès' texts forces us to confront the mimetic impropriety that resides at the heart of every being, for he shows that self-identity is dependent on the existence of an other, of an other's perception, or of an other's language without which no presencing, no manifestation of being would even be possible, but which at the same time sets in motion the processes through which that presence is also destroyed: "You can free yourself of an object, of a face, of an obsession," says one of Jabès' imaginary rabbis. "You cannot free yourself of a word. The word is your birth and your death" (*BQ*, 1: 101); "What the eyes seize is what death unveils little by little and what we can only possess in dying" (*BQ*, 2: 318).

The moment of revelation, whether it be primarily visual or

through the spoken word, can therefore never give us Being in its totality. Even the presence of God can only be perceived in the process of becoming distant from itself: "God is a synonym for dune... dune piled up, grain by grain, where the spirit blows across the desert. Our relations with God are so difficult because we are always at the mercy of a grain of sand" (*BQ*, 2: 318). God, the Jew, and his universe are indeed equally caught up in the temporal process of their own manifestation, and the possibility of an immediate contact, as a result, is perpetually deferred. Given that the process of revelation always involves some form of mediation, perception can thus be said to obey the law of language in the work of Jabès where the two become, in a sense, intertwined; the word renders visible (*donne à voir*) and perception transforms its object into a mere sign of its own existence: "The perception of the universe," Jabès states, "goes through words and we notice quickly that this perception is nothing other than our own metamorphosis, first unconscious, then accepted, in words. We become the word which gives reality to the thing, to being" (*DL*, 128). What is ultimately revealed, however, is not that Being simply *becomes* language, for Jabès is not creating a self-enclosed, purely linguistic universe here. Rather, Being cannot become *at all* without the aid of a supplement. Its existence depends, in other words, on the operations of a *technē* that fill up the void, complete an originary deficiency, so that *physis* can be brought to light. For this reason, the specificity of the Jew is throughout Jabès' fourteen volumes indissolubly linked to that of language, revealing an interconnectedness of *physis* and *technē* that undermines the self-contained status of each:

> So, with God dead, I found my Jewishness confirmed in the book, at the predestined spot where it came upon its face, the saddest most unconsoled that man can have. Because being Jewish means exiling yourself in the word and, at the same time, weeping for your exile. (*BQ*, 2: 143)

> I will have been a Jew for not being able to answer to any but myself, more of a stranger than anyone else, and close to the poorest in the losing word. (*BQ*, 2: 142–43)

> [E]very letter in the book is the skeleton of a Jew. (*BQ*, 2: 216)

The Jew in Jabès' text thus unwittingly becomes the ultimate subversive, for he undermines our most cherished assumptions about the purity and integrity of individual identity, with the originary presence of Being at the origin of its discourse contaminated by the secondariness of the word that represents it. Indeed, if the scream in Jabès' texts can be seen as a reaction to the loss of originary presence, to the sudden "flare-up of an ancient terror," which brings Lyotard's "'initial' shock" immediately to mind, it also reverses Lyotard's somewhat derivative chronology insofar as the scream is not simply a secondary consequence of an originary terror, it is itself at the origin. Indeed, God Himself, in His multiple manifestations, is associated with that scream. "Le cri de Dieu" is revealed as a fissure or crack in one of the "wooden wings" of the Holy Arc, which, to the human ear, remains inaudible. "Le cri de Dieu" is not only a book, whose "white pages" contain its multiple traces, but also the fading flower from which the book emerges in the painful process of its gestation. As that which comes, as a consequence, both earlier and later, the shrill voice of God is multiplied and disseminated like seeds planted in the desert, surging forth as an inaudible incision, a "scream of creation," that traces His absence as much as His presence and establishes a relation between being and language that brings them both into existence as they also tear each other apart. Indeed, every being bears the traces of that tearing; the echoes of its painful cries reverberate throughout the Jabesian universe, which for Jabès has become "a Jewish universe" (*un univers juif*) in which "the suffocated screams of our words of flesh" reveal "the entire extent of our human misery."[58]

The multiple traces of this inaudible tearing thus hark back to an "origin" that is no longer truly original, nor can it be defined in simple terms. Functioning neither as pure Being nor as pure Language, it has been transformed by Jabès into the resonating echoes of those screams, a disseminating game of mirrors whose images are both originary and secondary, multiple and dispersed. Indeed, God Himself emerges in Jabès' text as His own mirror image: "God is the mirror of a distance in tune with its reflection" (*BQ*, 2: 279). Like the stillborn child Elya, whose birth and death are reflected in the fissured surface of a broken mirror, the Creator, with whom Elya is at times identified, is traversed by mimetic duplicity, His image divided and refracted through the very sound of His name ("El," the Hebrew word for God), which resonates like so many scattered fragments in the names of three "central" characters, Yaël, Elya, and Aely. And if the fate of these characters becomes intertwined with that of their Creator, that is because God as well as His creation bear the marks of this originary duplicity, of the work of mimesis that brings them both into existence but originates itself from nothing. They have no center that is not already a multiplicity of refracted centers, a gaping wound or "abyss" out of which God, through the "broken mirror" of His words, emerges as His own fraudulent image, as the "lie," in Jabès' words, that exists at the "core of God's creation" (BQ, 2: 314).

The divine presence is thus contaminated at the very outset by the mimetic, by the originary violence of a *technē*, through which the absolute coincidence between God and His Word (*Logos*) finds itself disrupted by conflict; the two yet-to-be-formed entities, in their search for existence, cut into each other as they become divided and dispersed. Thus, as the words of a wise man in Jabès' *The Book of Dialogue* remind us: "Our relation to God is not as simple as it might seem. . . . Has He not from the beginning shown His suspicion of the Word . . . ? Two creators of equal power laying claim to [*se disputent*] creation."[59] Whether the word in its earliest manifestations takes the form of an originary scream or of a "blood-stained lancet," as it does in "The Return to the Book," it forms an "alliance with God" by participating equally in the same rupture, "secretly cutting" into the already "visible wound" inflicted in each.[60] Expelled, then, like the stillborn child, from the forgotten depths of this gaping "wound" at the "origin of life" (BD, 16), both God and His Word bear the marks of this violent beginning, their fragmented, bleeding images testify to an originary emptiness that produces, as one of the many voices in Jabès' texts graphically states, a "porous world" in which "blood oozes out everywhere" (BQ, 2: 98). It oozes from God who is described as a secret dawning "without ties and which bleeds" (BQ, 2: 132), and from the word, which leaves "red stains" of blood that only the Jew "recognizes because he remembers the wounds he suffered along these same roads" (BQ, 2: 315). Jabès' texts are permeated with references to this "inaugural" violence, and if the Jew forces us to confront that violence through his fragmented identity, the Jewish God through His inevitable withdrawal comes to stand for the emptiness of this forgotten wound at the origin. In revealing the originary "forgetting of God" out of which "God emerges," He allows us to remember "what is without memories" and thus to think the "unthought" as it arises through the "inaugural" confrontation with language (*BQ*, 2: 170, 148).

Although this may be seen as a form of response to Lyotard's call for a writing that exposes the forgotten non-origin, Lyotard would likely object, as did Lang, to Jabès' excessive focus on questions of the mimetic. It must be recognized, nevertheless, that the very problematization of mimesis in Jabès' texts, through the fore-grounding of the movement of deferral that both perception and language represent, brings us closest to the Lyotardian perspective. The forgotten "unrepresentable" at the "origin" of thought, which is neither pure Being nor pure Language but rather the condition of the relationship between the two, becomes in the Jabesian context a deep "pit without memory," an "unsoundable Emptiness" (*BD*, 33) that unveils while still veiling the catastrophic (non)presencing of Being. Indeed, Jabès shows that only through our understanding of the mimetic relation and of the fundamental interconnectedness of being and language can we come to a thought of this "terror without origin" (Lyotard). Mimesis is linked throughout the Jabesian corpus not only to violence in its more generalized sense ("I bleed with the echo"), but more specifically to the scorching flames of fire, carrying with it all its frighteningly holocaustal implications. In the reflections of the cracked mirror, through which we witness the birth of the stillborn God-child, Elya, we see the origin in flames, a "fire-God" who burns Himself up in His own simulated image. Jabès' divine "Master of mirrors" thus also becomes a "God of flames," serving as a metaphor for the self-incinerating, holo-caustal non-origin by functioning in a manner not unlike that of Derrida's differential trait. God, who is nothing but "difference," can "only create difference; a world estranged from the world and yet faithful to itself through its very strangeness" (*LH*, 73). God's word, referred to in Jabès' texts as the incendiary "trace of a trace" (*BQ*, 2: 188), becomes a point of convergence and also of conflict, bringing together both being and language, and thus giving them

each some measure of existence, while allowing neither to stand in
its full presence, sending nothing that has not been touched by the
scorching flames of fire: "To the incendiary letter we have granted
the right to set fire. The word is a world in flames. God burns
forever in the four fires of His Name."[61]

Existing only in their relation to the space of both an articulated
and an unarticulated word, God, man, and the universe are thus
drawn together in their fatal encounter with language (understood
here in its more restricted linguistic sense and in its extended
perceptual sense as well). They are joined in a shared state of
incompletion and finitude that is rendered particularly explicit by
Jabès' "univers juif," and although "we all suffer from this absence
of identity," the Jew in Jabès' texts, as one historically deprived of a
fixed point of origin or ultimate point of reference, is perhaps more
aware than others of this exile in language; he understands, as Jabès
states in a 1989 interview, that "if his word exists God exists and
that, by indirection, he [the Jew] does also" (DL, 175). If the fate of
the Jew and that of God thus become intertwined in Jabès' work, it
is because they share the same torment, for the Jew, like the One in
whose image he was created, is also a mimetic being: "Are we the
echo," someone asks in "The Book of Questions," "whose voice
centuries could not stifle?" (BQ, 1: 97). "[T]he Jew," someone adds
in "Aely," "lives in the lie of others. . . . Stepping out of himself he
does not see himself as they see him, but as he knows he can never
be seen" (BQ, 2: 299). It is in this expulsion from the self-identical
that Jewish "identity" paradoxically resides, an identity that, as we
have seen so many times before, is indissolubly linked to language.
As the following, oft-cited comment reveals, the entirety of the
Jewish experience, which is so central to Jabès' work, is assimilated
to the structure of writing, with both the word and the Jew wander-
ing aimlessly in exile with nothing to ground their movement. "I
have talked to you about the difficulty of being Jewish, which is the
same as the difficulty of writing. For Judaism and writing are but
the same waiting, the same hope, the same wearing out" (BQ, 1:
122).

Thus, in a text that deconstructs the traditional link between
word and thing, a curious correspondence is derived from this
shared state of exile, a sharing that is duplicitous in nature, for

Judaism and language form a unity in which difference and rupture are also inscribed. What this means, however, is that rather than constituting a self-contained, purely linguistic and therefore ahistorical universe, as so many critics of deconstruction would have us believe, this assimilation of the exile of language to that of the Jew, which is based on the loss of the referent, is what ultimately reinstates referentiality. Indeed, in opposition to Lang, who sees in Jabès' critique of representational discourse a certain bracketing of the event of the Holocaust itself, one can argue that Jabès' focus on the interconnectedness of being and language and on the fundamentally duplicitous structure of their sharing is what allows history and the memory of the Holocaust to be preserved. Although the process of representation becomes nothing more than a series of substitutions and replacements that ultimately depropriates what it seeks to represent, it also, as Jabès' texts clearly show, provides us our only possible contact with the world and with ourselves. Thus, as Jabès writes in *The Book of Shares*, every book is a book of history whose pages are "weighed down with centuries" (*BS*, 75). It is also a "book of ashes" whose words do not simply testify to the loss or destruction of the outside world and its history but become, like the smoldering remains of an earlier conflagration or like the wrinkles in an aging face, ineradicable traces of the past. Indeed, the memory of the Holocaust is indelibly embedded in *The Book of Shares*' burning pages that refer repeatedly to ashes and fire: "We were a people," Jabès writes, "[b]ut this people scattered. We are a book at the heart of the fire" (p. 73). "How can we read a page already burned in a burning book unless by appealing to the memory of fire?" (p. 95). In this case, both the Jew and the book, or the Jew *as* book, carry the indestructible traces of their history, bearing within their fragmented corporality the charred residues of an originary conflagration whose ties to a later more terrifyingly brutal incineration are also unmistakable.

Jabès stresses repeatedly throughout his work the interconnectedness of these two fundamentally unrepresentable "events" (the holocaustal "non-origin" and the Holocaust itself), beginning with his first text, "The Book of Questions," in which the burning pages of the book are linked specifically to the burning of "a human being close to the mass grave" (p. 146). And later, first in the "Book of

Yukel," where the fumes of a forgotten non-origin appear alongside
the gas chambers' blackened emissions, and then in "Elya," with its
reference to the "sparkling barbed wire of the void" (BQ, 2: 151).
What accounts for the interconnectedness of these two seemingly
unrelated events is the inability to tolerate the possibility of a Being
contaminated by that nothingness and the desire to eradicate the
"lack of being proper" in whatever form it might take through a
movement of repression that culminates at Auschwitz. For Ausch-
witz, as Jabès writes in his still untranslated last work, *Le Livre de
l'hospitalité*, is the "ultimate erasure," the "erasure of Nothing-
ness" and impropriety which "the jews," in the Lyotardian sense
but also in the Jabesian sense, have come to represent. By giving
bodily form and substance to this continual confrontation between
being and language, the Jew in Jabès' texts carries with him the
indestructible memory of that "nothingness" and becomes, as a
consequence, a victim of a far more radical extermination.

Thus, despite Jabès' constant questioning of the capacity of lan-
guage to represent history, references to the Holocaust permeate
the Jabesian corpus, even in the earlier volumes that became the
object of Lang's critique. Although Lang is correct that the story
of Sarah and Yukel is preserved in only fragmented form, Jabès'
volumes provide an unforgettable image of the causes of their suf-
fering, leaving ghostly imprints that take many different forms
throughout the texts. Like the initials "S.S." that Sarah Schwall
draws, one morning, in the sand or the images of the graffiti defam-
ing the Jews, they all refuse to let us forget the events surrounding
the Holocaust by testifying to its spectral presence. For those who
claim, then, that Jabès focuses excessively on the textual (and this
critique is implied even in Derrida's first essay on Jabès), a cursory
examination of merely three pages of "The Book of Questions"
suffices to dispel such objections.[62] Although historical events are
never developed in a logical, orderly sequence in Jabès' texts, the
reference is nonetheless unmistakable:

> We both have the number of our expiration tattooed on our fore-
> arms. At that time, barbed wire grew like ivy, but round, round
> and deep. . . . At that time, evidence was queen . . . the ashes of
> Jews sent to the ovens were used to season her meals. "Close

your eyes," advised the sensitive souls. "Do not look away," pleaded the victims. The door which opened onto the mass grave or onto life was the triangle formed by our conquerors' legs. You had to get down on all fours to go through it. Honor to those who were trampled there. Honor to those whose skulls were cracked by the boots of the enemy parading in rhythm to his hymns of glory. . . . And Serge Segal shouted at the prisoners around him, who would soon be scattered in the various extermination camps prepared for them, shouted as if in the name of the Lord to His assembled people [au nom du Seigneur à Son peuple rassemblé]: "You are all Jews, even the anti-Semites, because you are all marked for martyrdom." (*BQ*, 1: 162–63)

With echoes of the S.S. resonating both visually and audibly throughout the paragraph's closing lines, thus reinforcing the horror of its content, Jabès does not, as Berel Lang seems to suggest, subsume the memory of the Holocaust under a more generalized problematic of language; not only is Jabès *not* prevented from speaking out against the Holocaust but his very foregrounding of that problematic calls for a rethinking of mimesis (that is, of *technē*) in a way that ultimately subverts the very logic upon which the Holocaust and, indeed, all acts of intolerance are grounded. To exterminate the Jews in the name of racial purity is to exterminate the thought that no pure identity is possible. That thought, however, is what Jabès repeatedly resurrects. The fate of the book, which is never to be constituted as a unified entity, and the fate of the Jew are intertwined in such a way as to make the constitution of a purely textual world just as impossible as the purity of national or racial identity, for Jabès' many volumes bring the racial and the textual together in their experience of ashes and fire, joining being and language in a paradoxical structure of sharing that, as the verb "to share" (*partager*) itself implies, divides as much as it unites, carrying with it the recognition that no identity is safe from contamination by that which presumably remains outside it.

Through this "pyrotechnical" writing of fire and ashes, which marks the limits of mimesis itself, Jabès addresses the issue of the holocaust in the two senses of the term, as Lyotard's "originary terror" and as that singular, most terrifying of historical events. Indeed, the very word Holocaust, as the "all-burning," is itself caught up in the duplicitous structure of sharing, gathering together the multiple experiences of that atrocious event and permitting us to share in its memory while consuming it in its full presence, reducing it to ashes, leaving traces that nonetheless testify to the existence of a holocaustal fire.

A "Politics" of Community: Jabès and Jean-Luc Nancy

If one can say, then, that Jabès arrives at what Lyotard referred to as the "thought of 'the jews,' " one should add that Jabès also does much more than that by pointing, in a manner that takes it further than Lyotard was able to take it in his short treatise on Heidegger, to the sociopolitical consequences of that thinking, consequences that can be understood only in the context of the sharing made possible by the holocaustal "trait of flame." Out of that sharing comes not simply a solitary confrontation with the death residing at the heart of every being but the possibility of communal life, a curious experience of community, without which no political action, no collective involvement would even be possible, but which requires at the same time a reworking of the notion of the communal and of the political as well. The community that emerges in the work of Jabès has little to do with accepted notions of the communal as an immanent unity in which every member identifies with some internally defined communal essence. It challenges instead, through its remembrance of "the jews," all our most deeply embedded assumptions regarding the formation of a common political identity and responds, as a result, to Lyotard's demand for new ways of thinking community, where the political is conceived not in terms of a "fashioning of a people" or in the Heideggerian sense of an authentic destiny of the German *Volk* but in terms of a "people" whose unraveling of the traditional models of fashioning gives rise to a community of an entirely different sort. It leads to something resembling Jean-Luc Nancy's notion of the "unworked" or "unfashioned community" in which singular beings, as both guardians and "hostages" of the Forgotten, are exposed to their own limits. Such an unraveling of communal identity indeed gives rise to what Lyotard describes in *Heidegger and "the jews"* as a "people" dispersed in the desert, refusing to fashion themselves into a "people," or to project themselves according to what is proper to them alone, having learned that both unity and properness are neither in their power nor in their duty, that even the pretension to be the guardian of the Forgotten lacks consideration for it, since it is the Forgotten that holds the "people" hostage whatever their "fashion" of being-together. (p. 80)

What Lyotard envisions, then, is nothing other than a Jabesian community of "the jews," a gathering of finite beings whose very fragmented existence disrupts the traditional communo-political order not through a deliberate and willful act of subversion but by uncovering the "immemorial terror" in all social constructs and countering even the most vicious attempts by the totalitarian apparatus to eliminate it through countless purges, denunciations, and exterminations. As Lyotard later argues in his contribution to a collection of essays inspired in part by the work of Nancy, totalitarian politics fails to maintain order because the unmanageable "thing," a word that now signifies Lyotard's use of Freud's "unconscious affect," is not "manageable politically"; it inhabits the political community unconsciously, making the community itself its "hostage, unbeknownst to it."[63] If fascism, however, never let up in trying to "manage the unmanageable" and ultimately to destroy it in the name of some mythic community, the reason was that it carried to its ultimate conclusion the thinking that structures all dreams of political unity, a thinking that requires that the inherently intractable or disjunctive nature of community be forgotten so that the "phantasm of oneness and totality" can be affirmed.

Nancy also makes this point in *The Inoperative Community*, when he sees fascism's positing of the state as absolute, self-determining subject as one of the more "grotesque" manifestations of the West's "obsession with communion" (p. 17), one that "crystallized," according to Nancy, the nostalgia for a more archaic, more perfectly formed community that has structured the Western world's thinking about community from its very beginnings. Whether expressed as a longing for a more primitive, naturally harmonious, familial unity or for Christianity's communion with the body of Christ, that thinking has always been based on the assumption of a loss, on the belief in the disappearance of a more perfect communal order that is itself founded on an illusion, one that fails to recognize, has indeed forgotten, that the golden era of community never really took place. This idealized image of communality is, according to Nancy, one of the Western world's most ancient myths, and Nazism's reactivation and exploitation of its formative power not only allowed the Nazis to carry out, however imperfectly, their totalitarian objectives but also exposed the totalitarian essence of myth itself. If humanity, as Nancy indicates, is born to itself through its founding myths, it is at the same time subject to myth's organizing power, to its "will to mythation" that is totalitarian in content, gathering multiple existences together into a single, common identity. Indeed, the aim of mythic will is always one of communion, in Nancy's view. Whether it be the communion of man with God, of man with nature, or of man with the community of men, myth communicates itself "necessarily as a myth belonging to the community, and it communicates a myth of community: communion, communism, communitarianism, communication, community itself taken simply and absolutely, absolute community" (p. 57).

Although Nancy insists that the thinker of myth is not necessarily responsible for Nazism, Nazi Germany's reconstruction of itself through its mythicizing of the Aryan race clearly shows to what extent the invention of myth "is bound up with the use of its power," allowing for the "staging and setting to work [*mise en oeuvre*] of a 'Volk' and of a 'Reich,' in the sense that Nazism gave to these terms" (p. 46). As a fiction that fashions communitarian identity, and through which the community produces its own essence as its "work," myth presupposes the active adhesion of a people to the models it proposes, a total identification with the "dreamed image" through which the identity of the individual or of the state will find self-fulfillment. It is thus because myth can be defined as the instrument of this identification (that is, as the instrument of a *mimesis*, as "*the* mimetic instrument par excellence"), that German totalitarianism and its racist ideology became so caught up in its own mythic constructions. The mimetic process alone, according to Nancy, allows for the constitution of identity, and it does so, in this case, by covering over, in accordance with the most traditional mimetology, any reference to its own constituting mechanisms; it covers over, in other words, any reference to language (for the purity of the Aryan race was, as Nancy and Lacoue-Labarthe point out, linked to blood, not to language) as well as to the relationality implied in the very notion of community itself.[64]

If resistance is to come, then, it is not from the complete collapse of community but from the exposure of its inherently "disjunctive nature" through which community is revealed as "neither a work to be produced nor as a lost communion" but rather as a relational space of shared "singularities." It comes, in other words, from a Jabesian community of "the jews," in which the gathering of finite beings destines community to its own "unworking," underscoring the impossibility of constituting itself as a "pure collective totality." Indeed, as we have seen, there can be no totality in the work of Jabès. This is so, first of all, because his texts call into question the unifying function of myth itself. The multiple voices of the imaginary rabbis, which in large part structure the work, recall the Judaic tradition of scriptural exegesis, and yet their commentary reveals no Divine presence. All that is revealed is another commentary whose words, appearing in unconnected fashion, tell us little of the identities of those who speak them. The rabbis appear and disappear throughout the work as "visages effacés," as empty voices circling around a center that is never there, spewing forth a never-ending torrent of words in the form of citations, dialogues, and interminable interpretations. The rabbis' words, then, because they have no anchor, wander aimlessly throughout the text, becoming "paroles subversives," which bring myth's interruption by undermining the "manifestation of any presence" (*BR*, 1: 95), including the presence of the book itself. Although we become witnesses to the temporal process of the book's unfolding, that very process renders it forever inaccessible as a totality. An ever larger portion of each work is devoted to the time before the book, and the farther we move along within the two cycles making up *The Book of Questions*, the more inaccessible the book becomes. In "Aely," the section entitled "The Book," which is preceded by a seemingly endless sequence of "The Fore-Book" (*L'Avant-livre*) and "Before the Fore-Book" (*Avant l'avant livre*), does not appear until approximately twenty pages before the end, and even then we have not arrived; we are moved instead through a series of "approaches" to "Aely" without ever getting beyond that point. The book remains, then, forever at the threshold, always in language but never in the Book itself.

And yet despite the difficulties involved, the search for that "mythical book" (which "every book," according to Jabès, "tries in vain to reproduce"; *Book of Margins*, 175), continues; its language driven forward by the constant pursuit of a closure that only becomes another opening. By turning back on itself, "The Return of the Book" ends the first cycle, but, at the same time, that cycle is carried over to the next where the movement toward a point of finality is communicated by the title of the last book in the series, "El, or the Last Book." Here, the anagrammatic names have been reduced to the common element in each, "El," the Hebrew word for God. But this effort to close in on some ultimate "point" of convergence, whether it be God or the Book itself, only produces, as someone says in "El, or the Last Book," a "point drowned in a point" (*BQ*, 2: 371). Thus the reduction continues, but the point itself is never reached. The last book does not complete the cycle, nor does it bring an end to *The Book of Questions* as a whole, for the new series, *The Book of Resemblances*, opens with lengthy citations from each of the preceding works. Here, the characters from all seven volumes, the rabbis included, continue to appear with constant reference to their status as characters of fiction, but it is a fiction, in this case, that does not found a national identity; it is, rather, the means by which all notions of identity are undermined.

Indeed, nothing in the Jabesian universe appears as only itself. Words contain words, points contain other points, characters, as we shall see, emerge as composites of other characters, and books comprise a multiplicity of other books. In all these differential relationships, no single unit can be enveloped or revealed apart from the context that structures it. God, in the course of His revelation, undergoes the same process of transformation, and He emerges as little more than a play on words—"Dieu = Vide = Vie d'yeux. God = emptiness = life of the eyes" (*BQ*, 2: 410)—not, however, to be reduced to a purely linguistic entity, but to be brought forth as a being whose presence is both linguistically and perceptually deferred. With the "D" in "D'yeux," standing also, as Jabès writes in "Aely," for God's "Desire to see" and "be seen" by eyes that remain open to His unmediated presence, the link is made once again between language and perception, with the perceptual "eye of fire," like Derrida's "fire-words" or like thought itself, consuming what it also exposes, unveiling "little by little" what is at the same time "lost to our senses" as the spacing reveals it to an outside. God's image, as a result, like the book that circles around it, or indeed like the Jew who "withdraws in order to exist" (*BR*, 1: 19), never coincides with itself. In marking the "paths of the One toward the One," or "the Traces within the hollow of the Trace," God is instead "always *between*" (*BQ*, 2: 295), a "Providential gap./ Between fire and fire" (*BS*, 89) that exposes once again the incendiary operations of a *technē* in the disclosure/withdrawal of Being: " 'A flame,' you said, 'is, to the mind's eye, a mad rebirth of the world.' For us . . . everything started from there. And the book takes its ashes into account" (*BQ*, 2: 157), propelling itself forward, perhaps, by the desire to "save a few words from the fire smoldering inside us" (*BD*, 15). With this incendiary nonpresence at the heart of every being, all that issues from the blazing non-origin is thus influenced by the force of its movement constituting a world of resemblances, a shared existence in finitude made possible by this encounter with fire:

> Trouée providentielle.
> Entre feu et feu,
> où passent les hirondelles,
> où le passage est partage.
>
> Providential gap.
> Between fire and fire,
> where the swallow flies,
> where passage means sharing. (*BS*, 89)
>
> Tranche impunément dans le chair de l'indendie.
> Le partage a, pour lame, la flamme.
>
> Cut with impunity to the quick of the blaze.
> Shares are apportioned with a blade of flame.
> (*BS*, 93)

Out of the confrontation with this differential trait of flame, then, a strange form of alliance emerges. Its incendiary nonpresence provides the basis for a sharing that is as duplicitous and contradictory as the term "sharing" itself suggests, signifying not only division, a parceling out or dissociation, but also participation, belonging to a community or a partaking of the same. Every being in Jabès' "univers juif" is modeled in God's incendiary image, every reflection contains the flickering traces of His flame, with "all the secrets of the universe" becoming "buds of fire soon to open" (*BQ*, 1: 25), but whose "fatal scent" will, upon that opening, also bring death. As the process through which Being is brought forth to appearance but also extinguished in His revealing-concealing light, God thus becomes "the sum of our differences" (*BQ*, 2: 297), a movement of opening in which we all are implicated and through which we nourish the fire that gives life and unites us even as it sets us apart: "We are bound by the impossible." Our fate is "the flame made wedding band" (*BQ*, 1: 224, 202).

Community, then, does not disappear, as Nancy has argued. It instead resists; it is "in a sense, resistance itself: namely, resistance to immanence, . . . to all the forms and all the violences of subjectivity" (p. 35). This is primarily because the sharing through which community emerges is in itself incomplete. Indeed, the world of resemblances with which Jabès confronts us does not produce a fusional communion with some common identity; rather, it is one in which the identificatory mechanisms constituting social or individual identity have broken down. The entire second cycle of *The Book of Questions*, which is devoted to the characters Yaël, Elya, and Aely, is permeated with references to broken mirrors. When Yaël, about to give birth, throws an object at the threefold mirror standing before her, we see the arrival of her stillborn child Elya reflected in its fissured surface, with the child's deformed image, which continues to live on, becoming confused with that of the narrator himself:

> [I]n the room's half-light, the threefold mirror showed off its wound which in the faint rays announcing morning looked like a bloody vagina. Narrow crack of life and death which a woman in love offers him who takes her, I have seen a child come

out between its lips paired for the best and the worst. I have seen the child become an adolescent under my eyes, the adolescent find himself a man, me, with my face, but without name. (*BQ*, 2: 175)

In this interminably mimetic universe, which is constantly emerging but never fully present, the image of one element, brought forth as a fractured replica of itself, is reflected in the image of an other, producing no self-contained identity, no fusional communion, but an endless series of identifications through which one's identity is constituted but with which it never completely coincides: "Trying to unravel an enigma I have turned in vain all around my reflection. Which of us two is real?—as he is not I, I am no longer he, but another who surreptitiously stole my features in his desire to remain *the other*" (*BQ*, 2: 163). Whether the text is referring to the earliest structuring relations of the child's narcissistic identification with the self or to the future identifications allowing the social subject to emerge, it unceasingly calls attention to the ways the exposure of the self always involves a detour through the other, producing what Jabès has described as a "fusion in death" (*identification dans la mort*) (*BQ*, 2: 100), through which every constituted identity returns to itself, as Nancy would say, "broken," reflected in the image of the other but never completely identical with itself. Yaël is at the same time the mother of Elya, the narrator of the book and the narrator's lover. The ideal union between work and narrator, as between the two lovers, is unattainable because the relationship is always marked by conflict. They remain separated by another lover or by the narrator himself, who will always be "other" to Yaël. The effort, however, to suppress otherness by killing Yaël (or perhaps it is the suicide of the narrator himself) brings no resolution; they are dependent upon each other for their very existence, yet because of that dependence neither is able to affirm the totality of his identity: "I was at the same time Yaël, myself and *the other*" (*BQ*, 2: 72). Again life and death are intertwined. Identity is at the same time constituted by its relationship to the other and destroyed by it, unveiling what is for Jabès, citing Michel Leiris, "the deep sense of suicide" at the heart of being: "to become at the same time *one-self* and *the other*, male and female, subject and object, the killer and the killed—our only chance of communion with our-selves" (BQ, 2: 3).

The subversion of the metaphysics of community proceeds, therefore, not from the will of a fully constituted subject who attempts to break free of the constraints imposed by a presumably closed and oppressive communal order, but from the exposure of the very limits of the communal itself, which, in ceaselessly resist-ing completion and fusion, also resists any attempt to enclose it within the boundaries of a political program or context. Commu-nity in this intrinsically subversive sense is less a political end to be realized than the very condition not just of the political but of existence itself:

> Did I already know that opening and closing my eyes, lying down, moving, thinking, dreaming, talking, being silent, writing and reading are all gestures and manifestations of subversion? . . . Did I know further that there are degrees of subversion, that we are truly subversive in our relation with others only when we do not at all try for it, when in an atmosphere of non-suspicion fostered by our natural behavior, nobody notices? (BS, 54)

As the relational ground out of which being emerges, community cannot be thought in terms of political ends or origins, nor can it be seen as a common substance or being; it should be thought instead as the means by which being is made manifest, as a network or interweaving of singularities that brings being into existence by placing it in relation both to itself and to others in the movement of its "ex-posure" to the outside world. Nancy has described this process most succinctly:

> [Singular being] is what it is . . . only through its extension, through the areality that above all extroverts it in its very being . . . only by *exposing it to an outside*. This outside is in its turn nothing other than the exposition of another areality, of another singularity—the same other. This exposure, or this exposing-sharing, gives rise, from the outset, to a mutual interpellation of singularities prior to any address in language (though it gives to this latter its first condition of possibility). Finitude compears, that is to say it is exposed: such is the essence of community. (p. 29)

Although Nancy regards the "compearance" of singular beings as anterior to the speaking voice, it at the same time, as Christopher Fynsk convincingly points out in his introduction to Nancy's work, cannot be dissociated from language. The exposure that gives rise to the "mutual interpellation of singularities" is also what implies language in its extended sense, involving the articulation or communication of being in its finitude and by means of which that finitude compears: "Only in this communication," Nancy writes, "are singular beings given—without a bond *and* without communion, equally distant from any notion of connection or joining from the outside and from any notion of a common and fusional interiority. Communication is the constitutive fact of an exposition to the outside that defines singularity. In its being, as its very being, singularity is exposed to the outside" (p. 29). Thus, although the "mutual interpellation of singularities" may, as Fynsk argues, reside at the "limits of language" in a strictly linguistic sense, although it may even be the " 'origin' of language (in a Heideggerian sense of the term)," it "cannot be understood as other than language," for it is "always *of language*. Otherwise, there would be no *need* to write and no way to write it" (p. xxv).

Nancy himself seems to suggest this possibility when he makes the following claim: "A singular being ('you' or 'me') has the precise structure and nature of a being of writing, of a 'literary' being: it resides only in the communication—which does not commune—of its advance and its retreat. It offers itself, it holds itself in suspense" (p. 78). In stressing the communicative nature of being's advent and its withdrawal, Nancy clearly implicates language while taking great pains to distinguish it from the more restricted linguistic understanding of the term. The common exposure of singular beings implies no presence, no *thing* to be designated or represented linguistically, as if language were something that is to be added to an already constituted reality. Rather, singular being comes into being *in* language, communicating itself in/through and as what Nancy calls "writing" or "literature": "[S]ince being-in-common *is* nowhere, and does not subsist in a mythic space that could be revealed to us, literature does not give it a voice: rather, it is being *in* common that *is* literary (or scriptuary) . . . that has its very being in 'literature' (in writing, in a certain voice, in a singular music, but also in a painting, in a dance, and in the exercise of thought)" (p. 64).

While Nancy gives no indication as to the precise form that such a writing of finitude might take, there is no question that the multiple voices of his inoperative community can be heard in the work of Jabès, who shows to what extent the rethinking of community cannot be undertaken without a rethinking of our relationship to language. If, as Nancy claims, it is through writing or "literature" that being in its fundamentally shared (but also divided) essence exposes itself, then the literary and, more generally, language must be understood in a way that has nothing to do with the revelatory powers of mythic speech. It must bring myth's interruption by showing that the moment of revelation involves an exposure to alterity that threatens the self-contained identity of language itself: "My words rise out of a long absence of talk and compel like a scream" (BQ, 1: 385). "Drenched" with both "ink and blood" (BQ, 2: 290), the word, like all else in the Jabesian universe, is dislocated and dispersed in the course of its ex-position. It is also traversed by something outside it, indissociable from, and therefore also fragmented by, the very being it brings into existence:

> Is being language? [a voice asks in The Book of Shares] Is language recognition of being? Being holds language (which cannot encompass it) in check, but language likewise checks being (which cannot master it). Then being owes its possibility to be to language, and language owes to the meditation of being its possibility to exist. Bond of nothing and nothing. Of Void and Void. Of empty and empty. Hyphen of ashes [trait d'union en cendres]. (p. 70)

> My books bear witness to a practice of text tied to an experience of which I could not say to what point it is the experience of all words—so inseparable, so solidary are they in the face of risk. (BR, 2: 93)

And if the status of the word is, as we have seen, indissolubly connected to that of the Jew, if indeed the "Jewish word," like Derrida's "cinder word," marks the incendiary "destining" or "sending" of being, then it might be possible to understand "writing" as this impossible union of being and language or, more precisely, of *physis* and *technē* in the presencing/nonpresencing, working/un-working of Jabès' "univers juif." This coming together of the word and the Jew, neither of which exists independently of the other, constitutes the community of limits that emerges in the work of Jabès:

> Judaism warrants that the written belongs to the unwritten as well as the unwritten to the written. . . . Thus, the Jew tackles the difficult Jewish reality, having turned the word "Jew" into another word: a word of not-belonging beyond all belonging; affirming and, at the same time, subtly denying the latter. (*BD*, 57–58)

> One day I shall have to explain how this . . . not-belonging came to belong: my itinerary as a Jew. (*BR*, 2: 44)

Indeed, so interlaced are these two fragmented elements that the shifting movement of the individual characters as well as the complex interweaving of one text with another mimic the structure of writing itself in which all elements are placed in a differential relationship. Each term, every character, every object, and every text engenders another, but in so doing it becomes itself divided, caught up in the movement of life in death or death in life that sustains the work. Yaël gives birth to Elya, but the circumstances of Elya's birth become confused with Yaël's murder. Elya is stillborn, and yet he lives on in the following book as a multiple image of those who engendered him. In the third book, we are led through its labyrinthine structure in perpetual search for Aely, and yet he persists in eluding us. He, too, appears only as a composite of others, a shadow composed of the shadows which preceded him: "Aely . . . was perhaps always fused with [the shadow] of Yaël cradling Elya in her arms and, later, with that of Elya without Yaël. . . . Elusive down to his name which we never know how to pronounce" (*BQ*, 2: 325). Indeed, the anagrammatic names of the characters Yaël, Aely, and Elya call attention to the movement of differentiality that structures the Jabesian universe, and because every element must define itself in relation to what precedes or follows, it is always drawn into a network of relations, a community of "others" that undermines its self-sufficiency but that also allows it to exist: "We are bound to one another by a kind of complicity born of our not wanting to end it. . . . We are one and the

same victim. . . . How great our misery in its confounding relations"
(*dans sa confondante connexité*) (*BQ*, 2: 76, 112).

Out of this "confounding connectedness" between "being" and
"language," or between *physis* and *technē*, comes, however, not
simply an encounter with death and destruction but the possibility
of a strange kind of salvation, one that results from an experience of
sharing that cannot be fused into some idealized image of a unique
people or race but that carries with it, in its infinite resistance to all
forms of fusional identity, an irrepressible sense of accountability
and even commitment that stems from our involvement with an
other:

> There is word inside us stronger than all others—and more per-
> sonal. A word of solitude and certainty, so buried in its night that
> it is barely audible to itself. A word of refusal, but also of absolute
> commitment, forging its bonds of silence in the unfathomable
> silence of the bond. (*BS*, 1)

> Sharing has perhaps no other aim than to lift a corner of the
> heavy, dark curtain of our solitude . . . to exist means increasingly
> to open up to sharing. It means sharing our life with life, our joy
> with joy, our sorrow with sorrow, our death with death, in short,
> our moment with the moment. (*BS*, 93)

> The salvation of the Jewish people lies in severance, in solidarity
> at the heart of severance. (*BQ*, 1: 100)

The experience of sharing and its "unworking" of the identifica-
tory mechanisms constituting community in the traditional sense
thus respond to an exigency that goes far beyond a simple preoc-
cupation with the textual or with the "nihilistic" refusal of one's
ethico-political responsibility. Although such an experience may
expose the limits of the political, it clearly contains a notion of
responsibility toward others that imposes itself with considerable
ethical and political force. If, as Jabès has written, it was in the Nazi
camps that "the resemblance of creatures . . . had reached . . . its
zenith" (*BR*, 1: 47), if cultural and racial difference was extermi-
nated by their barbed enclosures of hatred, then the recognition of
this very otherness, this shared state of incompletion defining our
common existence, constitutes our ultimate and perhaps only de-
fense against the political acts of exclusion and intolerance. Jabès'

stories of impossible love and deadly identifications involve a rec-
ognition of the role of differentiality in the constitution of being, as
well as an acceptance of the other in the "sovereignty of its differ-
ence" (*DL*, 95), in its relation to an alterity in which every being is
implicated as it opens onto a world outside itself. Built into the
structure of Jabès' "univers juif" as an "unworked" community is
thus a notion of tolerance, a willingness to receive what is offered
as an impossible "gift" by means of which no "being" is given
without also being taken away. Such a gift carries what could easily
be interpreted as its own ethical imperative, demanding a response
and even responsibility from the one who receives it:

> —My responsibility toward you . . . is comparable to that of the
> sky toward the birds and to that of the ocean to its fauna and
> flora. . . .
> —I do not deserve the hospitality that I owe you.
> —Accept it. I will know that you have pardoned me. (*LH*, 18)

The generosity of spirit implied in the assumption of that re-
sponsibility is central to the notion of hospitality that dominates
the very last of Jabès' many volumes, *Le Livre de l'hospitalité*,
written just before his death in January 1991, in which the question
of responsibility is raised explicitly for the first time. In this vol-
ume, the voice of a journalist (which is that of Jabès himself, who
has reprinted one of his newspaper articles) openly condemns all
discourses of intolerance, a condemnation compelled, in part, by
one of the more frightening and incomprehensible anti-Semitic
acts in recent years—the desecration of Jewish tombstones in the
cemetery at Carpentras in the spring of 1989.[65] "To think . . . that
anti-Semitic discourse is less virulent today than it was before
the war of 1940, for example, is a serious error; for Auschwitz
soon followed. And the question to be raised is the following: How
could such a discourse still be tolerated? If the horror of Auschwitz
couldn't quell it, how can we think that Carpentras could?" (p. 36).
The journalist adds, however, that it is not enough to simply de-
nounce the events at Carpentras; we must recognize that we are all
implicated in such practices of intolerance and that the exclusion
of the other amounts ultimately to the exclusion of oneself, of the
other upon whom one's very existence depends: "The refusal of

difference leads to the negation of the other. Have we forgotten that to say 'I' is already to assert the *difference*? . . . [R]acism is simply the renewed expression of the negation of man, of every man in his richness and in his infinite poverty" (pp. 35–36).

In opposition to the anti-Semitic, racist discourses of exclusion, Jabès develops a more inclusive notion of "hospitality," pointing to the austere hospitality of the Bedouin host, who, in preserving the anonymity of the voyagers he welcomes into his community, remains open to difference and strangeness:

> Why did [our host] pretend not to recognize us? This attitude seemed abnormal, almost shocking, to us. How wrong we were! We obviously hadn't thought enough about what characterized the hospitality of the Bedouins. If our host received us while pretending not to know us, it was to indicate that, in his eyes, we remained each of us anonymous travelers he had to honor, in the name of the ancestral hospitality of his tribe, as we were because, otherwise, our unexpected visit would have quickly given the impression of a fleeting reunion. (*LH*, 85)

And given that the word *hôte* in French means both guest and host, the differences he preserves in the voyager are clearly his own as well. Hospitality thus comes to signify in Jabès' final work the ultimate act of tolerance. As a practice of openness and receptivity, it includes without subsuming the elements it brings into its community under a logic of sameness and identity, presupposing no transcendental notion of community, no idealized national identity or race to which the individual must conform. It exposes the communitary or relational ground that allows the individual to emerge in its strangeness and finitude as the other of the other and of itself. *Le Livre de l'hospitalité* thus provides a fitting subject for Jabès' last work, for the entire Jabesian *oeuvre* can be seen as a work of hospitality, as a practice of non-exclusion that opens onto being in its relation to alterity. Although that *oeuvre* has never been part of a political program, it has important political implications. In its disruption of community in the traditional sense, in its refusal to close itself off by affirming some clearly defined notion of individual or collective identity, it constitutes a resistance to any political program that depends on and is structured by the power of "immanence" as elaborated by Nancy.

Of Hospitality, Responsibility, and the Democratic "Ideal": Derrida's 'Specters of Marx'

The question to be raised now, of course, is: how is the lyricism with which Jabès describes his community of "the jews" to be translated into practical, real-world terms? Or, more precisely, how does one go about transforming the non-exclusionary practices of a Jabesian hospitality into more positive guidelines for the realization of concrete political objectives? In order to address these questions, I would like to return to the book mentioned briefly in the Introduction to this volume, Derrida's Specters of Marx, in which he articulates a Jabesian notion of hospitality and gives it more explicitly practical dimensions. In this work, Derrida elaborates a concept of community whose openness to the "spectrality" of the other constitutes more than just a resistance to the traditional models of fashioning as examined by Nancy. It points in an even more positive way, I would argue, to the possibility of political action by allowing for the affirmation of certain democratic "principles" from which we might draw institutional or organizational guidelines even as they resist our impulse to transform them into an inflexible political program or doctrine. Calling this new fundamentally "democratic" community the "New International," a label that paradoxically conjures up images of what is now assumed to be a defunct socialist utopia, Derrida envisions a practice of "absolute hospitality" whose aim is to withstand the propensity for closure to such an extent that it remains open to what is normally viewed as anathema to any notion of democracy by embracing the menacing "specter" of Marx. Rather than posing a threat, in this case, to certain democratic "values," the New International's incorporation of the "critical spirit" of Marxism allows for the affirmation of democracy's emancipatory ideals while working to prevent, through a process of constant critical analysis, the notion of "democracy" itself from solidifying into dogma.

Just how Derrida arrives at this point is worthy of consideration, particularly in light of the possibilities his New International presents for the integration of the non-exclusionary practices Jabès envisioned and, in a certain critical way, of the Marxist utopianism that is part of *Tel Quel*'s political legacy. Indeed, despite his long-standing opposition to a more conservative Marxist ontology which manifested itself, Derrida tells us, even in "the most vigilant and most modern reinterpretations" of Marx (including, I must add, those of the *Tel Quel* group which sought to dissociate Marx's theories from their more doctrinaire implications), Derrida offers, in his first "preliminary" analysis of the Marxist perspective, an acknowledgment, in unusually direct terms, of deconstruction's indebtedness to Marxism:

> [T]he deconstruction of the metaphysics of the "proper," of logocentrism, of linguisticism, phonologism, the demystification or the de-sedimentation of the autonomic hegemony of language . . . would have been impossible and unthinkable in a pre-Marxist space. Deconstruction never had any sense or interest, in my view at least, except as a radicalization, which is to say also *in the tradition* of a certain Marxism, in a certain *spirit of Marxism*. There has been, then, this attempted radicalization of Marxism called deconstruction. . . . But a radicalization is always indebted to the very thing it radicalizes. That is why I spoke of the Marxist memory and tradition of deconstruction, of its Marxist "spirit." It is not the only one and it is not just any one of the Marxist spirits, of course.[1]

Pluralizing the word "spirit" to stress the contradictory nature of Marxist thought, whose adoption of a perpetually self-critical posture did not protect it entirely from the conceptual demons it sought to expel, Derrida takes exception to the current "depoliticization" of Marxist theory by those who view it, following the collapse of Soviet communism, as a mere remnant of a bygone era. Indeed, the recognition of the political force of Marx's radical critique, which has provided the impetus for deconstruction's interrogation of authoritarian concepts of the state and of national sovereignty, is according to Derrida "more indispensable today than ever," for we are now faced with a dogmatism of a different sort, one whose modern-day incarnations are those of an increasingly pervasive, anti-Marxist rhetoric. Fueled by writings such as Francis Fukuyama's *The End of History and the Last Man*, which exults in the victory of capitalism and Western democracies over the Marxist state,[2] such rhetoric, in Derrida's view, not only de-emphasizes the very fragile character of that victory but also perpetuates what might be called our new "post-Marxist myth" whose discourse is no less dogmatic than the discourse it replaces. Repeated in the rhetoric of the West's politicians, in the discourses of its academic institutions, and disseminated by the mass media, the proclamations declaring the "end of Marxism" and the triumph of the new democratic "world order" have become for Derrida, borrowing from Marx, the "dominant discourse" of our post–Cold War era.

Without subscribing to Marx's notion of class struggle or to a simple opposition between an oppressive capitalist system and the social forces that oppose it, Derrida argues that the apparently uncritical acceptance of this anti-Marxist "conjuration" (a term signifying in French both "conspiracy" and "incantation" as used in the exorcising of demons) not only reveals a failure to recognize what might still be of value in Marx's political thought. In extolling the virtues of Western democracies and their economic liberalism, it tends to deny the many problems that also seem to be tearing these systems apart. Problems related to the trafficking in drugs, homelessness, and interethnic strife, to name only a few, require, however, not that our visions of a democratic society be abandoned, for that is hardly what Derrida is advocating here, but rather that the notion of democracy itself as the "ideal" or even "dogma" of the post–Cold War era be the object of critical analysis. This is why Marx, according to Derrida, still speaks to us today and why we must respond to his political injunction by remaining faithful to certain aspects of our Marxist heritage. Its components may have been contradictory—for there is no question that the more conservative aspects of Marxist theory served some of the most brutally repressive political apparatuses—but its spirit of critical analysis, which called for constant self-analysis as well, has left us a legacy that must be assumed:

> Here are two different reasons to be faithful to a spirit of Marxism. They must not be added together but intertwined. They must be implicated with each other in the course of a complex and constantly re-evaluated strategy. There will be no re-politicization, there will be no politics otherwise. Without this strategy, each of these two reasons could lead back to the worst, to worse than the bad, if one can put it that way, namely to a sort of fatalist idealism or abstract and dogmatic eschatology in the face of the world's evil. (p. 87)

With this call for a strategy that must be "constantly re-evaluated," we thus return to our point of departure, for a similar appeal was, as we have seen, made more than 25 years ago in the writings of *Tel Quel*. Kristevan semiology, it will be remembered, particularly as formulated in Kristeva's essay "Semiotics: A Critical Science and/or a Critique of Science," also attempted to incorporate Marx's spirit of self-criticism by advocating a perpetual critique of its own precepts. That the politics at *Tel Quel* interfered with the realization of Kristeva's objective—for the polemics unleashed by the journal illustrate vividly the extent to which critical Marxism had once been almost completely submerged—should not allow us to forget that the critical "spirit" of Marxism also eventually resurfaced, causing the group to revise its position and finally to dismantle the entire project. In this case, then, rather than ridiculing *Tel Quel* for its multiple changes in perspective, from Marxism to Maoism to a rejection of the political altogether, one could argue that *Tel Quel*'s frequent revisions were, in some respects, in conformity with a Marxist critique and illustrate in clearly practical ways the very point that Derrida is making. Once the group stopped identifying wholesale with a revolutionary ideal and once, as I have argued in the earlier sections of this book, it began to see the problematical nature of the structure of identification itself, it abandoned the dogmatic pronouncements of its politically militant period and came to a more open-ended notion of the collective and of the political as well. Indeed, we have seen the denials and prohibitions that accompany such attempts to identify with a revolutionary program or regulatory idea. In the context of Derrida's critique of the conservative "spirit" of Marxist ontology and its complicity with Marx's messianic, eschatological project, this argument is reinforced. Derrida shows in what way these "themes of the end," whether they are manifested in Marxist visions of a new, postcapitalist utopia or in the present-day celebrations of the end of Marxism and the arrival of a "capitalist paradise," ultimately constitute not simply a denial of history by assuming that our thinking will no longer be contaminated by the concepts and structures that are left behind. They also—and here we find ourselves returning once again to the central question of this book—deny mimetic impropriety, which, in Marx's case, takes the form of those "specters" of the past that continue to haunt revolutionary thought.

We need not go into all the details of Derrida's complex analysis of the spectral in Marx, which points to the "ghost" as a destabilizing simulacrum or mimesis in Marx's thought. What we should understand is that the totalitarian heritage of Marxist ontology, like the fascist totalitarianisms that preceded it, was shaped, according to Derrida, by its fear of the spectral and by the attempt to exorcise those "ghosts of the other," of the past as "other" that threaten the integrity of any social identity. By analyzing the many different manifestations of Marx's struggle against the spectral, Derrida shows, although he never addresses this question directly, that the paradoxical logic of the spectral that Marx uncovered is like that of mimesis itself: the search for the radically new takes imitation as its point of departure while trying ultimately to erase the traces of that process. When Marx argues, for example, in his analysis of Louis Napoleon's rise to power following the revolution of 1848, that past revolutionary crises are dependent on the models of the past, he makes the following comments:

> Men make their own history [*ihre eigene Geschichte*] but they do not make it just as they please [*aus freien Stücken*]; they do not make it under circumstances chosen by themselves, but under circumstances directly encountered, given and transmitted from the past [*überlieferten Umständen*]. The tradition of all the

dead generations [*aller toten Geschlechter*] weighs [*lastet*] like a
nightmare on the brain of the living. . . . And just when they seem
engaged in revolutionizing themselves and things, in creating
something that has never yet existed [*noch nicht Dagewesenes
zu schaffen*], precisely in such periods of revolutionary crisis they
anxiously conjure up [*beschwören sie ängstlich*] the spirits of the
past to their service [*die Geister der Vergangenheit zu ihrem
Dienste herauf*] and borrow [*entlehnen*] from them *names*, battle
cries [*Schlachtparole*] and costumes in order to present the new
scene of world history in this time-honored disguise and this
borrowed language [*mit dieser erborgten Sprache*].³

First appropriating the discourses of classical antiquity in order
to conceal what is for Marx the mediocrity of their bourgeois aspi-
rations, these revolutionary forces, once their mission is accom-
plished, then cast aside their ancient models (the "ghosts from the
days of Rome"), turning their backs on their Roman heritage in
order to constitute a new social order. Whether Marx is referring to
the French Revolution of 1789 or to a Napoleonic coup d'état, he
sees the same pattern repeating itself, involving first the "conjura-
tion" and then the "abjuration" of the specters of the past. By
underscoring in this way the mimetic processes necessary to the
constitution of modern bourgeois society, Marx exposes (although
he, of course, never discusses it in these terms) the traditional fear
of mimesis that structures our revolutionary heritage and whose
denial of spectrality was unwittingly reproduced, Derrida tells us,
in the writings of Marx as well. What might be construed as a
certain sensitivity to the inevitable contamination of revolution-
ary crises by the specter of past revolutions and their ancient mod-
els seems to dissolve, in Derrida's view, when Marx articulates his
vision of a new revolutionary program, one that breaks with the
anachronistic patterns of previous bourgeois revolutions by draw-
ing its "poetry"—indeed, its "spirit"—not from the models of the
past but from the future:

> Marx recognizes, of course, the law of this fatal anachrony and,
> finally, he is perhaps as aware as we are of the essential contami-
> nation of the spirit (*Geist*) by specter (*Gespenst*). But he wants to
> be done with it, he deems that one can, he declares that one
> should be done with it. He detests all ghosts, the good and the

bad, he thinks that one can break with this frequentation. It is as if he were saying to us, we who do not believe a word of it: What you think you are calling so subtly the law of anachrony is precisely anachronistic. That fate weighed on revolutions of the past. Those that are coming, *at present and in the future*, . . . those that are heralded already in the nineteenth century must turn away from the past, from its *Geist* as well as its *Gespenst*. In sum, they must cease to inherit. (p. 113)

In pitting the "social" revolution of the present and future, which actively forgets or purges itself of its "historical reminiscences," against the aborted revolutions of an earlier period, Marx denies the very processes that he himself helped to elaborate, and he does so for reasons that we have seen many times before, when the fear of the spectral as simulacrum or mimesis stems from the fear of the improper, of the dissolution of individual or social identity by the spectrality that constitutes it. As Derrida writes in the context of Marx's critique of the spectral in the writings of the German philosopher Max Stirner: "We see rise up [in Marx's *German Ideology*] the logic of this *fear of oneself* that is guiding our remarks," a fear of a self that, as Derrida states earlier, is

> inhabited and invaded by *its own specter*, . . . constituted by specters of which it becomes the host and which it assembles in the haunted community of a single body. Ego=ghost. Therefore "I am" would mean "I am haunted": I am haunted by myself who am (haunted by myself who am haunted by myself who am . . . and so forth). Wherever there is Ego, *es spukt*, "it spooks" [p. 133]. . . . The ipseity of the self is constituted there. No one will have escaped it, neither Marx, nor the Marxists, nor of course their mortal enemies, all those who want to defend the property and integrity of their home [*chez soi*]: the body proper, the proper name, nation, blood, territory, and the "rights" that are founded thereon. (p. 145)

What Marx thus chose to forget, like his present-day adversaries, who in their fear of the "specter of communism" joyously proclaim its demise, is that "a ghost," as Derrida tells us, "never dies"; it exceeds the revolutionary discourses opposing the past and the present by showing that no social order, whether traditional or modern, communist or democratic, exists fully in the present or in some idealized future as the plenitude of a self-presence; it exists in a time that is essentially "untimely" (*intempestif*), anachronistic, "out of joint." No matter how valiantly one might try to break free of the constraints of a certain tradition, its phantoms, as Derrida points out, and we have seen ample evidence of this, always return. Indeed, if *Tel Quel* engaged in the exorcising of those phantoms that its own theories helped to expose—by radicalizing *différance*, for example, to preserve the revolutionary *identity* of unmediated heterogeneity or by positing what its theory of intertextuality seems to preclude: a late-nineteenth-century "epistemological break" with the West's political, philosophical, and literary legacy—it also showed that its political struggle was haunted by the specter of that legacy, that the group's identification with a revolutionary ideal, which would not have been possible without a reaffirmation, via Marx, of the Enlightenment's emancipatory spirit, was structured by a logic, by an unacknowledged "mimetologic," that leaves no room for the spectral. Constituted, then, by a legacy that also undermined the integrity of its revolutionary identity, *Tel Quel*'s failed revolutionary experiment can be attributed in part to the contradictions implied in the mimetic relation itself, in the structure of identification whose paradoxical logic ("Be like me" / "Do not be like me") is, as Lacoue-Labarthe has pointed out, also part of our legacy. Thus, the *Tel Quel* experience signals not only the heritage of a mimetic *double bind* but also what Derrida describes as "the *double bind* of every heritage," which confronts us with a legacy that is unavoidable, even necessary, and yet at the same time impossible. Just as traditional models and precepts can never be completely avoided, neither can they be mechanically or unproblematically reproduced because, as Derrida has argued with reference to Marx, the spectral "is at work in any *tekhnē*" (p. 97), undermining our most air-tight constructions.

The fact that no heritage can either be absolutely affirmed or totally rejected should not, however, be taken to mean that all decisions and affirmations are essentially impossible. The paradoxical logic of the legacy does not dictate paralysis; it is, in fact, as Derrida suggests, the very condition of all responsible decisions. "[There is] no inheritance," Derrida writes, "without a call to responsibility" (p. 91), without a demand for action or a decision that does not (because it cannot) involve a mindless reproduction of the models inherited from the past (for even if such a thing were possible, it would determine everything in advance and thus end all decision making), but requires that we "reaffirm" our heritage while engaging with it critically, "transforming it as radically as will be necessary" by recognizing, in the spirit of critical Marxism, that our inheritance is "never a *given*, it is always a task" (p. 54). The necessity of this critical engagement is inscribed in the structure of the legacy itself, in the gaps and disjunctions of an impossible "gift" that disallows simple appropriations and identifications.

If Derrida thus accepted to speak out on Marx after years of relative silence, the reason was, first of all, he tells us, a desire "not to shirk a responsibility" but rather to examine the possible ways of responding to Marx's political injunction. All such responses would involve much more than a simple deconstruction of the "messianic eschatology" structuring Marx's political thought; they would require a rethinking of messianism itself through which a critical reaffirmation of the "emancipatory promise" that is also part of our Marxist legacy might become possible: "Not only must one not renounce the emancipatory desire, it is necessary to insist on it more than ever, it seems, and insist on it, moreover, as the very indestructibility of the 'it is necessary' ["*il faut*"]. This is the condition of a re-politicization, perhaps of another concept of the political" (p. 75; my bracketed insertion).

It is interesting to note at this point that if Kristeva's perspective in *Strangers to Ourselves*, with its affirmation of Enlightenment cosmopolitanism, began in certain ways to coincide more closely with that of deconstruction, so has Derrida moved closer to the position not just of Kristeva, but also, in some respects, to that of *Tel Quel* by making in *Specters of Marx* a more overtly "political gesture," one that embraces not only the critical spirit of Marxism but a revolutionary messianism as well. In this case, however, he goes beyond the more restrictive confines of *Tel Quel*'s revolutionary project by stressing repeatedly the limits of revolutionary discourse itself. Indeed, through what will always remain a guarded endorsement of the Enlightenment's emancipatory spirit, of which *Tel Quel* was also an inheritor, Derrida acknowledges deconstruction's indebtedness to those ghosts of past generations that revolutionary Marxism tried to foreclose, and he comes to a notion of the messianic that is neither Marxist nor anti-Marxist; it exposes instead the limitations of both positions by remaining, in a way that seems to have eluded *Tel Quel*, attuned to the spectrality of the "other" that haunts any utopian vision. Derrida's articulation of a messianism that exceeds its metaphysical determinations is not to be understood, then, as a renunciation of modern democracy's emancipatory ideal. As the experience of a promise that remains open to alterity, that allows for a thought of the phantom, of mimesis, and of *différance*, without which a "new" social order could never emerge, the messianic, as Derrida envisions it, could not be more "democratic" in its aspirations. Thus, Derrida's objective in reworking this notion is "to think and to put it into practice differently," to envision a democracy not as something that conforms to a regulative idea or a utopia to be realized in the plenitude of its self-presence, but as always "to come" (*à venir*), always open to the indeterminacy of its future (*avenir*), not as the product of some calculable program, but as a "democratic promise" that gives to the "other," to the ghost of the other as trace, iterability, and supplementarity, its voice.

The promise of Derrida's "a-theological messianism," of what is essentially a messianism "without messianism" in its metaphysical-religious sense, thus works to counter the highly polemical, exclusionary practices of collectives such as *Tel Quel* by functioning as the promise of "absolute hospitality." In its awareness of the inevitable contaminations within the communitarian ideal itself, such a promise remains open to the impossible gift of what is to come, anticipating the emergence of an "unanticipatable future" that can never appear *as such*, nor can it be rigidly programmed in advance, but that leaves a place for "the memory of the hope" or of the emancipatory promise, which for Derrida is "the very site of spectrality." Indeed, by welcoming in advance what he describes as "the absolute surprise of the new arrival [*l'arrivant*]," who comes shrouded in the clothing of a ghostly nonpresence and from whom "one will demand no compensation [*contrepartie*]," Derrida recalls the austere hospitality of Jabès' Bedouin host whose willingness to welcome the voyager in his foreignness opens the possibility not only of reworking traditional notions of the communal and of the political but also of responding to one of the most pressing of political ideals, that of the demand for justice. As a "hospitality without limits [*sans réserve*]," which Derrida views as "strange, strangely familiar and inhospitable at the same time (*unheimlich*, uncanny)" (p. 168), it exceeds calculation, rules, and political programs, and it offers, as a result, an experience of the future as an impossible gift without which there would be no justice, no possibility of taking responsibility for one's actions in a way that does not simply follow a system of rules and coded prescriptions. Derrida argues that such an application of codes might be in conformity with a principle or rule of law, but "it would not be just," for justice, as Derrida tells us in "Force of Law," is not the mere enactment of a preestablished program; it is instead "an experience of the impossible":

> A will, a desire, a demand for justice whose structure wouldn't be an experience of aporia would have no chance to be what it is, namely, a call for justice. Every time that something comes to pass or turns out well, every time that we placidly apply a good rule to a particular case, to a correctly subsumed example, according to a determinant judgment, we can be sure that the law [*droit*] may find itself accounted for, but certainly not justice. Law [*droit*] is not justice. Law is the element of calculation, and it is just that there be law, but justice is incalculable, it requires us to calculate with the incalculable; and aporetic experiences are the experiences, as improbable as they are necessary, of justice, that is to say of moments in which the decision between just and unjust is never insured by a rule.[4]

Out of Derrida's notion of "absolute hospitality," which, in the manner of Jabès' Bedouin host, requires nothing in return, which imposes no rules demanding recognition or gratitude, comes a possibility of justice beyond law and calculation, a possibility that, like the advent of democracy itself, is always in the future as that which is "yet to come":

> Justice . . . has an, it is *à-venir*, the very dimension of events irreducibly to come. It will always have it, this *à-venir*, and always has. Perhaps it is for this reason that justice, insofar as it

is not only a juridical or political concept, opens up for *l'avenir* the transformation, the recasting or refounding of law and politics. "Perhaps," one must always say perhaps for justice. There is an *avenir* for justice and there is no justice except to the degree that some event is possible which, as event, exceeds calculation, rules, programs, anticipations and so forth. Justice as the experience of absolute alterity is unpresentable, but it is the chance of the event and the condition of history.[5]

This notion of justice as the experience of alterity, as an emancipatory promise that gives to the other its voice, is not, however, to be understood as a simple affirmation of individual rights. Rather, it goes beyond the more proprietary uses of a term that traditionally support our sense of territorial or personal identity by understanding the relation to the other in the Levinasian sense as "the heteronomic relation to . . . the faces of otherness that govern me, whose infinity I cannot thematize and whose hostage I remain" (p. 22). Justice in this case, then, cannot be simply equated with established legal norms or moral principles affirming the rights of man; it exposes their limits, and, in so doing, it points to an "ideal" of democracy that understands the limits of the ideal itself, producing a notion of community that does not succumb to the demand for totality and therefore exclusion, nor does it enclose itself within boundaries determined by a rigid system of rules and legal restrictions. But, by recognizing the other as a possible contaminant within every enclosure, it remains forever open to the possibility of transformation, to a constant questioning (which never leads to a simple rejection) of the law and its governing principles:

> In short, for a decision to be just and responsible, it must, in its proper moment if there is one, be both regulated and without regulation: it must conserve the law and also destroy it or suspend it enough to have to reinvent it in each case, rejustify it, at least reinvent it in the reaffirmation and the new and free confirmation of its principle. Each case is other, each decision is different and requires an absolutely unique interpretation, which no existing, coded rule can or ought to guarantee absolutely. At least, if the rule guarantees it in no uncertain terms, so that the judge is a calculating machine, which happens, and we will not say that he is just, free and responsible. (p. 23)

Justice understood in this sense, then, does not dictate political and moral paralysis. On the contrary, as a movement of deconstruction within the law itself, it puts *more* of a strain on our decision-making powers not less and implies, as does the project of deconstruction itself, an increase not a decrease of responsibility. For if justice is what makes the project of deconstruction possible; if, that is, as Derrida has claimed, it is that from which deconstruction is indeed inseparable as the undecidable relation to an other undermining the purity of any legal, philosophical, or political concept, then the deconstructive project, far from operating in a nihilistic void or in the realm of theoretical abstractions, has important political implications. It has, as Drucilla Cornell has pointed out so convincingly, clearly practical applications as well, by presenting "the possibility of radical transformation within an existing legal system, including the new definition of right." Here, it is not the rights of the Jews that enter into Cornell's analysis but those of another group that has also served as the excluded "other" not simply of the fascist state but also of many presumably democratic societies:

> Homosexuals have been systematically persecuted, legally and otherwise, in the United States. Interestingly enough, the reading of deconstruction I have offered allows us to defend rights as an expression of the suspicion of the consolidation of the boundaries, legal and otherwise, of community. These boundaries foreclose the possibility of transformation, including the transformation of our current conceptions of "normal" sexuality as these norms have been reflected in the law and used as the basis for the denial of rights to homosexuals. What is "rotten" in a legal system is precisely the erasure of its own mystical foundation of authority so that the system can dress itself up as justice. Thus, Derrida can rightly argue that deconstruction "hyperbolically raises the stakes of exacting justice; it is sensitivity to a sort of essential disproportion that must inscribe excess and inadequation in itself and that strives to denounce not only theoretical limits but also concrete injustices, with the most palpable effects, in the good conscience that dogmatically stops before any inherited determination of justice." (p. 167)

Although this is not the place to go into the details of Cornell's analysis, her work offers a compelling argument in support of both the political and the practical dimensions of Derrida's thought. Derrida acknowledges her efforts, as well as those of Barbara Herrnstein Smith and others, to place deconstruction in a context that bridges what some see as a gap between the literary-philosophical side of deconstruction and its "politico-institutional" concerns, by claiming that such a conjunction responds "to the most radical programs of a deconstruction":

> [Deconstruction] would like, in order to be consistent with itself, not to remain enclosed in purely speculative, theoretical, academic discourses but rather . . . to aspire to something more consequential, to *change* things and to intervene in an efficient and responsible, though always, of course, very mediated way, not only in the profession but in what one calls the *cité*, the *polis* and more generally the world. Not doubtless, to change things in the rather naive sense of calculated, deliberate and strategically controlled intervention, but in the sense of maximum intensification of a transformation in progress, in the name of neither a simple symptom nor a simple cause (other categories are required here).[6]

Reinforcing this point in the context of Derrida's affirmation in *Specters of Marx* of the emancipatory and messianic promise of the democratic "ideal," Derrida adds:

> [A] promise must promise to be kept, that is, not to remain "spiritual" or "abstract," but to produce events, new effective forms of action, practice, organization, and so forth. To break with the "party form" or with some form of the State or the International does not mean to give up every form of practical or effective organization. It is exactly the contrary that matters to us here. (p. 89)

That Derrida has chosen to call this utopian promise the "New International," which also figures in the subtitle of his work on Marx, seems itself to stress the pragmatic, organizational, and even "revolutionary" implications of what is essentially a never to be fully realized communitarian ideal. As a promise of democracy, it gives us the principles necessary to the formation of institutional guidelines for action, guidelines that have concrete, practical applications even as we realize that, as with any ideal, perfection will never be fully attained. Indeed, although such an association of the pragmatic with the fundamentally unrealizable may seem paradoxical, to say the least, it is also perhaps necessary as one of the only ways of responding to the demand for a practical politics that has always been part of our political heritage, and of doing so while remaining constantly aware of the inflexible conceptualizations to which such demands have also given rise.

Hence, the importance of remembering the legacy of *Tel Quel*, whose rejection of conventional politics, through the formulation of a presumably unorthodox, undogmatic revolutionary praxis, did not prevent the group from embracing many of the most orthodox political strategies. That *Tel Quel's* revolutionary praxis became an instrument for conceptual mastery rather than self-criticism indeed underscores the difficulties inherent in any attempt to shed the more unsavory aspects of one's political heritage, difficulties that the group should have recognized from the start. The focus by Kristeva, Pleynet, and others on intertextuality as a complex set of relations in which social and historical complexity is also inscribed should have made them aware of the possibility, indeed, of the very inevitability of such contaminations. They would have then recognized the limitations of their own project by acknowledging that failure, contamination, the specter of the excluded "other" (that is, heterogeneity) were already inscribed within it. Had they understood this, they would have seen that deconstruction's focus on the limitations of the myths constructing our utopian visions of the future, its recognition of the very unattainability of the utopian ideal is what opens up the possibility for an engagement in real-world issues by allowing for a never entirely successful but, by the same token, never completely futile political struggle that might possibly resist (although never absolutely) the appropriations, identifications, and propensity for closure to which the *Tel Quel* group eventually succumbed.

If, however, *Tel Quel* was unable to remain faithful to the spirit of critical Marxism it initially embraced; if its visions of a postcapitalist utopia left, in a manner much like that of Marx himself, no room for the specters of the past, this does not mean that its writings are no longer pertinent or that they have nothing to say to us today. There is clearly much to be learned from *Tel Quel's* mistakes as well as from its positive contributions, both of which point to the necessity of rethinking the political and the communal by exposing the limits of the utopian ideal itself. These limits are indeed inscribed in Derrida's New International, whose boundaries are not closed off by some calculated program for the future but which, as the name itself indicates, acknowledges the future's indebtedness to the political specters of the past, to the spirit of Marx, to the spirit of *Tel Quel*, and even to a discourse of revolution that presumably forecloses such a possibility. As a community of "absolute hospitality," where *différance*, alterity, the heterogeneity of the other and of the past as other have been given their place and where the limits of the state and of national sovereignty have, as a consequence, been exposed, the New International is a revolutionary *potentiality* that goes beyond the restrictive confines of "revolution" as a regulative idea by announcing itself as a promise, not as the product of a revolutionary program, that envisions an emancipatory future while remaining constantly aware of its own limits:

> Open, waiting for the event *as* justice, this hospitality is absolute only if it keeps watch over its own universality. The messianic, including its revolutionary forms (and the messianic is always revolutionary, it has to be), would be urgency, imminence but, irreducible paradox, a waiting without horizon of expectation. One may always take the quasi-atheistic dryness of the messianic to be the condition of the religions of the Book, a desert that was not even theirs (but the earth is always borrowed, on loan from God, it is never possessed by the occupier, says precisely [*justement*] the Old Testament whose injunction one would also have to hear); one may always recognize there the arid soil in which grew, and passed away, the living figures of all the messiahs, whether they were announced, recognized or still awaited. (p. 168)

Derrida's New International indeed recalls the arid soil of the Jabesian desert whose austere hospitality remained open to a multiplicity of disparate voices, including in *Le Livre de l'hospitalité* not only those of the Jews but of the Palestinians as well: "Let the Palestinians," Jabès urges, "united behind the spokes-person of their choice, be heard. . . . Let the Israelis, who know that their only way out is through dialogue, mobilize. . . . The one who accepts a dialogue is no longer an enemy. . . . Let us not forget it. Our responsibility demands it" (p. 38). Obviously conscious of the legacy he was leaving in his final *adieu* to his readers, Jabès points to possibilities for the future while never letting us forget the future's ties to our shared heritage, recalling the tradition of biblical exegesis in the haunting refrains of the imaginary rabbis and reminding us, at the same time, of the evil that can always take place by giving voice to the Holocaust as a terrifying ghost of the past. The very thought of this contamination, of good by evil, of the future by the past, of being by language, of presence by mimesis, the improper or the spectral, opens up the possibility for future ethical or political relations not because we can now choose to believe dogmatically in phantoms but because we are encouraged to remain vigilant, to be on guard against the exclusionary thinking that turns our discourse into dogma. If Jabès' Jewish community of limits or Derrida's New International can thus be considered revolutionary in this sense, it is because they incorporate a spirit of hospitality as a practice of non-exclusion, as an acceptance of the *"différantielle* contamination" at the heart of being. In so doing, they offer a promise and an engagement in the future while remaining attuned to the specters of the present and of the past.

Reference Matter

Notes

Introduction

1. Jacques Derrida, *Spectres de Marx: L'Etat de la dette, le travail du deuil et la nouvelle Internationale* (Paris: Editions Galilée, 1993); *Specters of Marx: The State of the Debt, the Work of Mourning, and the New International*, trans. Peggy Kamuf (New York: Routledge, 1994).

2. A case for the political character of Derrida's thought was made as early as 1982 in Michael Ryan's *Marxism and Deconstruction: A Critical Articulation* (Baltimore: Johns Hopkins University Press). For a more recent study, see Drucilla Cornell's *The Philosophy of the Limit* (New York: Routledge, 1992).

3. Stressing the evasive tactics that deconstruction has employed when dealing directly with concrete political issues, Nancy Fraser was particularly critical in 1984, long before the publication of *Specters of Marx*, of Derrida's reticence with regard to Marxism. "Why," she asked, "despite the revolutionary rhetoric of his *circa* 1968 writings, and despite the widespread, taken-for-granted assumption that he is 'of the left' has Derrida so consistently, deliberately and dextrously avoided the subject of politics? Why, for example, has he danced so nimbly around the tenacious efforts of interviewers to pin him down on where he stands vis-à-vis Marxism? Why has he continued 'to defer indefinitely' the encounter of deconstruction with 'the text of Marx' which he has on occasion promised?" (pp. 127–28). Underscoring the "limitations of Derrideanism as an outlook seeking to confront the political," Fraser clearly viewed Derrida's refusal to declare his position on Marxism as another manifestation of deconstruction's avoidance of politics.

"The French Derrideans: Politicizing Deconstruction or Deconstructing the Political?" *New German Critique* 33 (Fall 1984): 127–54.

4. Simon Critchley, *The Ethics of Deconstruction: Derrida and Levinas* (Oxford: Blackwell, 1992).

5. The distinction between the "responsibility to act" and the "responsibility to otherness" is elaborated by Stephen K. White in *Political Theory and Postmodernism* (New York: Cambridge University Press, 1991). Although White sees in Derrida's recent writings "a concerted attempt to explore the turn from the responsibility to otherness to the responsibility to act," he claims that Derrida encounters "substantial impasses" in his effort to elaborate an acceptable approach to ethics and politics (pp. 76–84).

6. In a 1981 interview with Shuhsi Kao, Sollers states: "A collectivity consists of people who get together because they are rebelling against an established order. But as soon as this collectivity takes over, then it is no longer an interesting collectivity. *Tel Quel* was a collective up to the time when the movement threatened to become affirmative. If 'Telquelism' were to prevail, it would have to be contested right away; I would even be the first to take command of a Liberation Front against Telquelism." Kao, "Paradise Lost? An Interview with Philippe Sollers," *Sub-Stance* 30 (1981): 40.

7. Before the recent publication of Philippe Forest's *Histoire de Tel Quel 1960–1982* (Paris: Editions du Seuil, 1995), which offers the first truly comprehensive study of the *Tel Quel* experiment, the same could be said of European studies as well. Another study by Patrick French, entitled *Time of Theory: History of Tel Quel 1960–1983*, was published by Oxford University Press after the completion of the present volume. A recent issue of *L'Infini*, the journal that replaced *Tel Quel* following its dissolution, is also devoted to the history of *Tel Quel*. To commemorate the publication of the fiftieth issue of *L'Infini*, all those who were in some way involved in or affected by the *Tel Quel* "adventure" were invited to contribute. "*Tel Quel*: De *Tel Quel* à *L'Infini*," *L'Infini* 49/50 (Spring 1995).

8. See, for example, the collection of essays devoted to the question of the political in Kristeva's work, *Ethics, Politics and Difference in Julia Kristeva's Writing*, ed. Kelly Oliver (New York: Routledge, 1993). The introduction to Kelly Oliver's *Reading Kristeva: Unraveling the Double-bind* (Bloomington: Indiana University Press, 1993) also provides a brief elaboration of the different critical responses to Kristeva's work.

9. Oliver in *Reading Kristeva* takes a somewhat similar position, but her analysis focuses less on the modifications that emerge as one

passes through the different stages of Kristeva's writing than on the contradictions that can be found in the entire body of her work.

10. Jean-François Lyotard, *Heidegger and "the jews,"* trans. Andreas Michel and Mark S. Roberts (Minneapolis: University of Minnesota Press, 1990).

11. Philippe Lacoue-Labarthe, *Heidegger, Art and Politics*, trans. Chris Turner (Oxford: Basil Blackwell, 1990); Jacques Derrida, *Of Spirit: Heidegger and the Question*, trans. Geoffrey Bennington and Rachel Bowlby (Chicago: University of Chicago Press, 1989), and *Cinders*, ed. and trans. Ned Lukacher (Lincoln: University of Nebraska Press, 1991).

12. As a justification for this emphasis on the deconstructive nature of Jabès' poetic practice, it should be pointed out that, until Jabès' death in 1991, Derrida and Jabès had been engaged in an exchange of ideas that began in the 1960's. Some of the earliest indications of that exchange appeared in Derrida's *L'Ecriture et la différance* (Paris: Editions du Seuil, 1967), which included two essays on Jabès, "Edmond Jabès et la question du livre" and "Ellipse." Jabès, in turn, published an open letter to Derrida in a special issue of *L'Arc* in which he expressed his affinities for Derrida's deconstructive project. Referring here to what he described as "this fertile deconstruction," Jabès addressed the following comments to Derrida: "You always, and with unequaled rigor, question anything that is taken for granted. What immediately won me over in your writings and the resolve they convey, what commands our respect in your profound attempt to overcome all obstacles and grasp the ungraspable, is the total acceptance of risk that runs through all your work and quickly wears out those who would nail you down. It is precisely the kind of risk that the book in process of being made and unmade forces us to take at each stage of its evolution, its articulation, and its abandonment." *The Book of Margins*, trans. Rosmarie Waldrop (Chicago: University of Chicago Press, 1993), p. 44. Originally published as "Lettre à Jacques Derrida: Sur la question du livre," in *L'Arc*, reissued in 1990 by Librairie Duponchelle, pp. 59–64. The same French version also appears in Jabès' *Ça suit son cours* (Paris: Editions Gallimard, 1975), pp. 55–56.

13. Jacques Derrida, "Introduction: Desistance," introduction to Philippe Lacoue-Labarthe's *Typography: Mimesis, Philosophy, Politics*, ed. Christopher Fynsk (Cambridge, Mass.: Harvard University Press, 1989), pp. 6–7.

14. Jean-Luc Nancy, *The Inoperative Community*, ed. Peter Connor, trans. Peter Connor, Lisa Garbus, Michael Holland, and Simona Sawhney (Minneapolis: University of Minnesota Press, 1991).

15. Julia Kristeva, *Strangers to Ourselves*, trans. Leon S. Roudiez (New York: Columbia University Press, 1991), and *Nations Without Nationalism*, trans. Leon S. Roudiez (New York: Columbia University Press, 1993).

Chapter 1

1. "Déclaration sur l'hégémonie idéologique bourgeosie/révisionnisme," *Tel Quel* 1 (Spring 1960): 3. For an informative discussion of *Tel Quel* and its relationship to Sartrean engagement, see Danielle Marx-Scouras's "Requiem for the Postwar Years: The Rise of *Tel Quel*," *French Review* 64, no. 3 (February 1991): 407–16; and Suzanne Guerlac's "Transgression in Theory: Genius and the Subject of *La Révolution du langage poétique*," in *Ethics, Politics and Difference in Julia Kristeva's Writing*, ed. Kelly Oliver (New York: Routledge, 1993), pp. 238–57. Guerlac's translation of this passage was also consulted.

2. Philippe Sollers, "Le Réflexe de réduction," *Théorie d'ensemble* (Paris: Editions du Seuil, 1968), pp. 391–98. See also "Réponses à *La Nouvelle Critique*," pp. 384–90.

3. Sollers, "Le Réflexe de réduction," pp. 391–92.

4. See Julia Kristeva's "Mémoire," *L'Infini* 1 (Winter 1983): 39–54. The English translation, "My Memory's Hyperbole," appears in *The Female Autograph: Theory and Practice of Autobiography from the Tenth to the Twentieth Century*, ed. Domna C. Stanton (Chicago: University of Chicago Press, 1987), pp. 219–35. See also Marcelin Pleynet's "Dès tambours" in *Art et littérature* (Paris: Editions du Seuil, 1977), pp. 99–127.

5. An interview with Philippe Sollers in Jean Ristat's *Qui sont les contemporains?* (Paris: Editions Gallimard, 1975), pp. 158–68.

6. The following statement taken from the "Déclaration" of 1960 reveals the extent to which *Tel Quel* openly celebrated the eclectic and diverse nature of the group's activities: "One cannot expect a more precise definition of a group that is so diverse and formed (fortunately) by contradictory personalities. . . . Nothing, in fact, would please us more than to be accused of eclecticism." *Tel Quel* 1 (Spring 1960): 4.

7. Ristat, *Qui sont les contemporains?*, p. 162.

8. Reprinted in Philippe Sollers's *Logiques* (Paris: Editions du Seuil, 1968), pp. 9–14.

9. Ristat, *Qui sont les contemporains?*, p. 163. The most thorough and informative discussion of the early years at *Tel Quel* that has been provided to date is that by Philippe Forest, *Histoire de Tel Quel 1960–1982* (Paris: Editions du Seuil, 1995). For other useful discussions of *Tel*

Quel's early years, see Lawrence Kritzman, "The Changing Political Ideology of *Tel Quel*," *Contemporary French Civilization* 2, no. 3 (Spring 1978): 405–21; Michel Condé, "*Tel Quel* et la littérature," *Littérature* 44 (December 1981): 21–32; and Stephen Bann, "The Career of *Tel Quel*: *Tel Quel* Becomes *L'Infini*," *Comparative Criticism* 6, ed. E. S. Shaffer (Cambridge, Eng.: Cambridge University Press, 1984), pp. 327–39.

10. Julia Kristeva, *Séméiotiké: Recherches pour une sémanalyse* (Paris: Editions du Seuil, 1969), pp. 27–42; "Semiotics: A Critical Science and/or a Critique of Science," trans. Seán Hand, in *The Kristeva Reader*, ed. Toril Moi (New York: Columbia University Press, 1986), pp. 74–88.

11. Kristeva, *Séméiotiké*, pp. 34–40.

12. Julia Kristeva, "Pratique signifiante et mode de production," *Tel Quel* 60 (Winter 1974): 30.

13. Julia Kristeva, *La Révolution du langage poétique* (Paris: Editions du Seuil, 1974); *Revolution in Poetic Language*, trans. Margaret Waller (New York: Columbia University Press, 1984).

14. Louis Althusser, *For Marx* (London: Verso, 1990), pp. 166–67. First published as *Pour Marx* (Paris: François Maspero, 1965).

15. Philippe Sollers, "Sur la contradiction," *Sur le matérialisme: De l'atomisme à la dialectique révolutionnaire* (Paris: Editions du Seuil, 1974), p. 141. This particular essay was initially presented at a conference in 1971.

16. Sollers, "Sur la contradiction," p. 137; Althusser, *For Marx*, p. 101.

17. Sollers's critique became particularly acerbic in the footnote added to the text in 1973, after *Tel Quel*'s break with the French Communist Party, which accused Althusser of embracing a dogmatic, mechanistic conception of the dialectic: "Before '68, Althusser's perception of Mao could play a progressive role. The same cannot be said today. . . . Althusser is the victim of his political passivity, of the rigidity of academic discourses and, theoretically, of an underestimation of Freud." "Sur la contradiction," p. 141 n. 4.

18. See George Elliott's *Althusser: The Detour of Theory* (London: Verso, 1987), which offers a thorough and very useful account of Althusserian Marxism as well as this "standard Soviet" definition of dialectical materialism (p. 104). Philippe Sollers also cites a slightly different version that views the dialectic as a "science of the general laws of movement governing the external world as well as human thought." "Lenine et le matérialisme philosophique," *Sur le matérialisme*, pp. 106–7. The essay was originally written in 1970.

19. Sollers, "Ecriture et révolution: Entretien de Jacques Henric avec

Philippe Sollers," *Théorie d'ensemble*, p. 70; Althusser, *For Marx*, pp. 171–72.

20. Defined initially in *For Marx* (pp. 231–35), ideology is linked more explicitly in a subsequent essay to Jacques Lacan's "mirror stage" when the infant sees reflected in the mirror a falsely coherent image of itself. Using Christian religious ideology to exemplify this mirroring function, Althusser writes: "We observe that the structure of all ideology, interpellating individuals as subjects in the name of a Unique and Absolute Subject is *speculary*, i.e. a mirror-structure, and *doubly* speculary: this mirror duplication is constitutive of ideology and ensures its functioning. Which means that all ideology is *centred*, that the Absolute Subject occupies the unique place of the Centre, and interpellates around it the infinity of individuals into subjects in a double mirror-connexion." "Ideology and Ideological State Apparatuses," *Lenin and Philosophy and Other Essays*, trans. Ben Brewster (New York: Monthly Review Press, 1971), p. 180.

21. Both of these essays can be found in Althusser's *Lenin and Philosophy*.

22. Althusser, "Lenin and Philosophy," ibid., p. 68.

23. Philippe Sollers, "De quelques contradictions," *Tel Quel* 38 (Summer 1969): 2–3.

24. Althusser, "Ideology and Ideological State Apparatuses," p. 174.

25. Signed "Mouvement de juin 1971," "Le Dogmatisme à la rescousse du révisionnisme," *Tel Quel* 48/49 (Spring 1972): 187–88.

26. Philippe Sollers, "Critiques," *Tel Quel* 57 (Spring 1974): 135–36.

27. Bernard Sichère, "Sur la lutte idéologique," *Tel Quel* 52 (Winter 1972): 99.

28. Ibid., p. 100.

29. Marcelin Pleynet, *Lautréamont par lui-même* (Paris: Editions du Seuil, 1967).

30. Fredric Jameson, for example, who sees the foundation of the *Tel Quel* journal as an important "sign-post" in the emergence of structuralism in the 1960's, claims that *Tel Quel*'s "script-oriented interpretations" reflect structuralism's privileging of the linguistic model and its "drive toward formalism." *The Prison House of Language: A Critical Account of Structuralism and Russian Formalism* (Princeton: Princeton University Press, 1972), pp. 195–96. More recent analyses of *Tel Quel* and its relationship to postmodernism tend to link the various members of the group to the French poststructuralists. They generally agree, however, with Jameson's view that *Tel Quel*'s focus on writing brings them much closer to the formalist or modernist tradition. See, for example, Andreas Huyssen, *After the Great Divide* (Bloomington: Indiana University Press, 1986), pp. 206–16; Steven Connor, *Post-*

modernist Culture: An Introduction to the Theories of the Contemporary (New York: Basil Blackwell, 1989), p. 107; and Linda Hutcheon, *The Politics of Postmodernism* (New York: Routledge, 1989), p. 27.

31. Marcelin Pleynet, "Lautréamont politique," *Tel Quel* 45 (Spring 1971): 23–45. By focusing in his own analysis on the intertextual nature of Lautréamont's text, Sollers underscores both implicitly and explicitly some of the problems in Pleynet's study. He argues that the biographical subject, whose traces, according to Pleynet, are ultimately "erased" by Lautréamont's subversive textual practice, is replaced in the course of Pleynet's analysis by a purely linguistic subject, one who emerges unproblematically as the product of the writing itself ("La Science de Lautréamont," *Logiques*, pp. 253–54). I offer a more detailed analysis of Pleynet's reading of Lautréamont in "A Question of Privilege: Marcelin Pleynet and Lautréamont," *French Forum* 15, no. 3 (September 1990): 329–42.

32. Marcelin Pleynet, *Stanze: Incantation dite au bandeau d'or I–IV* (Paris: Editions du Seuil, 1973). Discussing his work in an interview following its publication, Pleynet pointed to the influence of Mao Tse-tung's poetry, some of which had been translated into French by Philippe Sollers. Pleynet claimed that after the completion of *Stanze's* first canto, he acquired from Mao's poems a renewed sense of the "globality" of the text whose connections to the social and historical complex allowed it to be "situated in concrete history" and thus turned into a "revolutionary force." "Dès tambours," p. 113.

33. Cited in François Bruzzo's "Clé pour l'anatomie du singe," *Tel Quel* 77 (Autumn 1978): 72.

34. Sollers, "De quelques contradictions," pp. 5–6.

35. Cited in Patrick Combes's *La Littérature et le mouvement de mai 68* (Paris: Editions Seghers, 1984), which includes Pleynet's addendum to *Tel Quel's* "La Révolution ici maintenant." Combes's informative analysis should be consulted by anyone interested in the activities of *Tel Quel* during the events of May 1968.

36. Signed "Mouvement de juin 1971," "Le Dogmatisme à la rescousse du révisionnisme," *Tel Quel* 48/49 (Spring 1972): 189.

37. Ibid.

38. *Tel Quel* 46 (Summer 1971): 101.

39. See, for example, *Tel Quel* issues 39 (Fall 1969), 40 (Winter 1970), and 43 (Fall 1970).

40. Jean-Pierre Faye, "Le Camarade 'Mallarmé,'" *L'Humanité*, September 12, 1969.

41. *L'Humanité*, October 10, 1969.

42. *L'Humanité*, September 19, 1969, reprinted in *Tel Quel* 39 (Fall 1969): 102.

43. *Tel Quel* 43 (Fall 1970): 91–92, 90.

44. Ibid., 89.

45. Maurice Clavel and Philippe Sollers, *Délivrance* (Paris: Editions du Seuil, 1977), pp. 132–33. See also Philippe Forest's discussion of *Tel Quel*'s Maoism in *Histoire de Tel Quel*, pp. 377–80, 408–13.

46. Sollers, *Sur le matérialisme*, p. 121.

47. Julia Kristeva, "How Does One Speak to Literature?" *Desire in Language: A Semiotic Approach to Literature and Art*, ed. Leon S. Roudiez, trans. Thomas Gora, Alice Jardine, and Leon S. Roudiez (New York: Columbia University Press, 1980), p. 123 n. 17.

48. *Tel Quel* 61 (Spring 1975): 5 n. 1. A particularly aggressive critique of Derrida, entitled "O mage à Derrida," was written by the members of the *Tel Quel* group and published in the *Bulletin du mouvement de juin 71 2/3* (April 30, 1972).

49. *Tel Quel* 58 (Summer 1974): 5–6.

50. *Tel Quel* 59 (Fall 1974): 4.

51. *Tel Quel* 53 (Spring 1973): 3–4.

52. *Tel Quel* 58 (Summer 1974): 5.

53. Kristeva, *Séméiotiké*, p. 41.

Chapter 2

1. Julia Kristeva, "Problèmes de la structuration du texte," *Théorie d'ensemble* (Paris: Editions du Seuil, 1968), pp. 297–316; "Le Texte clos," *Séméiotiké: Recherches pour une sémanalyse* (Paris: Editions du Seuil, 1969), pp. 113–42; "The Bounded Text," in *Desire in Language: A Semiotic Approach to Literature and Art*, ed. Leon S. Roudiez, trans. Thomas Gora, Alice Jardine, and Leon S. Roudiez (New York: Columbia University Press, 1980), pp. 36–63.

2. Kristeva, "The Bounded Text," p. 42; "Le Texte clos," p. 121.

3. Kristeva, *Séméiotiké*, p. 112.

4. Julia Kristeva, *Polylogue* (Paris: Editions du Seuil, 1977), p. 235.

5. Kristeva, "The Bounded Text," p. 55; my emphasis.

6. Kristeva, *Séméiotiké*, p. 324.

7. Kristeva, "The Bounded Text," p. 57.

8. Julia Kristeva, "Pratique signifiante et mode de production," *Tel Quel* 60 (Winter 1974): 23–24.

9. Julia Kristeva, *La Révolution du langage poétique* (Paris: Editions du Seuil, 1974), p. 457. Not included in the English translation.

10. Kristeva, "Pratique signifiante et mode de production," pp. 21–22.

11. Kristeva, *La Révolution du langage poétique*, p. 440.

12. Ibid., p. 400.

13. Kristeva uses the term "ideologeme" to emphasize the text's "intertextual function," the fact that the text is structured by the social and historical context in which it is produced. The concept of the text as "ideologeme" is not, therefore, "an interpretive step coming after analysis in order to explain 'as ideological' what was first 'perceived' as 'linguistic,'" for it "determines the very procedure of a semiotics that, by studying the text as intertextuality, considers it as such within (the text of) society and history" ("The Bounded Text," pp. 36–37).

14. See, for example, Jennifer Stone, "The Horrors of Power: A Critique of Kristeva," *The Politics of Theory: Proceedings of the Essex Conference on the Sociology of Literature, July 1982*, ed. Francis Barker, Peter Hulme, Margaret Iversen, and Diana Loxley (Colchester: University of Essex, 1983), pp. 38–48; Judith Butler, "The Body Politics of Julia Kristeva," *Hypatia* 3, no. 3 (Winter 1989): 104–18; and Jacqueline Rose, who writes in her essay "Julia Kristeva—Take Two": "It is . . . almost impossible not to assign the status of origin to the semiotic once it is defined as beyond language in this way" (*Sexuality in the Field of Vision* [London: NLB/Verso, 1986], p. 152). Reprinted along with Judith Butler's article in *Ethics, Politics and Difference in Julia Kristeva's Writing*, ed. Kelly Oliver (New York: Routledge, 1993).

15. Kristeva, "From One Identity to an Other," *Desire in Language* (New York: Columbia University Press, 1980), p. 133.

16. Kristeva, "Du sujet en linguistique," *Polylogue*, p. 303. First published in *Langages* 24 (December 1971).

17. *Tel Quel* 46 (Summer 1971): 101.

18. See the notice on the back cover of the book in which this text appears and which also bears the same title: *Le Mécrit* (Paris: Editions du Seuil, 1972). "Le mécrit" is a neologism formed by combining the term "écrit" (writing or written) with the privative prefix "mé" (un-, mis-, non-), which conveys the idea of wrong writing or "miswriting." Roche's text is characterized by this kind of play with verbal form, particularly with the visual and sonorous properties of language, which can easily be lost in translation. Consequently, some of my translations of Roche's text will be accompanied by the original French.

19. See Barbara Herrnstein Smith's *Poetic Closure* (Chicago: University of Chicago Press, 1968), for an analysis of the apparent tendency in much contemporary poetry toward anticlosure and for an outline of a number of anticlosural techniques.

20. Denis Roche, *Eros énergumène* (Paris: Editions du Seuil, 1968), p. 11.

21. See Carlos Lynes's article "Ecrire/mécrire (Poétique et antipoétique chez Denis Roche)," *French Forum* 2, no. 1 (January 1977): 70–89,

for an interesting discussion of the struggle for cultural revolution that structures "Le Mécrit." Sarah N. Lawall also examines "Le Mécrit" from this point of view, underlining the "utopian ideal of social perfectibility" that informs the poetry of both Roche and Marcelin Pleynet: "The Poem as Utopia," *French Forum* 1, no. 2 (May 1976): 153–76.

22. See Wolfgang Iser's *The Implied Reader* (Baltimore: Johns Hopkins University Press, 1974) for an explicit and informative discussion of this tendency within the modern text to encourage and to frustrate the reader's attempts at "consistency building." His analysis of the reading process, particularly as it relates to the modern literary work, proved useful to the following analysis of "Le Mécrit." Marcelin Pleynet's essay on Roche, "La Poésie doit avoir pour but . . . ," in *Théorie d'ensemble* (pp. 94–126), also analyzes the role of the reader in Roche's earlier works.

23. This pattern of changing substitutions for "&" was pointed out by Sarah Lawall in her essay on Bonnefoy and Roche in *About French Poetry from Dada to "Tel Quel,"* ed. Mary Ann Caws (Detroit: Wayne State University Press, 1974), pp. 69–95. I would disagree, however, with her implication that the pattern remains consistent throughout the texts.

24. "Programme," *Tel Quel* 31 (Autumn 1967): 4. Also appears in Philippe Sollers, *Logiques* (Paris: Editions du Seuil, 1968), p. 10.

25. Denis Roche, *Louve basse: Ce n'est pas le mot qui fait la guerre c'est la mort* (Paris: Editions du Seuil, 1976), pp. 55–56.

26. Serge Gavronsky, *Poems & Texts* (New York: October House, 1969), pp. 176–77.

27. Kristeva, *Séméiotiké*, p. 342.

28. Julia Kristeva, *Revolution in Poetic Language*, trans. Margaret Waller (New York: Columbia University Press, 1984), p. 103 (my emphasis).

29. Kristeva, "Le Sujet en procès," *Polylogue*, p. 66.

30. Kristeva, *Séméiotiké*, p. 341.

31. Ibid., p. 308.

32. Kristeva, "Semiotics: A Critical Science and/or a Critique of Science," trans. Seán Hand, in *The Kristeva Reader*, ed. Toril Moi (New York: Columbia University Press, 1986), p. 86.

33. Kristeva, *Revolution in Poetic Language*, pp. 81–82. Given that Kristeva posits the occurrence of an "epistemological break" toward the end of the nineteenth century, it is important to point out that the English translation erroneously renders "la deuxième moitié du XIXe siècle" in *La Révolution du langage poétique* as "the first half of the nineteenth century."

34. Kristeva, "Semiotics: A Critical Science," p. 86.

35. Kristeva, *La Révolution du langage poétique*, p. 356.
36. Kristeva, *Séméiotiké*, p. 338.
37. Denis Roche, *Notre antéfixe* (Paris: Flammarion, 1978), pp. 31–32.
38. Michael Riffaterre, *Semiotics of Poetry* (Bloomington: Indiana University Press, 1978), p. 4.
39. Kristeva, *Séméiotiké*, pp. 359–60.
40. Roche, preface to "Le Mécrit."

Chapter 3

1. Shuhsi Kao, "Paradise Lost? An Interview with Philippe Sollers," *Sub-Stance* 30 (1981): 49.
2. Philippe Sollers, "Malraux," *Tel Quel* 69 (Spring 1977): 103.
3. Consider, for example, the following comments by Kristeva: "The intellectuals . . . have used their superior historical perspective inherited from the nineteenth century to devote themselves to a cause whose ideal of social and economic equality is evident but which serves both to swallow up the particular characteristics of intellectual work and to perpetuate the myth of a successful society whose messianism, when not Utopian, has turned out to border on totalitarianism." "A New Type of Intellectual: The Dissident," trans. Seán Hand, in *The Kristeva Reader*, ed. Toril Moi (New York: Columbia University Press, 1986), p. 293. Guy Scarpetta confirms this view in "Dissidence et littérature": "To hear the discourse of the dissidents . . . is to learn to challenge all dreams of the 'good society,' to learn to see in what way murder is inscribed in *all* social bonds" (*Tel Quel* 76 [Summer 1978]: 48).
4. Kristeva, "A New Type of Intellectual," pp. 294–95.
5. "We are more revolutionary today than when we were Maoists precisely because we have abandoned this division between political proclamations, on the one hand, and the search for an experience that opposes it" (Sollers, *Tel Quel* 84 [Summer 1980]: 26).
6. Scarpetta, "Dissidence et littérature," pp. 48, 46.
7. Julia Kristeva, "From One Identity to an Other," *Desire in Language: A Semiotic Approach to Literature and Art*, ed. Leon S. Roudiez, trans. Thomas Gora, Alice Jardine, and Leon S. Roudiez (New York: Columbia University Press, 1980), p. 125.
8. Kao, "Paradise Lost?" p. 50.
9. Julia Kristeva, *Tales of Love*, trans. Leon S. Roudiez (New York: Columbia University Press, 1987). *In the Beginning Was Love: Psychoanalysis and Faith*, trans. Arthur Goldhammer (New York: Columbia University Press, 1988).

10. Kristeva, "My Memory's Hyperbole," *The Female Autograph: Theory and Practice of Autobiography from the Tenth to the Twentieth Century*, ed. Domna Stanton (Chicago: University of Chicago Press, 1987), p. 234. Translated from the French "Mémoire," *L'Infini* 1 (Winter 1983): 39–54.

11. Julia Kristeva's theories have aroused the interest and occasionally the ire of a number of writers concerned with feminist issues. See, for example, Gayatri Chakravorty Spivak, "French Feminism in an International Frame," *In Other Worlds: Essays in Cultural Politics* (New York: Routledge, 1988), pp. 134–53; Ann Rosalind Jones, "Julia Kristeva on Femininity: The Limits of a Semiotic Politics," *Feminist Review* 18 (Winter 1984): 56–73; Jennifer Stone, "The Horrors of Power: A Critique of Kristeva," in *The Politics of Theory: Proceedings of the Essex Conference on the Sociology of Literature, July 1982*, ed. Francis Barker, Peter Hulme, Margaret Iversen, and Diana Loxley (Colchester: University of Essex, 1983), pp. 38–48; and Jane Gallop, "The Phallic Mother: Fraudian Analysis," *The Daughter's Seduction: Feminism and Psychoanalysis* (Ithaca: Cornell University Press, 1982), pp. 113–31.

12. Let us recall that Kristeva's distinction, as initially formulated in *Revolution in Poetic Language*, trans. Margaret Waller (New York: Columbia University Press, 1984), placed the semiotic within the prelinguistic space of drives and energy charges that precedes but also participates in the construction of the speaking subject. Associated with the term "chora," meaning "receptacle" or "womb," which Kristeva borrowed from Plato's *Timaeus*, the structure of the semiotic was essentially instinctual and dual for Kristeva. As a period of indistinction between itself and its mother's body, the infant was without a sense of "otherness," without object (for the object is seen as identical to the self), and without the intervention of a paternal third party who separates and differentiates. Despite her claim that the semiotic is a heterogeneous space before the constitution of identity and, therefore, without an ontologically feminine specificity, it has been, as her critics point out, consistently linked throughout her work to the maternal as opposed to the paternal. The symbolic, on the other hand, has always been equated with the paternal realm of identity and of communicative language. It places the subject within a normalizing triadic relationship in which the paternal third party becomes an agent of separation and difference constituting an object for the subject and vice versa. Here, the needs of bodily impulses are repressed in order for the discursive, representational function of language and the identity of the individual to be established, with the child finding itself weaned from its attachment to the mother so that it may become conscious of its

own existence as a distinct and separate identity. This process (which later provided the basis for Kristeva's discussion of the "abject," in *Powers of Horror*, which, as a form of defilement, must be cut off and thrust aside) occurs when the child has mastered normal patterns of speech, and only then is the individual as an integrated being actually formed.

13. See, for example, Jacqueline Rose's discussion of "Kristeva's reversals from celebration of the semiotic to abjection and back to a (now paternal) ideal," in "Julia Kristeva—Take Two," *Ethics, Politics and Difference in Julia Kristeva's Writing*, ed. Kelly Oliver (New York: Routledge, 1993), p. 58.

14. Julia Kristeva, *Powers of Horror: An Essay on Abjection*, trans. Leon S. Roudiez (New York: Columbia University Press, 1982), pp. 1–2.

15. Kristeva, "My Memory's Hyperbole," p. 225.

16. Kristeva, *Tales of Love*, pp. 380–81.

17. An elaboration of the ethical dimension of Kristeva's thinking can be found in her much discussed essay "Stabat Mater," in *Tales of Love*, which first appeared as "Héréthique de l'amour" in *Tel Quel* 74 (Winter 1977): 30–49. Through an examination of the cult of the Virgin Mary and its paradoxical role in sustaining traditional representations of motherhood and countering them at the same time through the integration of "a pre-conscious acknowledgement of a maternal feminine" (p. 254), Kristeva finds the possibility of a new "heretical ethics" or "herethics" of love that is founded on the inscription of the maternal body. By claiming that the process of giving birth takes the mother out of her "oneness" and installs the possibility of the ethical in this motherly "reaching out to the other" (pp. 259–60), Kristeva has clearly not abandoned her essentializing appropriations of the maternal. And yet her analysis of the complexities within the structure of Christian doctrine stands in stark contrast to her earlier condemnations of its uniformly repressive practices, for we find, in Kristeva's words, the "return of the repressed in monotheism" itself: "[The Virgin Mary] adds to the Christian trinity and to the Word that delineates their coherence the heterogeneity they salvage. . . . Christianity is perhaps also the last of the religions to have displayed in broad daylight the bipolar structure of belief: on the one hand, the difficult experience of the Word—a passion; on the other, the reassuring wrapping in the proverbial mirage of the mother—a love" (pp. 250, 252).

18. Julia Kristeva, "Psychoanalysis and the Polis," trans. Margaret Waller, *The Kristeva Reader*, p. 304.

19. Marilyn Edelstein, "Toward a Feminist Postmodern Poléthique: Kristeva on Ethics and Politics," *Ethics, Politics and Difference in Julia Kristeva's Writing*, p. 202.

20. Kristeva, "Mémoire," p. 52; "My Memory's Hyperbole," p. 234.
21. *L'Infini* 1 (Winter 1983): 3.

Chapter 4

1. Jacques Derrida, "La Différance," *Théorie d'ensemble* (Paris: Editions du Seuil, 1968), pp. 41–66. Reprinted in *Marges de la philosophie* (Paris: Editions de Minuit, 1972), pp. 1–29; and in *Margins of Philosophy*, trans. Alan Bass (Chicago: University of Chicago Press, 1982), pp. 1–27. An abbreviated form appears in *A Derrida Reader: Between the Blinds*, ed. Peggy Kamuf (New York: Columbia University Press, 1991), pp. 59–79.

2. Criticizing Derrida for aligning himself, on the one hand, with the conservative position of the PCF and the university system and, on the other hand, for refusing to accept "the more innovative aspects of Marxist theory," Sollers writes: "As far as Derrida is concerned, let us say that he exploits to the hilt the classical situation where the French Party asks intellectuals to accept above all its party line without becoming involved in politics and least of all in Marxism" ("Critiques," *Tel Quel* 57 [Spring 1974]: 136–37). See also *Tel Quel* 66 (Summer 1976): 103–4, and *Tel Quel* 61 (Spring 1975): 5.

3. Julia Kristeva, *Revolution in Poetic Language*, trans. Margaret Waller (New York: Columbia University Press, 1984), p. 142.

4. Ibid., pp. 142–43. See also Toril Moi's discussion of Kristeva's attempt "to account for the subject and the splitting (the *coupure* of the thetic) which produces it," in her introduction to *The Kristeva Reader*, ed. Toril Moi (New York: Columbia University Press, 1986), p. 16.

5. Julia Kristeva, "From One Identity to an Other," *Desire in Language: A Semiotic Approach to Literature and Art*, ed. Leon S. Roudiez, trans. Thomas Gora, Alice Jardine, and Leon S. Roudiez (New York: Columbia University Press, 1980), p. 131.

6. Kristeva, *Revolution in Poetic Language*, p. 148.
7. Ibid., pp. 143–44.
8. Moi, *The Kristeva Reader*, p. 16.
9. Tilottama Rajan, in "Trans-Positions of Difference: Kristeva and Post-structuralism," confirms my view when she states that the "notion of a signifying material that operates outside the symbolic is crucial . . . to Kristeva's project of remobilizing as irruption and the heterogeneous what grammatology reduces to the trace and différance." We differ, however, in that she appears to support Kristeva's effort to counter Derrida's "neutraliz[ation]" of the "political effectiveness of *différance*" by putting it back into the realm of "pre-symbolic

immediacy." *Ethics, Politics and Difference in Julia Kristeva's Writing*, ed. Kelly Oliver (New York: Routledge, 1993), p. 225.

10. Kristeva, *Revolution in Poetic Language*, p. 144.

11. "Interview with Jean-Louis Houdebine and Guy Scarpetta," *Positions: Jacques Derrida*, trans. Alan Bass (Chicago: University of Chicago Press, 1981), pp. 37–96.

12. An expression used by Geoffrey Bennington with reference to the *Tel Quel* position, in Geoffrey Bennington and Jacques Derrida, *Jacques Derrida* (Paris: Editions du Seuil, 1991), p. 32.

13. In *Positions*, Derrida explicitly rejects the discourse of transgression by claiming that "even in aggressions or transgressions, we are consorting with a code to which metaphysics is tied irreducibly, such that every transgressive gesture reencloses us . . . within this closure" (p. 12).

14. Although the term has been discussed, defined, interpreted, and misinterpreted many times over, a brief review of its function is in order here, given that it serves as one of the major points of contention between Derrida and *Tel Quel*. Understood in Saussurian terms as a movement of differentiality in which the value of a word is determined not by its "natural" attachment to some preexisting concept but by its difference from the other words within the signifying chain, Derridean *différance* draws out the consequences of Saussurian theory by showing that the play of differences within language is a process that not only constitutes meaning and conceptuality but also undermines the unity of the concept it produces. It shows that the concept comes to signify only as it is drawn into the system of referral from one term to the other. The signified concept, as a result, can never be "present in and of itself" because it is composed solely of these relations and differences, caught up in the process of differentiation and referral that allows it to signify (and that is indeed the condition of signification) but only by depriving it of the self-contained unity of its content. What permits the establishment of the differences that place each element in relation to another is what Derrida has come to call "spacing," a movement or interval that separates, differentiates, and divides each element while at the same time producing its meaning. As Derrida writes: "An interval must separate the present from what it is not in order for the present to be itself, but this interval that constitutes it as present must, by the same token, divide the present in and of itself, thereby also dividing, along with the present, everything that is thought on the basis of the present, that is, in our metaphysical language, every being, and singularly substance or subject. In constituting itself, in dividing itself dynamically, this interval is what might be called *spacing*, the

becoming-space of time or the becoming-time of space (*temporization*)." "Différance," *A Derrida Reader*, p. 66.

15. Jacques Derrida, *Limited Inc* (Evanston: Northwestern University Press, 1988), p. 8.

16. Cited in ibid., p. 26.

17. Derrida, *Positions*, p. 28.

18. Ibid., p. 92.

19. Judith Butler makes a similar case when she indicates that the failure of Kristeva's political strategy stems from her "uncritical appropriation of drive theory" (p. 166) and from an "exclusively *prohibitive* conception of the paternal law" which fails to "take into account the full complexity and subtlety of the law" itself: "If subversion is possible," she writes, "it will be a subversion from within the terms of the law, through the possibilities that emerge when the law turns against itself and spawns unexpected permutations of itself." "The Body Politics of Julia Kristeva," in *Ethics, Politics and Difference*, p. 178.

20. Thus, I would disagree with Suzanne Guerlac's endorsement of Kristeva's strategy to " 'revolutionize' *différance*," which, in linking it to the transgressive movement of negativity (*le rejet*) that sets into motion the mechanisms pulverizing the speaking subject, perpetuates the illusion that such an unproblematized, unified, phenomenal subject actually exists. "Transgression in Theory: Genius and the Subject of *La Révolution du langage poétique*," in *Ethics, Politics and Difference*, p. 242.

21. Julia Kristeva, *Strangers to Ourselves*, trans. Leon S. Roudiez (New York: Columbia University Press, 1991).

22. In the introduction to Julia Kristeva's *Lettre ouverte à Harlem Désir* (Paris: Editions Rivages, 1990), p. 9. The letter was included without the introduction in *Nations Without Nationalism*, trans. Leon S. Roudiez (New York: Columbia University Press, 1993).

23. Sigmund Freud, *Totem and Taboo* (1913), Standard Edition of the Complete Psychological Works of Sigmund Freud, trans. and ed. James Strachey (London: Hogarth Press, 1953–74), 13: 89. Hereafter abbreviated S.E. with appropriate volume and page numbers.

24. Sigmund Freud, *On Narcissism: An Introduction* (1914), S.E., 14: 77.

25. Sigmund Freud, *Beyond the Pleasure Principle* (1920), S.E., 18: 51.

26. Sigmund Freud, *The Ego and the Id* (1923), S.E., 19: 46.

27. See Jacques Lacan's essays on narcissism "Sur le narcissisme" and "Les Deux Narcissismes" in *Le Séminaire, Livre I: Les Ecrits techniques de Freud* (Paris: Editions du Seuil, 1975), pp. 125–47. This

is, in fact, the fundamental lesson of Freud's concept of identification, which he links to narcissism, in *Mourning and Melancholia*. Here, Freud claims that the "other," the object of the subject's affection, is absorbed through "narcissistic identification" into the subject's own ego, thus giving the subject a new and different identity. *Mourning and Melancholia* (1917 [1915]), S.E., 14: 248–49.

28. In a separate essay on Lacan, Kristeva claims that Lacan's notion of *la langue* put forth in his seminar of 1972–73 introduces a "fundamental refinement into the relation between the unconscious and language previously elaborated," for it accounts to a greater extent for the role of the instinctual and the heterogeneous in the unconscious. See Julia Kristeva, "Within the Microcosm of 'the Talking Cure,'" in *Interpreting Lacan*, ed. Joseph H. Smith and William Kerrigan (New Haven: Yale University Press, 1983), pp. 33–48.

29. Using Lacan's theory to describe the emergence of the thetic phase, defined by Kristeva as "the break which produces the positing of signification [and, one could add, of the speaking subject]," she claims that the first break occurs at the mirror stage, equated here with primary narcissism: "Captation of the image and the drive investment in this image, which institute primary narcissism, permit the constitution of objects detached from the semiotic *chora*. Lacan maintains, moreover, that the specular image is the 'prototype' for the 'world of objects.'" The second separation, castration, "puts the finishing touches on the process of separation that posits the subject as signifiable, which is to say, separate, always confronted by an other." *Revolution in Poetic Language*, pp. 46–47.

30. It will be remembered that in *Totem and Taboo*, Freud described narcissism in the following way. "Manifestations of the sexual instincts can be observed from the very first, but to begin with they are not yet directed towards any external object. . . . This stage is known as that of auto-erotism and it is succeeded by one in which an object is chosen. Further study has shown that it is expedient . . . to divide the first stage, that of auto-erotism into two. At this intermediate stage . . . the hitherto isolated sexual instincts have already come together into a single whole and have also found an object. But this object is not an external one, extraneous to the subject, but it is his own ego, which has been constituted at about this same time. . . . [W]e have given [this new stage] the name of 'narcissism'" (pp. 88–89).

31. Julia Kristeva, *Powers of Horror: An Essay on Abjection*, trans. Leon S. Roudiez (New York: Columbia University Press, 1982), p. 62.

32. Kristeva, "Place Names," in *Desire in Language*, p. 281.

33. Kristeva, *Powers of Horror*, p. 44.

34. See Jean Laplanche and J. B. Pontalis, *Vocabulaire de la psychanalyse* (Paris: Presses Universitaires de France, 1973), pp. 264–65, for a brief critique of certain aspects of the Freudian conception of primary narcissism.

35. Julia Kristeva, *Tales of Love*, trans. Leon S. Roudiez (New York: Columbia University Press, 1987).

36. Sigmund Freud, *New Introductory Lectures on Psycho-Analysis* (1933), S.E., 22: 95.

37. In the early formulation of his libido theory, Freud made a distinction between "sexual instincts," which were directed toward objects, and "ego instincts," which served the self-preservation of the individual. Recognizing, however, that narcissistic libido took the self as a sexual object, Freud came to see the original opposition as "inadequate," for it was clear that the ego instincts also had a sexual component. Freud thus abandoned the original distinction and put the opposition between life instincts and death instincts in its place. See Freud's discussion of these revisions, in *Beyond the Pleasure Principle* (1920), S.E., 18: 50–61.

38. Kristeva, "The Bounded Text," in *Desire in Language*, p. 41.

39. For a useful analysis of the problematic of otherness and its implications for a feminist ethics, see Ewa Ziarek, "Kristeva and Levinas: Mourning, Ethics and the Feminine," in *Ethics, Politics and Difference*, pp. 62–78.

40. See also Suzanne Clark and Kathleen Hulley, "An Interview with Julia Kristeva: Cultural Strangeness and the Subject in Crisis," *Discourse* 13, no. 1 (Fall-Winter 1990–91), in which she addresses directly the question of gender: "[I]f we insist on the fact that the feminine differentiates the individual, we may arrive at a new form of homogeneity. . . . I would emphasize not the notion of gender, but the notion of singularity. Of the irreducibility of individuals—whether they be men or women" (p. 166).

41. Kristeva, *Strangers to Ourselves*, p. 3.

42. Jacques Derrida, *The Other Heading: Reflections on Today's Europe*, trans. Pascale-Anne Brault and Michael B. Naas (Bloomington: Indiana University Press, 1992), pp. 78–79.

43. An expression taken from Michael Naas's introduction to Derrida's *The Other Heading*. He states succinctly that the "identity of politics has always been complicitous with a certain politics of identity" (p. xix).

44. Ibid., p. 57.

45. Derrida, *Positions*, p. 62.

46. Jacques Derrida, "Some Statements and Truisms about Neologisms, Newisms, Postisms, Parasitisms, and Other Small Seismisms,"

trans. Anne Tomiche, *The States of "Theory": History, Art and Critical Discourse*, ed. David Carroll (New York: Columbia University Press, 1990), pp. 85–86. Reissued in 1994 by Stanford University Press.

47. See Nancy Fraser's critique of the double strategy implicit in Nancy's and Lacoue-Labarthe's attempt to rethink the political from the standpoint of deconstruction's "re-trait du politique." In claiming that deconstruction's "withdrawal" from any direct involvement in political struggle (that is, politics, *la politique*) is a fundamentally political gesture, involving the "re-tracing" of the political through the interrogation of the very essence of the political (*le politique*) itself, Nancy and Lacoue-Labarthe reveal, according to Fraser, "all the more starkly the limitations of Derrideanism" (p. 142), for its goal is to produce "profound, new, politically relevant insights without dirtying any hands in political struggle." "The French Derrideans: Politicizing Deconstruction or Deconstructing the Political?" *New German Critique* 33 (Fall 1984): 150. Taking his cue from Fraser's critique, Simon Critchley raises similar objections by claiming that Lacoue-Labarthe's and Nancy's "reduction of *la politique* to *le politique*" amounts to the "exclusion of politics itself": "Is there not," he asks, "an inextricable contamination of *le politique* by *la politique*, and vice versa? ... [I]s not this reduction of *la politique* itself a refusal of the 'dirty hands' that must accompany any intervention in political struggle?" *The Ethics of Deconstruction: Derrida and Levinas* (Oxford: Blackwell, 1992), p. 215. In response to Critchley's question, I would argue that precisely because they are aware of the likelihood of contamination and of the impossibility of maintaining a rigorous distinction, even between such concepts as *la* and *le politique*, the theorists in question have embraced the deconstructive perspective.

48. Derrida, "Some Statements and Truisms," p. 77.

49. Derrida, *Limited Inc*, p. 116.

50. Derrida, *The Other Heading*, p. 41.

51. Ibid., p. 6.

Chapter 5

1. Victor Farias, *Heidegger et le nazism* (Paris: Editions Verdier, 1987).

2. *Newsweek*, February 15, 1988, p. 65.

3. Jacques Derrida, "Like the Sound of the Sea Deep within a Shell: Paul de Man's War," trans. Peggy Kamuf, *Critical Inquiry* 14, no. 3 (Spring 1988): 127–64. Revised and reprinted in *Responses: On Paul de Man's Wartime Journalism*, ed. Werner Hamacher, Neil Hertz, and

Thomas Keenan (Lincoln: University of Nebraska Press, 1989); and in *Memoires for Paul de Man*, rev. ed. (New York: Columbia University Press, 1989).

4. David Carroll, "The Temptation of Fascism and the Question of Literature: Justice, Sorrow, and Political Error (An Open Letter to Jacques Derrida)," *Cultural Critique* 15 (Spring 1990): 54–55, 63.

5. John Brenkman and Jules David Law, "On Jacques Derrida's 'Paul de Man's War': Resetting the Agenda," *Critical Inquiry* 15, no. 4 (Summer 1989): 805.

6. Defining "French Heideggerianism" with a formula that they admit is rather "crude, even shocking," Ferry and Renaut write: "If according to the formula we have explained, *Foucault = Heidegger + Nietzsche*, and if, as we will show later, we can say that *Lacan = Heidegger + Freud*, French Heideggerianism can be defined by the formula *Derrida = Heidegger + Derrida's style*." In a footnote on the same page, they add: "We have also mentioned Lyotard's work as a manifestation of French Heideggerianism. We prefer here the example of Derrida because his work is more consistently established within this connection to Heidegger. In Lyotard, this connection becomes fully explicit only with *Le Différend* (Ed. de Minuit, 1983)." *French Philosophy of the Sixties: An Essay on Anti-humanism*, trans. Mary H. S. Cattani (Amherst: University of Massachusetts Press, 1990), p. 123.

7. *The Heidegger Controversy: A Critical Reader*, ed. Richard Wolin (Cambridge, Mass.: MIT Press, 1993), p. xviii.

8. Richard Wolin, "French Heidegger Wars," ibid., pp. 283–84.

9. The original version of Derrida's interview appeared as "L'Enfer des philosophes," in *Le Nouvel Observateur*, November 6–12, 1987. An English translation, "Philosophers' Hell: An Interview," was provided by Wolin in the first edition of *The Heidegger Controversy* (New York: Columbia University Press, 1991), pp. 264–73. Derrida's withdrawal of the translation from the second edition of Wolin's book was taken by Wolin as an "act of self-criticism" on Derrida's part stemming from the recognition of the problematical nature of the interview's "defense" of Heidegger's position. This conclusion was soundly refuted, however, by Derrida, who claimed in a recent interview that his withdrawal of "Philosophers' Hell" was inspired by the fact that it was published without Derrida's authorization and by the poor quality of Wolin's translation. A second, authorized translation of the interview appears in the volume in which Derrida discusses this controversy. *Points...Interviews, 1974–1994: Jacques Derrida*, ed. Elisabeth Weber, trans. Peggy Kamuf and others (Stanford, Calif.: Stanford University Press, 1995), pp. 422–54.

10. Jacques Derrida, *Of Spirit: Heidegger and the Question*, trans. Geoffrey Bennington and Rachel Bowlby (Chicago: University of Chicago Press, 1989), p. 39.

11. Ibid., p. 40.

12. See also Gillian Rose, "Of Derrida's Spirit," in *Of Derrida, Heidegger, and Spirit*, ed. David Wood (Evanston: Northwestern University Press, 1993), pp. 56–72.

13. Jean-François Lyotard, *Heidegger and "the jews,"* trans. Andreas Michel and Mark S. Roberts (Minneapolis: University of Minnesota Press, 1990), pp. 75–77.

14. The word "impropriety" is derived from the French *propre*, signifying property or the state of being in possession of one's own and proper identity.

15. See Eric Gould's introduction to *The Sin of the Book: Edmond Jabès*, ed. Eric Gould (Lincoln: University of Nebraska Press, 1985), p. xv.

Chapter 6

1. Berel Lang, "Writing-the-Holocaust: Jabès and the Measure of History," in *The Sin of the Book: Edmond Jabès*, ed. Eric Gould (Lincoln: University of Nebraska Press, 1985), pp. 191–92.

2. Published English translations of these volumes were used whenever possible. The seven texts that make up *Le Livre des questions* are included in *The Book of Questions*, vols. 1–2, trans. Rosmarie Waldrop (Hanover: Wesleyan University Press, 1991). The first volume contains three works that were originally published as separate texts: "The Book of Questions," "The Book of Yukel," and "Return to the Book." The second volume includes the originally separate works "Yaël," "Elya," "Aely," and "El, or the Last Book." Each volume will be hereafter cited in the text as *BQ*, 1 or *BQ*, 2.

3. Jacques Derrida, "Shibboleth," in *Midrash and Literature*, ed. Geoffrey Hartman and Sanford Budick (New Haven: Yale University Press, 1986), p. 327.

4. Cited in the foreword to Jean-François Lyotard's *Heidegger and "the jews,"* trans. Andreas Michel and Mark S. Roberts (Minneapolis: University of Minnesota Press, 1990), pp. xxvii–viii. The original French version appears in " 'Il faut bien manger' ou le calcul du sujet: Entretien (avec J.-L. Nancy)," *Cahiers Confrontation* 20 (Winter 1989): 113.

5. Edmond Jabès, *The Book of Shares* (hereafter cited in the text as *BS*), trans. Rosmarie Waldrop (Chicago: University of Chicago Press, 1989), p. 83.

6. Paul Auster, "Book of the Dead: An Interview with Edmond Jabès," in *The Sin of the Book*, pp. 18–19.

7. Quoted by Jason Weiss in "The Questions of Edmond Jabès," *International Herald Tribune*, July 21, 1983. See also Warren F. Motte's discussion of Lang's critique of Jabès in *Questioning Edmond Jabès* (Lincoln: University of Nebraska Press, 1990), pp. 89–91.

8. Edmond Jabès, *Du Désert au livre: Entretiens avec Marcel Cohen* (Paris: Pierre Belfond, 1991), p. 93. Hereafter cited in the text as *DL*.

9. Philippe Lacoue-Labarthe, *Heidegger, Art and Politics*, trans. Chris Turner (Oxford: Basil Blackwell, 1990).

10. Martin Heidegger, *The Question Concerning Technology and Other Essays*, trans. William Lovitt (New York: Harper & Row, 1977), p. 135.

11. That reference, which according to Lacoue-Labarthe was made by Heidegger in 1949 in one of a series of four lectures on the subject of technology, reads as follows: "Agriculture is now a motorized food industry, the same thing in its essence as the production of corpses in the gas chambers and the extermination camps, the same thing as blockades and the reduction of countries to famine, the same thing as the manufacture of hydrogen bombs" (*Heidegger, Art and Politics*, p. 34).

12. Heidegger, *The Question Concerning Technology*, p. 152.

13. Jean-Luc Nancy, *The Inoperative Community*, ed. Peter Connor, trans. Peter Connor, Lisa Garbus, Michael Holland, and Simona Sawhney (Minneapolis: University of Minnesota Press, 1991), pp. 51, 45.

14. Philippe Lacoue-Labarthe and Jean-Luc Nancy, "The Nazi Myth," trans. Brian Holmes, *Critical Inquiry* 16, no. 2 (Winter 1990): 291–312.

15. Martin Heidegger, *An Introduction to Metaphysics*, trans. Ralph Manheim (New Haven: Yale University Press, 1959), p. 191.

16. Lacoue-Labarthe, *Heidegger, Art and Politics*, p. 69.

17. Martin Heidegger, *Nietzsche, Volume III: The Will to Power as Knowledge and as Metaphysics*, ed. David Farrell Krell, trans. Joan Stambaugh, David Farrell Krell, and Frank A. Capuzzi (San Francisco: Harper & Row, 1987), p. 95.

18. Philippe Lacoue-Labarthe, *Typography: Mimesis, Philosophy, Politics*, ed. Christopher Fynsk (Cambridge, Mass.: Harvard University Press, 1989).

19. Lacoue-Labarthe, *Heidegger, Art and Politics*, p. 80.

20. Heidegger, *Introduction to Metaphysics*, p. 184.

21. Ibid., p. 185.

22. Lacoue-Labarthe, *Heidegger, Art and Politics*, p. 81.

23. Lacoue-Labarthe, *Typography*, p. 115.

24. Philippe Lacoue-Labarthe, "La Transcendance finit dans la politique," in *Rejouer le politique*, ed. Michel Delorme (Paris: Editions Galilée, 1981), pp. 171–214. Collected in *L'Imitation des modernes: Typographies II* (Paris: Editions Galilée, 1986), pp. 133–73. A translation in English by Peter Caws appears in *Social Research* 49 (Summer 1982): 405–40; and in *Typography*, pp. 267–300.

25. Lacoue-Labarthe, *Typography*, p. 297.

26. Ibid., p. 118.

27. Ibid., pp. 297–98.

28. Richard Wolin, "French Heidegger Wars," in *The Heidegger Controversy*, ed. Wolin (Cambridge, Mass.: MIT Press, 1993), p. 293. See also David Farrell Krell's discussion of Dominique Janicaud's *L'Ombre de cette pensée: Heidegger et la question politique* (Grenoble: Jerome Millon, 1990), in which he applauds Janicaud's demonstration that "the destinal historialism of Lacoue-Labarthe outdoes that of Heidegger himself." Citing Janicaud, he writes: " 'At no moment does Lacoue-Labarthe doubt this interpretation of the destiny of the Occident,' to wit, that ever since Plato's *Republic* it was bound for Auschwitz." Krell goes further than Janicaud in criticizing Lacoue-Labarthe's "*emblematic* use of Auschwitz," which constitutes, in his view, a "peculiar form of the *ontotypological representation* that Lacoue-Labarthe himself is always at pains to unmask in others," but he finds Janicaud's judgment that " 'national aestheticism' is a mere 'alibi for National Socialism' " too harsh. Krell argues that "[i]t is potentially much more than that, and very much worth pursuing, as moreover, Janicaud himself later in his book seems to concede." *Daimon Life: Heidegger and Life-Philosophy* (Bloomington: Indiana University Press, 1992), pp. 169–70.

29. Derrida also makes this point in his introduction to *Typography*, where he claims that Lacoue-Labarthe "dislocates the epochal history scanned by the Heideggerian deconstruction" by making "an abyss appear in (the truth of adequation or *homoiosis*)," that is, by marking "a disturbing and destabilizing power that draws from a pre-originary mimesis" (p. 28). In making this point, however, he also inserts a cautionary note, one aimed more directly at this current text than at Lacoue-Labarthe's later work, by warning of the "irresistible temptation to generalize the mimesis condemned by Plato or to rehabilitate it in conferring upon it the noble status of an originary mimesis. The line to be crossed, for such a temptation, seems so subtle that no one—I would say not even Lacoue-Labarthe—can constantly mind it" ("Introduction: Desistance," p. 21).

30. Heidegger, *Introduction to Metaphysics*, p. 203.

31. Heidegger's Rectoral Address, entitled "The Self-Assertion of the German University," in *The Heidegger Controversy* (1993), p. 30.

32. Lacoue-Labarthe, *Typography*, p. 299.

33. Heidegger, *The Question Concerning Technology*, pp. 10–11, 13.

34. Although the term *Ge-stell* was not initially linked to representation and its forgetting of Being (see, for example, "The Origin of the Work of Art," in *Poetry, Language, Thought,* trans. Albert Hofstadter [New York: Harper & Row, 1971], pp. 15–87), it came in Heidegger's writings on technology to incorporate all the possible meanings of the verb *stellen* (to place or set) and its potential for obfuscation, including, as the translator, William Lovitt, explains in *The Question Concerning Technology*: "*bestellen* (to order, command, to set in order), *vorstellen* (to represent), *sicherstellen* (to secure), *nachstellen* (to entrap), *verstellen* (to block or disguise), *herstellen* (to produce, to set here), *darstellen* (to present or exhibit), and so on" (p. 15 n. 14).

35. Heidegger, *Introduction to Metaphysics*, p. 114.

36. Jacques Derrida, *The Postcard: From Socrates to Freud and Beyond*, trans. Alan Bass (Chicago: University of Chicago Press, 1987), pp. 65–66.

37. Lacoue-Labarthe, *Typography*, p. 255.

38. Lacoue-Labarthe, *Heidegger, Art and Politics*, p. 84.

39. Martin Heidegger, "The Way to Language," in *On the Way to Language*, trans. Peter D. Hertz (San Francisco: Harper & Row, 1971), p. 121.

40. Jacques Derrida, "The *Retrait* of Metaphor," *Enclitic* 2, no. 2 (Fall 1978): 4–33.

41. As Heidegger describes it in "The Origin of the Work of Art," the rift as trace, as "inaugural" conflict, allows for the establishment of truth in the work of art while it is at the same time caught up in truth's conflictual structure, becoming itself veiled in the course of Being's (un)veiling: "Truth," he writes, "establishes itself as a strife [between lighting and concealing in the opposition of world and earth] within a being that is to be brought forth only in such a way that the conflict opens up in this being, that is, this being is itself brought into the rift-design. The rift-design is the drawing together, into a unity, of sketch and basic design, breach and outline. Truth establishes itself in a being in such a way, indeed, that this being itself occupies the Open of truth. This occupying, however, can happen only if what is to be brought forth, the rift, entrusts itself to the self-secluding factor that juts up in the Open. The rift must set itself back into the heavy weight of stone, the dumb hardness of wood, the dark glow of colors. As the earth takes the rift back into itself, the rift is first set forth into the Open and thus placed, that is, set, within that which towers up into the Open as self-closing and sheltering" (pp. 63–64).

42. Derrida, "The *Retrait* of Metaphor," p. 29.

43. Lacoue-Labarthe, *Heidegger, Art and Politics*, p. 85.
44. Martin Heidegger, "Aletheia (Heraclitus, Fragment B 16)," *Early Greek Thinking*, trans. David Farrell Krell and Frank A. Capuzzi (San Francisco: Harper & Row, 1975), p. 117.
45. Ibid., pp. 122–23.
46. Heidegger, "Language in the Poem," in *On the Way to Language*, p. 179.
47. Jacques Derrida, *Of Spirit: Heidegger and the Question*, trans. Geoffrey Bennington and Rachel Bowlby (Chicago: University of Chicago Press, 1989), p. 84.
48. Heidegger, "Language in the Poem," p. 179.
49. Ibid., pp. 181, 183.
50. Referring to Heidegger's *Kehre*, Lyotard writes: "The 'turning'... revolutionizes, so to speak, the very principle of all political, 'spiritual,' National Socialist or populist-ontological revolution inasmuch as a revolution is always an incarnation." In pointing out that at this moment in Heidegger's thinking, through his readings of Hölderlin, the thinker is no longer seen as "*Führer*" but as "*Hüter*, guardian: guardian of the memory of forgetting" or of a meaning that is "interminably deferred," Lyotard asserts: "Here, I would say, is the 'moment' in Heidegger's thought where it approaches, indeed, touches the thought of 'the jews.' If there is a *mimèsis* in this art of waiting, it can only be acted out there, it would seem, as a prohibition" (*Heidegger and "the jews,"* p. 79). At the same time, however, Lyotard continually stresses the inadequacy of this turn, claiming that the failure to "watch (over) the Forgotten" lingers even in Heidegger's later writings. Heidegger's "turning," he writes, "turns short. And this is not the fault of the spirit (nor of work), but rather, I venture to say, the very fault of deconstruction, in itself. The existential-ontological 'approach' itself, which would appear so attentive to what I have developed as the unconscious affect and the sublime. . . . [I]t is this approach that, according to its boldest turn, continues to, by itself, keep Heidegger away from the question that his 'affair' reawakens today, distances him from it to such a point that he said nothing and has nothing to say about this question, the question (that Adorno) called 'Auschwitz' " (p. 76).
51. See also Herman Rapaport's reading of the Holocaust in Derrida's texts in *Heidegger & Derrida: Reflections on Time and Language* (Lincoln: University of Nebraska Press, 1989). He writes: "[My] reading of *De l'esprit* takes into account that the text incorporates a vocabulary suggesting holocaust (at one point Derrida remarks that *Geist* in Hegel is equivalent to *le gaz*) and ends with some very pointed and unusually direct remarks on what has silently contributed to nazism" (pp. 163–64). Avital Ronnell makes a similar claim while providing a list of the

many texts by Derrida in which a "reading of the Holocaust and the metaphysics of race" can be found. "The Differends of Man," *Diacritics* 19, no. 3–4 (Fall-Winter 1989): 63–75.

52. Jacques Derrida, *Glas*, trans. John P. Leavey Jr. and Richard Rand (Lincoln: University of Nebraska Press, 1986), pp. 238–39. First published in France as *Glas* (Paris: Editions Galilée, 1974).

53. Jacques Derrida, *Cinders*, ed. and trans. Ned Lukacher (Lincoln: University of Nebraska Press, 1991), pp. 35, 73.

54. Jacques Derrida, "Feu la cendre," *Anima* 5 (December 1982): 45–99. The article was later revised and published both as a book and as a cassette recording in the series "Bibliothèque des Voix" (Paris: Editions des femmes, 1987).

55. Lacoue-Labarthe, *Heidegger, Art and Politics*, p. 110.

56. Edmond Jabès, *The Book of Resemblances* (hereafter cited in the text as *BR*), vol. 1, trans. Rosmarie Waldrop (Hanover: Wesleyan University Press, 1990), p. 110.

57. Edmond Jabès, *The Book of Resemblances II: Intimations The Desert*, trans. Rosmarie Waldrop (Hanover: Wesleyan University Press, 1991), p. 44.

58. Edmond Jabès, *Le Livre de l'hospitalité* (Paris: Editions Gallimard, 1991), p. 43. Hereafter cited in the text as *LH*.

59. Edmond Jabès, *The Book of Dialogue* (Middletown: Wesleyan University Press, 1987), p. 11. Hereafter cited in the text as *BD*.

60. Edmond Jabès, "The Return to the Book," *The Book of Questions*, 1: 365; translation slightly modified.

61. Edmond Jabès, *The Book of Margins*, trans. Rosmarie Waldrop (Chicago: University of Chicago Press, 1993), p. 37.

62. Jacques Derrida, "Edmond Jabès and the Question of the Book," *Writing and Difference*, trans. Alan Bass (Chicago: University of Chicago Press, 1978), pp. 64–78.

63. Jean-François Lyotard, "A L'Insu (Unbeknownst)," *Community at Loose Ends*, ed. Miami Theory Collective (Minneapolis: University of Minnesota Press, 1991), pp. 42–48.

64. This is why Nancy saw the concentration camps as an expression of Nazism's will to destroy community in its relational sense and to bring about a political fusion that could, in truth, never be fully realized, for the suppression of relationality would mean the "suicide" of the Aryan nation, the death of community itself. Absolute community should thus be perceived not so much as a fully realized, "total fusion of individuals," but as the "will of community: the desire to operate, through the power of myth, the communion that myth represents and that it represents as a communion or communication of wills" (*The Inoperative Community*, p. 57).

65. Edmond Jabès, "Quand notre responsabilité est mise à l'épreuve" (When our responsibility is put to the test), *Libération*, June 28, 1990.

Chapter 7

1. Jacques Derrida, *Specters of Marx: The State of the Debt, the Work of Mourning, and the New International*, trans. Peggy Kamuf (New York: Routledge, 1994), pp. 92–93.

2. Francis Fukuyama, *The End of History and the Last Man* (New York: Free Press, 1992).

3. Cited by Derrida in *Specters of Marx*, p. 108, this passage was taken from *The Eighteenth Brumaire of Louis Bonaparte*, in Karl Marx and Friedrich Engels, *Collected Works*, vol. 11 (New York: International Publishers, 1979). Derrida's brackets and emphasis.

4. Jacques Derrida, "Force of Law: The 'Mystical Foundation of Authority,'" trans. Mary Quaintance, in *Deconstruction and the Possibility of Justice*, ed. Drucilla Cornell, Michel Rosenfeld, and David Gray Carlson (New York: Routledge, 1992), p. 16. See also Drucilla Cornell's discussion of Derrida's definition of justice as an experience of aporia, in *The Philosophy of the Limit* (New York: Routledge, 1992).

5. Derrida, "Force of Law," p. 27.

6. Ibid., pp. 8–9.

Index

In this index an "f" after a number indicates a separate reference on the next page, and an "ff" indicates separate references on the next two pages. A continuous discussion over two or more pages is indicated by a span of page numbers, e.g., "57–59." *Passim* is used for a cluster of references in close but not consecutive sequence.

Abject (abjection), 108f, 132, 135, 266n12
Adorno, Theodor, 170, 176
Alētheia, 182, 189, 192
Alterity, 1, 70, 119–23, 146, 230, 233f, 244, 246, 250
Althusser, Louis, 3, 19, 24–37, 61f, 72–73, 123, 259n17
Anaesthetics, 169, 209
Aporia, 154f, 245, 281n4
Archi-trace, 195
Arendt, Hannah, 170
Aristotle, 178, 183, 194
Artaud, Antonin, 16
Auschwitz, 8, 166, 169, 171, 175–80 *passim*, 211, 233, 277n28, 279n50. *See also* Holocaust

Bakhtin, Mikhail, 38
Barthes, Roland, 3, 17, 19, 38
Bataille, Georges, 171

Baudry, Jean, 19
Beckett, Samuel, 170
Being (being): according to Heidegger, 56, 178, 182, 184–85, 189; Lacoue-Labarthe's critique of Heideggerian notion, 190–95; Nancy and singularity of being, 11, 220, 223, 228–30, 233; relation between being and language, 211–19, 230–33; retreat of Being, 197–99, 206–8, 224–27
Benjamin, Walter, 170
Butor, Michel, 17, 53

Caesura, 205
Carpentras, 233
Carroll, David, 161, 170, 209
Cayrol, Jean, 57
Celan, Paul, 170
Céline, Louis-Ferdinand, 77, 171
Char, René, 171

Christianity, 104–5, 108, 137–38, 179, 221, 267n17
Combes, Patrick, 55
Community, 9, 11f, 124, 136–46 *passim*, 155, 181–87 *passim*, 220–35, 245–50 *passim*, 280n64. *See also* New International
Contradiction, Marxist concept of, 26–28, 72
Cornell, Drucilla, 247–48
Cosmopolitanism, 136–43, 243
Critchley, Simon, 1, 2, 273n47
Cultural Revolution, 59, 61, 101, 112

Deguy, Michel, viii
De Man, Paul, 114, 160–62
Democracy (democratic values), 144, 146, 235ff, 244–48 *passim*
Derrida, Jacques, 171, 256n5; and Heidegger, 10, 163–66, 198, 200, 202–5 (*see also* Works: *Of Spirit*); and Jabès, 215, 218, 225, 230, 244–45, 250–51, 257n12; and Marxism, 1, 2, 23, 114, 118–19, 159, 235–44, 255n3, 268n2 (*see also* Works: *Specters of Marx*); and *Tel Quel*, 2–7 *passim*, 19, 23, 55–57, 63, 113–24, 147–55, 236, 244
—Works: *Cinders*, 8, 208–9, 230; *L'Ecriture et la différance*, 218, 257n12; "Force of Law," 245–48; *Glas*, 63, 206–7, 208; "Introduction: Desistance," 10, 277n29; *Memoires for Paul de Man*, 160–61; *The Other Heading*, 144–46, 154–55; "La Parole soufflée," 17; *Positions*, 118–21, 148–49; *The Postcard*, 194; "The *Retrait* of Metaphor," 197; "Shibboleth," 174–75, 177; "Signature Event Context," 121–22; "Some Statements and Truisms," 149–53; *Specters of Marx*, 1, 3, 235–45, 248, 250–51; *Of Spirit*, 8, 163–66, 200–206

Derridean grammatology, *Tel Quel*'s critique of, 114–21, 122
Descartes, René, 180
Désir, Harlem, 124, 143
Destinal historialism, 190, 277n28
Dialectical materialism, 23–36, 53, 60, 62, 123
Diderot, Denis, 139
Différance, 2, 6–7, 114–24, 146, 148, 195, 242, 244, 250, 269n14
Dissidence, 102–3, 265n3

Ecriture, 11, 38
Eidos, 184, 189
Enframing, *see* Ge-stell
Enlightenment, 137–45, 242–43
Envoi, 194
Ereignis (appropriating event), 198–200, 207–8
Es gibt, 207–8. *See also* Gift
Ethics: and deconstruction, 1–2, 9, 154–55, 162, 232f, 251, 256n5; and Kristeva, 6, 12, 111, 113, 124, 137, 139, 141–42, 267n17
Evil, 200–205 *passim*, 238, 251

Farias, Victor, 159f, 162
Father of individual pre-history (archaic father), 108, 110, 131–34
Faye, Jean-Pierre, 53, 55–58, 63, 114
Ferry, Luc, 162, 274n6
Fire (flame), 198–210 *passim*, 215–20 *passim*, 225–26. *See also* Trait
Flaubert, Gustave, 170
Foreignness (foreigner), 124, 135–45, 244. *See also* Other
Forgotten, the, 167–70, 196, 199, 201, 215–21 *passim*, 279n50. *See also* Unrepresentable
Foucault, Michel, 3, 17, 19, 274n6
Fraser, Nancy, 1, 2, 255n3, 273n47
French Communist Party (PCF), 28, 34, 53–64 *passim*
"French Heideggerians," 7, 10, 162, 202, 274n6
Freud, Sigmund, 26ff, 31, 124–26,

169f, 274n6; and Kristeva, 21, 70, 102, 106, 108–10, 117, 127–43 *passim*; and *Tel Quel*, 18f, 23–24, 42, 44, 53, 59f, 63, 114

Fukuyama, Francis, 237

Fynsk, Christopher, 229

Geist, see Spirit

Genotext, 73–74, 89–94

Ge-stell (enframing), 193, 278n34

Ghost, *see* Spectrality

Gift, the, 207–8, 233, 243, 245

Goebbels, Joseph, 181

Hallier, Jean-Edern, 63

Heidegger, Martin, 8, 10, 159; and Nazism, 56, 163–67, 168, 177–80, 188–95 *passim*, 203–4, 205; silence on Auschwitz, 166, 168, 179–80, 202, 209 —Works: "Aletheia," 198–99; *An Introduction to Metaphysics*, 182–83, 185–86, 191, 197–98; *Nietzsche, Volume III*, 184; *On the Way to Language*, 196, 200–201, 203; "The Origin of the Work of Art," 189–90, 196, 278n41; *The Question Concerning Technology*, 179–80, 192–93

Heraclitus, 198–200

Heritage, 146, 237–42 *passim*, 249, 251. *See also* Legacy

Heterogeneity: according to Derrida, 118–23, 250; according to Kristeva, 21–22, 71, 73, 77, 104, 109–10, 116–17, 128–34 *passim*, 138–43 *passim*, 170, 266n12; according to *Tel Quel*, 8, 22–23, 41, 44, 118–23, 242, 249. *See also* Semiotic; Unconscious

Holocaust, 168, 175, 202f, 205, 209, 279n51; and Jabès, 9, 171–77, 210, 215, 217–20, 251; as originary terror, 206–10 *passim*, 215, 219–20. *See also* Auschwitz

Homoiōsis, 186, 189, 277n29

Hospitality, 138, 146, 233–35, 244–45, 250–51

Houdebine, Jean-Louis, 118–20, 122

Idea, 179, 184–86, 189

Identification, 20; and deconstructive approach, 8–9, 10, 144–45, 178, 186–87, 191, 222, 226–27, 232f, 243; narcissistic, 105–10, 124–38 *passim*, 146, 270n27; and *Tel Quel*, 4, 6f, 52, 88, 154–55, 238, 242, 249. *See also* Mimesis

Ideology, 148, 162, 164, 222; Althusser's concept of, 25–27, 30–37; and *Tel Quel*, 16, 19, 22–23, 68, 77, 87, 102–3, 147

Immanentism (immanence), 11f, 181f, 187, 226, 234

L'Infini, 16, 112

Intertextuality, 38–39, 82, 97, 153, 242, 249, 263n13

Jabès, Edmond, 7–11 *passim*, 171–77 *passim*, 210–20, 223–36 *passim*, 244f, 250–51

Jakobson, Roman, 17

Jetty, the, 149–53

Joyce, James, 16, 65

Justice, 245–47

Kafka, Franz, 65, 171

Kehre (turning), 163, 201, 279n50

Krell, David Farrell, 277n28

Kristeva, Julia: and deconstruction, 2, 6, 114–18, 120, 122, 143–46, 243; on dissidence, 102–3, 265n3; on poetic language, 74–77, 91–94, 128; and psychoanalysis, 6, 21–22, 103–12, 124–46 *passim*, 170; on religion, 103–4, 108, 110, 267n17; and *Tel Quel*, 2–7 *passim*, 16ff, 19–23, 38–41, 51, 60–65 *passim*, 81–82, 101–3, 238, 249 —Works: "From One Identity to an

Other," 74–75; *In the Beginning Was Love*, 104; *Nations Without Nationalism*, 12, 124; "Place Names," 129; *Powers of Horror*, 109, 111, 129–30, 136; "Pratique signifiante et mode de production," 70–71; "Psychoanalysis and the Polis," 111–12; *Revolution in Poetic Language*, 21–23, 62, 70–73, 89, 106, 114–18, 127–28; *Séméiotiké*, 19f, 38–39, 70, 73, 89, 90–93, 97; "Semiotics: A Critical Science and/or a Critique of Science," 19, 23, 238; *Strangers to Ourselves*, 12, 76, 123–24, 129, 135–45 *passim*, 243; "Du Sujet en linguistique," 76; *Tales of Love*, 76, 104–11, 129, 130–35, 142, 267n17; "Le Texte clos," 66–69, 80

Lacan, Jacques, 3, 21, 24, 106, 118, 126–28, 132–33, 143, 274n6
Lacoue-Labarthe, Philippe, 7, 10, 105, 144, 162–63, 164, 171, 209f, 242, 273n47; *Heidegger, Art and Politics*, 8, 177–92 *passim*; and Lyotard, 195–96, 205–6, 209; "The Nazi Myth," 8–9, 180, 182, 186, 223; in *Rejouer le politique*, 188; *Typography*, 184–85, 189–90
Lang, Berel, 172–77 *passim*, 215, 217ff
Lautréamont, le Comte de, 16, 38f, 65f, 70, 89, 92
Legacy, 3f, 236, 238, 242–43, 249, 251. *See also* Heritage
Leiris, Michel, 227
Lenin, Vladimir Ilyich, 26–31 *passim*, 53f, 58–59, 63
Levinas, Emmanuel, 1, 246, 272n39
Logos, 56, 198–201, 205, 214
Lucretius, 60
Lyotard, Jean-François, 7, 162, 166–71, 195–96, 202–15 *passim*, 219, 220–21

Mallarmé, Stéphane, 16, 59f, 65f, 70, 89, 92, 170
Maoism, 18, 24, 26, 28, 52, 59–63, 72, 113, 238, 261n32, 265n5
Marxism: and Derrida, 1, 3–4, 114, 118–19, 148, 151, 159, 235–44, 248, 268n2; and Pleynet, 42–46, 49; and *Tel Quel*, 2ff, 18–37, 39–42, 53–54, 58–63, 70, 114, 123, 147, 150, 236, 238, 249; *Tel Quel*'s critique of, 101–4, 112. *See also under* Derrida
Marxist-Leninist theory, *Tel Quel*'s endorsement of, 26, 53–54, 58–59, 63
May 1968, 2, 18, 53–55
Messianism, 239, 243–44, 248, 250, 265n3
Mimesis, 277n29; and cultural identity, 4, 7, 9, 144–45, 178, 183–91, 195–96, 201, 211, 222; in Jabès, 210, 213–15, 219, 227, 251; and language, 4–5, 8, 10, 20–21, 22, 39f, 76, 80, 95, 97, 123, 155; in Marx, 239–42, 244; mimetic impropriety, 189, 191, 194–95f, 204–6, 239; and psychic identity, 4, 6, 105–6, 125f. *See also* Identification; Representational language
Mimetology, 183, 185, 188–90, 194–95, 205, 223, 242
Mirror stage, 115, 126–29, 131
Montesquieu, Baron de La Brède et de, 139f
Movement of June '71, 59–60
Myth, 11, 126, 131, 133, 181–84, 210, 222f, 230, 237, 249. *See also* Nazi Myth

Nancy, Jean-Luc, 7ff, 10, 105, 144, 171, 175, 273n47; *The Inoperative Community*, 11f, 181–82, 187, 220–30 *passim*, 234f
Narcissism: and Freud, 104, 124–35 *passim*; and Kristeva, 6, 104–11, 124–40 *passim*, 146, 271n29; and

Lacan, 126–27, 128, 132–33, 271n29
National aestheticism, 180–81, 277n28
National Socialism (Nazism), 8, 55–56, 177, 180–82, 187, 203, 209, 222, 277n28; and de Man, 160–62; and Heidegger, 56, 159–68 passim, 177–80, 188–95 passim, 203–4
Nazi myth (German myth), 8, 180–82, 184, 209, 222, 280n64
Nerval, Gérard de, 92
New International, 235–36, 248, 250–51
Nietzsche, Friedrich, 164, 178, 184
Nihilism, 178–79, 192

Object relations, 125–34 passim
Oedipal triangle, 105–10 passim, 127–32
Onto-ideo-logy, 185, 187
Onto-typo-logy, 185, 187–88, 277n28
Other (otherness), 1, 3, 11, 113, 125–27, 128, 154, 249; and deconstruction, 2, 7, 120–21, 144–45, 235, 239, 244–50 passim, 256n5; and Jabès, 227, 231, 233–34; and Kristeva, 105–6, 109–11, 123–24, 127–36, 141–43, 266n12; in Stanze, 44, 46–47, 50. See also Foreignness
Overdetermination, 26–28

PCF, see French Communist Party
Phantom, see Spectrality
Phenotext, 73–74, 89–94
Physis, 182–85 passim, 189–95 passim, 199, 231–32
Plato, 178f, 183–89, 191, 195, 277nn28, 29
Pleynet, Marcelin, 5, 16ff, 37–54 passim, 63–64, 77f, 142, 153, 249, 261n32
Polemos, 198
Ponge, Francis, 17, 63–64

Poststructuralism, vii–viii, 2
Pre-Oedipal phase, 43–44, 105f, 108–10, 127–34

Rectoral Address (Heidegger), 163, 191f, 202–3
Renaut, Alain, 162, 274n6
Representational language, 8, 45, 50, 78–79, 98, 173–74, 193, 195, 201, 209, 217; Kristeva and/or Tel Quel's concept of, 4–5, 7f, 20–21, 30, 40–42, 76, 105f, 266n12. See also Mimesis
Responsibility, 2f, 7–8, 145, 154, 159, 174–75, 176, 232–33, 242–51 passim, 256n5
Ricardou, Jean, 17
Riffaterre, Michael, 96
Rimbaud, Arthur, 170
Riss (rift), 189, 195–97, 205, 278n41. See also Trait
Robbe-Grillet, Alain, 17
Roche, Denis, 5, 17f, 37, 51, 77–89, 94–98
Roche, Maurice, 57
Rosenberg, Alfred, 188
Roy, Claude, 58

Sade, Marquis de, 16
Sartre, Jean-Paul, 15, 18, 53f
Saussure, Ferdinand de, 20, 76
Scarpetta, Guy, 102–3, 118, 121f
Searle, John R., 121–22
Semiotic, the, 5, 6–7, 44, 49, 70, 73–76, 108–11, 127–35, 154–55, 266n12
Sichère, Bernard, 34–35
Simon, Claude, 17
Smith, Barbara Herrnstein, 248
Sollers, Philippe, 26–34 passim, 77, 89–97 passim, 123, 268n2; and critique of Tel Quel, 3, 9, 101–2, 103, 104, 151, 153, 256n6; and history of Tel Quel, 2, 16–18, 22, 37, 39, 52f, 57, 61f, 86–87, 146
Spectrality, 200–204 passim, 236–44 passim, 249ff

Spirit: of critical Marxism, 1, 3, 23, 59, 236–43 *passim*, 249f; in Heidegger, 163, 200–205, 206

Symbolic, the, 5, 7, 49, 70, 73–76, 108–11, 127–36, 143, 154–55, 266n12

Technē, 8, 178–83 *passim*, 190–98 *passim*, 205, 209–14 *passim*, 219, 225, 231–32, 242. *See also* Fire; *Riss*; Trait

Technology, 178–80, 188, 190, 192–95, 278n34

Thibaudeau, Jean, 58, 63

Trait, the, 195–97, 204–9, 215, 220, 226. *See also* Fire; *Riss*; *Technē*

Trakl, Georg, 200–204 *passim*

Translinguistic, the, 11, 38–39

Uncanny, the, 136, 139–40, 142, 245

Unconscious, the: and Freud, 21, 106, 127, 133, 135–36, 140; and Kristeva, 21–22, 75, 92, 102, 104ff, 117, 127, 133, 135–36, 140, 142f; and *Tel Quel*, 22, 44, 46, 48, 114; "unconscious affect," 169–70, 201, 221, 279n50

Undecidable, the, 2, 148, 153–54, 161f, 247

Unrepresentable, the, 167–70, 172, 205, 215, 217

Volk, 190–92, 220, 222

Wolin, Richard, 162–66, 171, 190

Library of Congress Cataloging-in-Publication Data
Brandt, Joan Elizabeth.
Geopoetics : the politics of mimesis in poststructuralist French
poetry and theory / Joan Brandt.
    p. cm.
Includes bibliographical references and index.
ISBN 0-8047-2760-0 (cloth)
ISBN 0-8047-2761-9 (pbk.)
1. French poetry—20th century—History and criticism.   2. Mimesis
in literature.   3. Politics and literature—France.   I. Title.
PQ443.B73   1997
841'.91409358—dc20   96-23400
                                                              CIP

⊛ This book is printed on acid-free, recycled paper.

Original printing 1997

Last figure below indicates year of this printing:

06 05 04 03 02 01 00 99 98 97

DATE DUE

DATE DUE			
JUL 21 '03 F			
MAY 0 5 2003			
MAY 2 3 2011			
GAYLORD			PRINTED IN U.S.A.